GHOST
HUNTERS

GHOST HUNTERS

A GUIDE TO INVESTIGATING THE PARANORMAL

YVETTE FIELDING &
CIARÁN O'KEEFFE

HODDER &
STOUGHTON

Copyright © 2006 by Yvette Fielding and Ciarán O'Keeffe

First published in Great Britain in 2006 by Hodder & Stoughton
A division of Hodder Headline

The right of Yvette Fielding and Ciarán O'Keeffe to be identified
as the Authors of the Work has been asserted by them in
accordance with the Copyright, Designs and Patents Act 1988.

A Hodder & Stoughton Book

1

A CIP catalogue record for this title
is available from the British Library

ISBN 0 340 89978 6

Typeset in Minion by Hewer Text UK Ltd, Edinburgh
Printed and bound by Mackays of Chatham Ltd, Chatham, Kent

Hodder Headline's policy is to use papers that are natural,
renewable and recyclable products and made from wood grown
in sustainable forests. The logging and manufacturing processes
are expected to conform to the environmental regulations of the
country of origin.

Hodder & Stoughton Ltd
A division of Hodder Headline
338 Euston Road
London NW1 3BH

'True love is like ghosts, which everybody talks about
and few have seen.'

FRANÇOIS DE LA ROCHEFOUCAULD

CONTENTS

INTRODUCTION: Do Ghosts Exist?

Once upon a midnight dreary, while I pondered, weak and weary
Over many a quaint and curious volume of forgotten lore,
While I nodded, nearly napping, suddenly there came a tapping,
As of someone gently rapping, rapping at my chamber door.
'Tis some visitor,' I muttered, 'tapping at my chamber door;
Only this, and nothing more.'

EDGAR ALLAN POE: THE RAVEN (1845)

Ghost stories have always been popular for sleepovers, campfires and Hallowe'en. But do they really have any validity or are they just a timeless form of entertainment?

Ghosts aren't just a subject for campfire stories these days, but for on-site investigations and lecture hall discussions by avid hobbyists, academics and scientists. From Ouija boards, Stephen King's books and the *X Files* to the Society for Psychical Research and Living TV's *Most Haunted*, ghost hunting today isn't just about superstition but about data, investigations, theories and experiments – all attempting to answer the question: do ghosts exist?

Cynics and believers alike are eager to put forward their theories either proving or disproving the existence of ghosts. Are ghosts psychological projections stemming from our subconscious fear of death? Are they hallucinations? Are they just stories? Are they an elaborate hoax? Are they departed spirits or the visions of past events? The aim of this book is to present these theories and discuss them even-handedly so that you can make up your own mind.

WHERE WE'RE COMING FROM

When it comes to investigating ghosts the first thing you need isn't high-tech equipment or a qualification in parapsychology but an open mind. The next is a desire and a love for this type of work.

If you've seen us working together on Living TV's *Most Haunted* you'll know that we are open-minded and dedicated to our work. As paranormal investigators we complement each other well. Yvette doesn't claim to be psychic but is scared of the dark and highly sensitive to changes in atmosphere, moods, strange noises and smells. Ciarán draws on his background in science and parapsychology to provide the voice of the sceptic, the scientist in search of knowledge. Put us together and we represent two different approaches united by a passionate desire to uncover the truth.

There are dozens of books available that focus on hauntings, ghosts, mediumship or the paranormal. These books fall into three main categories: biographies or autobiographies of psychics (i.e. life stories), 'how to' texts (i.e. ghost hunting for beginners), and historical texts from a biased perspective (i.e. either sceptical or believer). What has been missing is a book that discusses the evidence for ghosts from the point of view of both sceptic and believer – and this is it. Here you'll find a veritable compendium of all aspects of the phenomena seen from both perspectives. From the first séances and reported apparitions, through to recent investigations carried out in haunted locations exclusively for this book, you'll be taken on a gripping and informative guided tour through the paranormal world.

So make sure your doors are locked, grab a snack and settle into your favourite chair and enjoy. Oh – and if you happen to feel a sudden chill while you're reading don't panic, it might just be a passing draught.

The book is divided into two parts:

Part One, 'Setting the Scene for Paranormal Investigation', presents an overview of hauntings. We'll outline the history of hauntings, explain the difference between hauntings and poltergeist activity and investigate three important cases in detail. We'll also examine famous evidence captured in photographs and on tape and video recordings. Chapter Seven, 'The Dark Side', should not be read after dark by those with a nervous disposition as it looks at 'evil' cases of spirit possession, Ouija boards and so on. The section ends with a discussion of typical investigative techniques, in which we look at the pros and cons of the methods available and, drawing on our experiences, offer advice to those who want to pursue their own paranormal investigations.

Part Two, 'Haunting Case Files', is our favourite part of the book because it's where we take you from an impartial observer to first-hand participant. Exclusively for this book we have selected five 'new' cases never examined before and carried out our own investigations. These are recorded, along with all our findings, and it is our hope that you'll share the thrill of our experiences.

There are also a couple of appendices. For the serious student they contain important information. Appendix A lists the names and addresses of major psychical research and paranormal investigation societies. You'll also find some useful website listings, including Ciarán's parapsychology website. Appendix B is a list of recommended reading about ghosts, spirits and hauntings including information about *Most Haunted* DVDs and videos.

PART ONE

SETTING THE SCENE FOR PARANORMAL INVESTIGATION

INTRODUCTION

'To himself everyone is an immortal. He may know that he is
going to die, but he can never know that he is dead.'

SAMUEL BUTLER: IMMORTALITY

Surveys indicate that around one in three of us thinks that
ghosts, phantoms and other supernatural apparitions
really exist. That's a lot of people.

For what reason do one third of us believe in ghosts?
Why are two thirds not convinced? What is one side not
seeing, feeling or sensing? These are questions we'll attempt to tackle, but first we need to take a look at some
simple but often misunderstood vocabulary, specific to the
study of ghosts, to make sure we're all on the same page.

WHAT DO YOU MEAN BY A GHOST?

Most people use the word **ghost** to mean any spirit
phenomenon when what they really mean is the spirit
of a dead human being. Is there a difference? Yes. Paranormal investigators generally prefer to use the word ghost
to mean the visual appearance of a person who has died
and the more general word apparition to mean all types of

phantoms, both human and non-human. A ghost there-fore is only one kind of apparition. For example, if you were lucky enough to see an angel floating in your garden you would call this an apparition, not a ghost.

Most ghost hunters tend to avoid the word **super-natural** as it carries the suggestion that some divine, occult or demonic power is causing the event. To avoid this connection they prefer to use the word **paranormal,** which means something that is beyond the range of everyday human experience or scientific explanation.

A **haunting** is perhaps the most frequently used para-normal term. A haunting happens when one or more ghosts inhabit a space or make themselves known to the living. The word has a negative association, but not all reported hauntings are harmful or negative.

Someone who sees an apparition is called the **percipient** and the apparition that is seen is called the **agent**. A **ghost hunter** (who by the way prefers to be called a **paranormal investigator**, or **ghost researcher**) looks for proof or evidence that ghosts exist. He or she does not necessarily believe in ghosts and may approach the investigation with an open mind. It's worth pointing out that many para-normal investigators also have an interest in psychic phenomena. The related scientific field of **parapsychology** studies Extra Sensory Perception (ESP) and Psycho Kin-esis (PK). ESP covers telepathy, precognition and clair-voyance. **Telepathy** is mind-to-mind communication. **Precognition** is essentially predicting the future. **Clair-voyance** is the ability to perceive objects or people not visible through any of the five ordinary senses. PK covers any phenomenon that shows alleged action of the mind on inanimate objects.

A **ghost buster** is someone whose job is to get rid of spirits or at least to stop a haunting, and to do that he or she must believe in ghosts. Sometimes a paranormal investigator may act as a ghost buster – for example, a member of his or her team with psychic abilities may ask a ghost to leave, or to explain its business so that it can leave – but it is important to remember that paranormal investigation (ghost hunting) and ghost busting are not the same thing.

Exorcism is the expulsion of unwanted, and often evil, demons, spirits and ghosts thought to be in possession of a person or haunting a location. It could be described as the ultimate ghost busting. Chances are slim that you'll ever come up against evil or demonic forces on a paranormal investigation and even slimmer that you'll ever need an exorcism, but if you want to know more about 'the dark side', Chapter Seven has plenty of grisly details.

Now that we've made sure we're all speaking the same language the next step is to put everything in context so that you can see the bigger picture. The brief history of hauntings that follows takes you back in time to when humankind first attempted to communicate with the dead. Then it fast forwards to some of the first recorded accounts of hauntings in the West and, centuries later, medium mania, the birth of spiritualism and full-blown paranormal investigations.

So, if you're ready for about two thousand years of ghost history – let's get started.

1

AN INTRODUCTION TO HAUNTING PHENOMENA

SPIRITS OF THE DEAD

'It is wonderful that five thousand years have now elapsed since the creation of the world, and still it is undecided whether or not there has ever been an instance of the spirit of any person appearing after death. All argument is against it; but all belief is for it.'

BOSWELL: LIFE OF JOHNSON

It seems that ghosts have always been present in human history. Almost every social culture has had a belief in ghosts or some form of existence after death.

In early days, ancestor-worship became a form of religion; primitive people had no doubt that their ancestors survived death and had powers to affect the living for good or ill. Therefore due reverence was shown to them in order to incur favour, and the wise men of the tribe, who were thought to possess psychic powers (the equivalent of modern mediums), would attempt to communicate with them.

To foretell the future, ancient seers would call up spirits of the dead using a specific type of divination that involved fasting, secret rituals and incantations known as necromancy. One of the best-known cases of necromancy can be found in the Old Testament (I Samuel 28: 7–16). Even though the Law of Moses forbade necromancy, Soul Saul was desperate. David (of Goliath fame) had gathered an army together against him and Soul Saul needed advice fast. He visited the so-called Witch of Endor, who conjured up Samuel, a deceased King, but Samuel was so angry at being 'disquieted' that he refused to help Soul Saul or give him advice.

Early nineteenth-century engraving showing 'the Witch of Endor conjuring up the spirit of Samuel at the request of Saul'.

The Witch of Endor was probably not a witch at all but some kind of oracle, similar to the oracles in ancient Greece, of which the oracle of Apollo at Delphi was the most famous. The oracle, usually a female set up in a temple dedicated to a particular god, would enter a trance to deliver messages from the gods and sometimes from the dead. So there is nothing new in the concept of a spiritual world inhabited by ghosts or in the use of special powers to communicate with spirits.

THE FIRST GHOST STORIES

It's unclear whether the earliest written records of hauntings were based on first-hand experience or legends.

In the *Iliad* and the *Odyssey*, the epic poems of the eighth century BC attributed to the Greek poet Homer, ghosts don't bother the living much, and even though they plot and scheme they are harmless and occasionally consoling. Around the time of the Greek philosopher Socrates (469–399BC), beliefs about ghosts and their nature began to change. After centuries of being called upon by seers to do their bidding, ghosts finally turned the tables on the living and started to make their own demands. Ghosts were still thought to be helpful most of the time, but they could also be restless beings that might attack or kill someone who upset them. It was believed that the ghost of a person might linger near its grave, and the ghost of someone who had committed suicide or died violently or prematurely was said to be especially dangerous.

The first extant report of a haunted house comes from a letter written by the Roman orator Pliny the Younger (AD61–115). He wrote to his patron, Lucias Sura, about a villa in Athens that nobody would rent because of a resident ghost. In this first ever account of a haunting we see some classic ingredients: the chain-clanking ghost, the restless corpse and even the beckoning finger. The translation below is a slightly revised version of the one published by William Melmoth in 1746:

There was in Athens a house, spacious and open, but with an infamous reputation, as if filled with pestilence. For in the dead of night, a noise like the clashing of iron could be heard. And if one listened carefully, it sounded like the rattling of chains. At first the noise seemed to be at a distance, but then it would approach, nearer, nearer, nearer. Suddenly a phantom would appear: an old man, pale and emaciated, with a long beard, and hair that appeared driven by the wind. The fetters on his feet and hands rattled as he moved them.

Any dwellers in the house passed sleepless nights under the most dismal terrors imaginable. The nights without rest led them to a kind of madness, and as the horrors in their minds increased, on to a path toward death. Even in the daytime—when the phantom did not appear—the memory of the nightmare was so strong that it still passed before their eyes. The terror remained when the cause of it was gone.

Damned as uninhabitable, the house was at last deserted, left to the spectral monster. But in hope that some tenant might be found who was unaware of the malevolence within it, the house was posted for rent or sale. It happened that a philosopher named Athenodorus came to Athens at that time. Reading the posted bill, he discovered the dwelling's price. The extraordinary cheapness raised his suspicion, yet when he heard the whole story, he was not in the least put off. Indeed, he was eager to take the place. And did so immediately.

As evening drew near, Athenodorus had a couch prepared for him in the front section of the house. He asked for a light and his writing materials, then dismissed his retainers. To keep his mind from being distracted by vain terrors of imaginary noises and apparitions, he directed all his energy toward his writing.

For a time the night was silent. Then came the rattling of chains. Athenodorus neither lifted up his eyes nor laid down his pen. Instead he closed his ears by concentrating on his work. But the noise increased and advanced closer till it seemed to be at the door, and at last in the very chamber. Athenodorus looked round and saw the apparition exactly as it had been described to him. It stood before him, beckoning with one finger.

Athenodorus made a sign with his hand that the visitor should wait a little, and bent over his work. The ghost, however, shook the chains over the philosopher's head, beckoning as before.

Athenodorus now took up his lamp and followed. The ghost moved slowly, as if held back by his chains. Once it reached the courtyard, it suddenly vanished.

Athenodorus, now deserted, carefully marked the spot with a handful of grass and leaves. The next day he asked the magistrate to have the spot dug up. There they found—intertwined with chains—the bones that were all that remained of a body that had long lain in the ground. Carefully, the skeletal relics were collected and given proper burial, at public expense. The tortured ancient was at rest. And the house in Athens was haunted no more.

WHY COME BACK?

The ancients suggested a number of reasons why ghosts would return to this side of the veil. One of the most popular was to demand proper burial rites. For example, it was said that the ghost of the infamous Roman emperor Caligula, who had been murdered and cremated, haunted the Lamian Gardens, where his ashes were buried, until burial rites befitting an emperor were held.

Other reasons were to offer help and advice or to express gratitude to the living. Those who had been murdered sometimes returned to harm their murderers or to help the living find their murderers and bring them to justice. The Roman poet Ovid (17BC–AD43) mentions the spectre of Remus returning to haunt his assailant.

Today ghost experts continue to hypothesise about why spirits return. Here are some of the reasons suggested – you'll notice that a few haven't changed over the centuries:

- To give warning, or to help, comfort and advise humans
- To request a proper burial so that they can rest in peace
- To seek revenge, right a wrong or obtain justice – especially if they have been murdered
- To tell heirs where treasure is hidden
- To guard, protect or watch over property or a person
- To return to a place that is loved or loathed or in some way closely associated with them during life
- To confess their guilt
- In some cases the ghost has no idea it is dead and is just hanging around, unaware that it doesn't belong there.

PURGATORY

Christianity has its share of ghost stories. All saintly apparitions, for example, are ghost sightings, and Christian writers acknowledged life after death. It wasn't until the thirteenth century, however, when the concept of purgatory was established, that a decision was made about exactly what happens to a soul after death. Purgatory in Roman Catholic theology is an ethereal realm in which the souls of people who have died must suffer while being cleansed of, or atoning for, their sins before entering heaven. Belief in this realm was confirmed at the Council of Trent in the sixteenth century.

Ghostly sightings of pale and sad apparitions marked by

burns and scars inflicted on them in purgatory were frequent throughout the Dark and Middle Ages. Almost always these apparitions warned the living to obey the laws of the Church so as to reduce the number of years they would have to spend in purgatory.

In addition to ghosts of the dead it was also thought that satanic spirits existed and that they could take the form of loved ones. If a ghost appeared as an animal, had a harsh voice or tried to hurt, flatter or tempt you, the chances were that it was a satanic spirit. To protect yourself you needed to say the Lord's name and make the sign of the cross on your forehead. To make sure it didn't appear again, you needed to spend the rest of your life obeying the laws of the Church.

By the end of the fifteenth century Christian writings were describing how unseen ghosts would announce their presence by knocking or tapping on a table or solid object. Sorcerers would ask spirits to knock to make themselves known, and centuries later this form of spirit communication would be adopted by the early spiritualists.

Beliefs about ghosts and purgatory were challenged in the sixteenth century by Protestant writers of the Reformation. In 1572 one of the best-known Protestant books on ghosts was published in English as *Of Ghostes and Spirites walking by nyght, and of strange noyses, crackes and sundry forewarnynes.* (Now that's a title!) The author, Louis Lavator, a Swiss reformer, believed that most ghost sightings could be explained away as being the result of human error, trickery or natural causes. He also dismissed any sightings by women, because they were for the most part 'given to fear more than men' and inclined to see and hear things that weren't there!

Despite attempts by Protestants to inject a healthy scepticism most people continued to believe in ghosts, as a belief in the reality of purgatory had now become deeply ingrained.

HEADLESS AND HOMELESS

Several collections of ghost stories were assembled in seventeenth-century England following the restoration. The best-known stories are those collected by Joseph Glanvil (1636–1680), an Anglican minister to Charles II, who investigated a famous poltergeist case called the Drummer of Tedworth.

Accounts of ghosts at this time portray them as normal in voice and behaviour. They didn't pass through walls but were polite and knocked on doors. They showed no signs of having been tortured in purgatory and seemed to linger with no apparent purpose or reason. Rather gruesomely, a ghost would often resemble the corpse at the time of death. It wasn't unusual, for example, for a ghost that had been beheaded in life to be seen carrying a bloodied head under its arm in death.

In the eighteenth century there was a general scepticism and disbelief in ghosts. Then during the romantic era of the late eighteenth century and early nineteenth centuries things came full circle and society once again turned towards a belief in the existence of ghosts.

VISIONS OF AN UNSEEN WORLD

As beliefs about science and religion changed, so did beliefs about the afterlife, the existence of ghosts and the ability to communicate with the dead. It was against this backdrop that the Swedish scholar and scientist Emanuel Swedenborg (1688–1772) made his mark. In 1743 Swedenborg claimed to have had conversations with angels, which he believed were spirits of the dead. He began to deliver messages from the dead by automatic writing, a technique in which you hold a pencil and allow spirits to move your hand over a paper.

Swedenborg's mystical teachings and revelations eventually evolved into a religion, the 'New Church', which is still practised today. He also had a great impact on the emerging spiritualism movement which embraced many of his ideas, such as the belief that a spirit survives death with its earthly memories intact, and the use of automatic writing to communicate with spirits in place of the tedious rappings they had previously used.

MESMERISE ME

The next important figure to emerge in the history of hauntings was Austrian-born physician Anton Mesmer (1734–1815). Mesmer would put his patients into a trance state in order to treat them (and yes, that is where the word mesmerise comes from) and discovered that, once mesmerised, some of his patients could diagnose and heal themselves.

Although many traditional doctors were keen to dismiss Mesmer as a quack, before long physicians all over Europe were attempting the same technique. British surgeon James Briad (1795–1860), who coined the term hypnotism, discovered that patients when hypnotised were highly suggestible. There were reports of incredible phenomena exhibited by hypnotised subjects, such as the ability to perform impossible physical feats, recall past events and even display telepathic powers.

It didn't take long before believers began to see that putting people into a trance state might be a way for them to see the spirit world – or for spirits to use someone in a trance to communicate with the world. There were countless reports of contact with the spirit world while mesmerised.

Anton Mesmer (1734–1815)

Very soon, the lights would be dimmed and a person would go into a trance. 'Hush. Did you see something? What was that? Is there anybody there?' The stage was set for medium mania and the birth of the spiritualist movement.

THE BIRTH OF SPIRITUALISM

Modern spiritualism is generally considered to date from the events which occurred at Hydesville, New York State, USA, on 31 March 1848, when two sisters, Margaretta and Catherine Fox, allegedly established intelligent communication with a spirit entity via a series of raps and knocks. The publicity which this aroused and the numerous investigations carried out at the time encouraged a frenzied fascination with ghosts, hauntings and the possibility of life after death.

In a short space of time many societies of spiritualists were formed in America and Britain. These societies were interested not merely in the psychic phenomena produced but also in the philosophical significance of communicating with spirits.

MEDIUM MANIA

Spurred on by the success of the Fox sisters, hundreds of mediums – people claiming to be able to communicate with the dead – came forward all across the United States and England, some of them gaining a large following. It became a common practice for people to meet informally in their homes trying to contact spirits for themselves, and the popularity of these home circles reached its peak in the late nineteenth and early twentieth centuries.

Almost from the start mediums were accused of using magicians' tricks to produce spirit phenomena. Although fraud was undoubtedly the order of the day, there were certain mediums who captured the public's imagination and even impressed the scientists with their apparent ability to display genuine paranormal phenomena. These included the Edinburgh-born D.D. Home (1833–1873) – who produced physical feats at séances, such as floating in the air and handling hot coals – and British medium Florence Cook (1856–1904), who was renowned for producing full materialisations of spirit in well lit conditions. Medium mania didn't end with Home and Cook –other popular individuals appeared over the years and decades that followed. Today there are still celebrity mediums like James van Praagh, Tony Stockwell and Sylvia Browne who claim to be able to talk to the dead.

THE SÉANCE

When spiritualism was at its height séances were all the rage. Some were entertaining as well as amazing – offering everything from musical instruments that played themselves to full-form spirits that appeared from nowhere.

Professional mediums were not essential for holding a séance. In the 1870s *The Spiritualist*, a weekly English magazine, published suggestions on how to set up your own home circle, or private séance. Some of the tips included:

- Keep the room cool and dark, as spirits most often appear in these conditions
- Don't invite people who don't like each other to take part, as the bad vibration may inhibit spirit materialisation

- Pick someone to lead your séance who has mediumistic potential. The best mediums are genial, impulsive and affectionate
- Keep the circle down to a maximum of ten people: five men and five women is ideal
- Use the same room each time for a séance, so the spirits can grow familiar with it.

Typically séances would be held after dark. The lights would be turned down and the séance conducted by candle-light or moonlight. The members would gather round a table holding hands or with their palms on the table. Some groups simply sat on chairs arranged in a circle. Sometimes mediums would have their hands and feet tied to prevent the possibility of fraud.

Most mediums worked through a spirit called a **control,** which acted as a guide or intermediary to the other world. Controls often had their own unique personalities, separate and distinct from that of the medium. A **drop-in communicator** was the term used for an uninvited spirit that would make its presence known suddenly and unexpectedly at a séance.

At first table tipping was the standard way for spirits to communicate. Mediums claimed that spirits moved the table, but before long this wasn't enough. People wanted spirits to talk to them. The Fox sisters worked out a rapping code with which the spirits could communicate. No raps meant no and one rap meant yes. After a while the rappings were replaced by automatic writing into the séance room. The medium would hold a pen and let the spirits take possession of her hand and write their answers to questions.

Sometimes a Ouija board would be used to receive answers to questions (more about that in Chapter Seven), but the biggest leap forward was direct writing, where the script would simply appear on a piece of paper or on a surface. It no longer took forever to get answers, and soon direct writing became a favourite tool for mediums.

Communication was speeded up further when mediums allowed their controls to speak through them, in a form of mediumship now called channelling. The spirit took possession of the medium's vocal cords and talked through the medium's mouth, almost always sounding different from the medium's voice.

Soon mediums began to produce direct voice phenomena, i.e. speech from a spirit that didn't seem to emanate from the medium's mouth. Usually the ghost's voice would seem to come from a point slightly above or to the side of the medium's head.

But written words and voices in the dark simply weren't enough for sitters at séances. They wanted more, and before long mediums began to manifest real and solid objects from thin air, such as flowers, books or fruit. An object that appears from nowhere in the presence of a medium is called an **apport** (as opposed to an **asport,** where an object disappears). Spirits supposedly assembled some apports from invisible matter; others were allegedly teleported from another location.

Going one step further, some mediums even claimed to be able to materialise spirit essence or matter. Ectoplasm is the term used to describe spirit substance that would appear as a shapeless material oozing from one or more of the medium's orifices. Although fluid and shapeless at first, ectoplasm was said to mould itself into spirit faces and limbs and bodies.

If you thought ectoplasm was bizarre and incredible, think again. Some sitters actually got to see spirits. At first spirit faces appeared, but before long full-form manifestations would appear. The first medium to produce full-form spirits with regularity was Florence Cook, and it made her an overnight sensation.

Florence Cook lies in a trance, with a spirit form behind her, during a séance at the home of William Crookes (1874).

The potential for trickery during the height of spiritualism was clearly enormous, and the exposure of several prominent mediums as frauds by an increasingly sceptical and informed public undoubtedly contributed to a downturn in popularity in the 1930s. Séances never completely went out of fashion, however, and they are still performed today, but with much less of the hype, phenomena, tricks and sensationalism of those heady days. Modern séances tend to be altogether calmer affairs, with mediums quietly delivering messages from the other side to members of an audience.

SPIRIT PHOTOGRAPHY

Another important development took place in the mid to late nineteenth century: the discovery that spirits could be photographed. Photography was a fairly new science when medium mania was at its height. It was only a matter of time before spiritualists saw its potential for proving the existence of ghosts and spirits.

Spirit photography was originally used in posed sittings to capture on film the image of a ghost, usually a loved one, beside a living person. It is generally credited to William Mumler, a jewellery engraver and amateur photographer in nineteenth-century Boston. In 1861 Mumler took a self-portrait and, when he developed it, he saw a ghostly face next to his. On examination he realised it was a double exposure, but he also realised the potential and began working as a medium specialising in spirit photography.

Spirit photography remained popular well into the twentieth century despite the obvious potential for trickery. To date there has never been a fully authenticated spirit photograph. Most are obvious fakes, with patent flaws in the development or oddities caused by natural means, but around ten per cent of the pictures taken that have been examined by both photographic and paranormal experts cannot be dismissed as fraudulent or caused by natural means. The famous picture of the Brown Lady of Raynham Hall, which was published in the 1 December 1936 edition of *Country Life* magazine, is one such example. It has to date not been proven to be a fake and is still the subject of debate.

Today spirit photography is a term used to describe the capturing on film of any ghost, spirit or sign of paranormal activity. It can be a useful tool for the modern paranormal investigator, and because of this a whole chapter has been devoted to it later in the book. (See page 126.)

THE FIRST GHOST HUNTERS

Both the phenomena and the teachings of spiritualism attracted the attention of eminent scientists and intellectuals in the first half of the nineteenth century. The impetus for this serious investigation was the claim that mediums were producing spirits in the séance room. The spectres weren't just spotted now and again; they were being summoned on a regular basis.

Proof of the afterlife was also being provided by cross correspondences. Cross correspondences were a rare phenomenon in which separate mediums at different times and locations received the same or interrelated bits of information from one or more spirits. To understand the communication all these bits of information had to be joined together.

With mediums, séances and cross correspondences hitting the headlines, what better time to find out whether ghosts existed or not? Two serious societies were founded in the nineteenth century for just this purpose, and are still running.

In 1882 the Society for Psychical Research (SPR) was formed in London. The society dedicated itself to the examination of spirit activity in the light of scientific knowledge and religion. In addition to ghosts and poltergeists the SPR also studied hypnosis, ESP and other paranormal powers.

The key members of the society in its early days were Trinity College Cambridge fellows Henry Sidgewick, Frederick W.H. Myers and Edmund Gurney. Other leading members included G.N.M. Tyrell, who became known for his study of apparitions, chemist and physicist Sir William Crookes, author Sir Arthur Conan Doyle and, years later, psychoanalyst Sigmund Freud and psychiatrist Carl Jung.

An early SPR survey called a Census of Hallucinations divided ghosts into three categories: apparitions of the living, apparitions of the dying, and apparitions of the dead. The first question asked was: 'Have you ever, when believing yourself to be completely awake, had a vivid impression of seeing or being touched by a (spectral) being or inanimate object, of hearing a voice; which impression, as far as you could discover, was not due to any external physical cause?' Of 17,000 people sampled roughly ten per cent said yes, and most of those who said yes were women.

The London Ghost Club was another society formed in the nineteenth century, and predates the SPR. It was started in 1862 as a private organisation that investigated ghost phenomena. In 1885 the SPR also prompted the founding of the American Society for Psychical Research in Boston. In the beginning their main difference was that most of the members were spiritualists, whereas SPR members tended to come from a scientific background.

Although many SPR and ASPR members contributed to the field of paranormal investigation, perhaps the most famous ghost hunter of the first half of the twentieth century was Harry Price (1881–1948). Price joined the SPR in 1920 and was sent on a number of investigations. He wrote voluminously about the cases and today the Harry Price Library of Magical Literature is in the Senate House Library in the University of London. Throughout his career his methods, his investigations and even his honesty were frequently questioned, but he was one of the most colourful figures in the history of psychical research and the author many popular books on the subject.

Prior to 1930 psychical research was typically carried out outside the science laboratory. Mediums would be investigated under controlled conditions, and evidence of spontaneous phenomena, such as ghosts, would mostly consist of eye witness accounts and interviews. Then along came pioneer researcher J. B. Rhine, and the era of controlled laboratory experiments and statistical evaluation began. Founder and Director of the Parapsychology Laboratory at Duke University,

Rhine is often called the father of modern parapsychology. He is credited with adopting the term parapsychology from the German term *Parapsychologie* to describe the scientific study of the paranormal that he pioneered. Prior to that parapsychology was referred to as psychical research. He also coined the term extrasensory perception, and indeed much of the terminology still used in the field today dates back to Rhine's research at Duke University. Rhine's era lasted until 1965.

GHOST HUNTING CONTINUES

Early investigators had to rely on eyewitness accounts, photographs and their own observation skills, but in the last few decades increasingly high-tech and expensive equipment has been used to help investigators with their research. Psychical researcher Harry Price was one of the first paranormal investigators to use modern technology in ghost investigations, the most famous being that of Borley Rectory (which you'll hear more about in Chapter Four). Between 1929 and 1938 Price created a high-tech laboratory in the Rectory complete with telescope, portable phone, felt overshoes, steel tape measures, cameras and fingerprinting equipment.

Today, ghost hunting is increasingly sophisticated and precise, aided not only by the passion and commitment of ghost-hunting specialists, clubs, websites and societies all over the world but by laboratory experiments, statistical evaluation and high technology. Since the mid-1990s, high-tech equipment has dramatically changed the nature of ghost investigation, especially in America.

Some ghost investigators are worried about relying too much on high-tech equipment. While such gadgets can detect environmental changes, they tend also to detract from important eyewitness observations. The equipment is also extremely expensive and finance is often a problem for most ghost investigators. Others argue that ghost investigation relies too heavily on eyewitness accounts and it is also virtually impossible to rule out ESP as a factor influencing a haunting. The use of high technology and computer programs to investigate hauntings is controversial, but it does enable researchers to record phenomena and witness them in real time without being present at a site. And one day we believe it may just prove crucial if there is ever to be any conclusive proof of ghosts and the afterlife.

WAS THAT A GHOST?

Ghost investigators typically estimate that up to 98 per cent of all reports of haunting phenomena are false or have logical explanations. But what about the two per cent of cases that can't be explained?

There are many theories that attempt to explain these remaining cases. You'll find some of them briefly outlined below and we'll be referring to them in the rest of the book. We're not endorsing any one of them – all we want to do at this stage is show you what's on offer:

Telepathy

The now largely discredited theory of SPR founding members Frederic Myers and Edmund Gurney suggested that spirits of the dead sent mental (telepathic) messages to the living rather than physically returning as ghosts. The person's brain then started to interpret this message and used it to produce an external hallucination that resembled a ghost. German psychiatrist Hans Berger originally invented the electroencephalograph (EEG) in 1929 as a tool to study whether telepathy might be explained by brain waves.

The trouble with this theory is that it doesn't explain why, if a phantom is a personal hallucination, more than one person can sometimes see the same ghost. Even if the ghost could send out collective thought waves, why would everyone imagine the ghost to look the same? Wouldn't everyone create an individual hallucination?

Gurney suggested that collective apparitions were caused by the telepathic sharing of information from one medium to all of the people who see the ghost. The problem with this is that you must believe that telepathy exists and so far there is no documented proof that it does.

Super ESP

In the late 1950s the American sociologist and psychical researcher Hornell Hart (1888–1967) coined a term to cover a theory that was put forward by others at the time and has been constantly debated ever since. That term is super ESP, and it refers to an extraordinarily powerful form of telepathy (mind reading) that allows a medium to pick up information about the dead from other living beings. The idea was that mediums with super ESP could mentally project this information in the form of a hallucination that could be seen by others as a ghost. The medium might not even be aware that he or she is doing it.

Super ESP does not prove or disprove the existence of ghosts, but its existence could explain a number of ghost sightings.

Believers in precognition (seeing visions of the future) and retro-cognition (seeing visions of the past) say that super ESP is the answer to the ghost phenomenon. They believe that anyone can see a glimpse of the past or future at any time. Today paranormal investigators are likely to be just as sceptical about the concept of super ESP as they are about the concept of ghosts. Think about it: which is harder to believe – that people can read minds and/or see into the future or the past, or that ghosts are real?

I see dead people
The traditional view of ghosts is that they are the spirits of dead people that for some reason are 'stuck' between this plane of existence and the next, often as a result of some tragedy or trauma. Some psychics believe that such earth-bound spirits don't know they are dead. Ghosts exist in a kind of limbo in which they haunt the scenes of their deaths or locations that were pleasant to them in life. Very often, these types of ghosts are able to interact with the living. They are, on some level, aware of the living and react to being seen on the occasions when they materialise.

Some psychics claim to be able to communicate with them, and when they do, they often try to help these spirits to understand that they are dead and to move on to the next stage of their existence.

This is the most common interpretation when someone is confronted with a visible apparition, and it certainly does fit many hauntings where the apparition is more or less recognisable as someone who is deceased. For most of us, this theory is also comforting, as it hints at a life after the physical body is gone.

One common example of this type of manifestation is when an individual suddenly becomes aware of the death of a loved one through one or more senses. This type of occurrence is often visual, but may just be a sudden 'feeling', as if conveyed telepathically, or it may even come in the form of a vivid dream. Typically, this type of manifestation relays important information to the observer.

Residual hauntings or recordings
Some ghosts appear to be mere recordings on the environment in which they once existed. A Civil War soldier is seen on repeated occasions staring out of a window at a house where he once stood guard. A dead child's laughter is heard echoing in a hallway where she often played. There are even cases of ghost cars and trains that can still be heard and sometimes seen, even though they are long gone. These types of ghosts do not interact with or seem to be aware of the living. Their appearance and actions are always the same. They are like spirit-level recordings – residual energies – that replay over and over again.

Followers of this theory believe that a traumatic moment in time leaves an indelible impression on the building or area, replaying itself for eternity. This could be anything from a 'glimpse of the past' – a recreation of some traumatic or emotion-laden event – to footsteps up and down a hallway. Although most agree that these types of apparitions do appear to be 'recorded' somehow in the surroundings, there is disagreement on how exactly we as observers perceive these recordings. One side says that it is something within the observer that sets the recording in motion, and that the recording 'plays inside our heads'. The other side says that the recording is being played externally for all to see, but that only those with the right 'antenna' can experience it.

Thus, as frightening as this type of manifestation may be, the apparition is not a thinking entity, and it is no more of a threat to the observer than a character on a television show. This is all very intriguing but, even if it were true, vital questions still need to be answered, such as what causes these recordings to be made and how and why they are played back.

Naturally occurring electrical, magnetic or electromagnetic conditions

Some people believe that ghosts of the dead are the residual energy left behind by an emotionally strong person or event. More energy and electrical impulses are expended during periods of high trauma or excitement, and that energy can linger indefinitely.

Everything is composed of energy. Our thoughts, feelings, sensations, experiences, and indeed our very souls are all forms of energy. The theory is that when the physical body dies, this energy continues on in some form and can be tapped by living persons sensitive enough to perceive it. This may also be the energy that travels in out-of-body experience or near-death experiences or ghostly doubles of the living. Animals seem to be quite sensitive to this type of energy, and many very reliable reports of them avoiding certain rooms, chasing unseen prey, or sitting contentedly as if being stroked and petted have been recorded throughout history – another indication that this type of phenomenon is quite interactive.

Modern ghost hunters equip themselves with devices that locate and track energy sources. Many serious paranormal researchers believe that measurable properties such as electricity or magnetism play a part in why we experience ghostly encounters.

A number of different variations on this theme have been suggested to do with the 'feelings' reported by observers in the vicinity of paranormal phenomena. Feelings of 'magnetism' are often reported, as are sensations that the hair is 'standing on end', a common occurrence around fields of high electricity. Temperature fluctuations are often reported, as are vague feelings of the area being 'energised' by some unknown process.

Many different theories have been offered as to how naturally-occurring elements may interact to allow for paranormal phenomena. These include such exotic ones as ley lines emitting energy, natural geologic fault lines creating bursts of it, or some kind of natural vibration or earth harmonic.

One of the few things we do know for sure is that paranormal phenomena are more likely to be experienced at night, and there may be a scientific explanation for this. In short, the earth is covered by a fluctuating membrane that we all know as the atmosphere, which is constantly being bombarded by a strong solar wind from the sun. During the day, this membrane is at its thinnest and densest because it is being directly hit by the solar wind. However, at night, when sheltered from the sun, it expands much farther into space and has much less resistance. This explains why television and radio stations come in better at night, and why you can tune into stations much farther away than is possible during the day. Therefore, the reason we see more paranormal activity at night is because there is much less resistance to every kind of magnetic and electrical current or force, making it easier for energy-based manifestations to appear. Indeed, the best time to go on ghost hunts is widely believed to be between 9 p.m. and 3 a.m., with midnight being optimal. For these same reasons, since ancient times, total eclipses of the sun have been the source of many legends and tales of paranormal occurrences.

Messengers
These kinds of ghosts may be the most commonly reported and they are often linked to a strong belief in the existence of an afterlife and/or heaven, depending on religious conviction. These spirits usually appear shortly after their deaths to people close to them. They are aware of their deaths and can interact with the living. They most

often bring messages of comfort to their loved ones, to say that they are well and happy, and that there is no need to grieve for them. These ghosts appear briefly and usually only once. It is as if they deliberately return with their messages to help the living cope with their loss.

Poltergeists and psychokinesis

Many believe that poltergeists are proof of an afterlife or a non-physical world inhabited by ghosts. However, a poltergeist (German for noisy spirit) is not a ghost, because it is not an apparition of a dead human being. Although poltergeists are seen – very rarely – they are usually described as invisible spirits. They can be playful and mischievous, but also malicious, vicious and even dangerous. Sometimes ghosts and poltergeists are confused with one another as their activities are similar. For example, both like to make thumping and rapping noises, but in general poltergeists tend to be more aggressive and destructive in their behaviour.

Stories featuring poltergeists typically focus heavily on raps, thumps, knocks, footsteps, and bed-shaking, all without a discernible point of origin. Many accounts describe objects being thrown about the room, furniture being moved, and sometimes people being levitated. A few poltergeists have even been known to speak. Throwing or raining stones is an activity often associated with poltergeists. According to eyewitnesses, the stones start flying through the air suddenly and inexplicably, as if from nowhere, and cease just as abruptly.

Although poltergeist stories date back to the first century, most evidence to support the existence of poltergeists is anecdotal. The most famous poltergeist investigations include:

- The Drummer of Tedworth (1661)
- The Bell Witch (1817)
- The Haunting of the Fox sisters (1848), which started the Spiritualism movement
- The Borley Rectory phenomena (1929) (see Chapter Four)
- The Enfield Poltergeist (1977) (see Chapter Two)

Poltergeist activity tends to occur around a single person called an agent or a focus (typically a prepubescent female), and this has led to the hypothesis among parapsychologists that the 'poltergeist effect' is most likely caused by a person who is unknowingly using paranormal powers to produce the phenomena. This is sometimes referred to as repressed psychokinetic energy, or psychokinesis. According to some parapsychologists the 'poltergeist effect' is the outward manifestation of psychological trauma. In many cases poltergeist activity occurs in a house where there is a child just entering puberty. It has been suggested that if an adolescent is experiencing emotional and physical trauma, it might unconsciously display itself in the form of poltergeist activity. This is all fascinating, but overlooks the fact that many famous poltergeist cases do not involve children. Also, if it were true, wouldn't every household with a teenager harbour a poltergeist?

Sceptics believe that the phenomena are hoaxes perpetrated by the agent. Indeed, many poltergeist agents have been caught by investigators in the act of throwing objects. A few of them later confessed to faking. The longevity of and consistency between poltergeist stories ensure that the matter remains open for debate within the parapsychology community.

Another theory about poltergeists is the 'wrath theory'. When a person dies in a powerful rage, that person is believed by some to come back to take revenge. In some cases, the need is so strong that the ghost is unable to let go or forgive. It then becomes a poltergeist, capable of moving solid objects, sometimes to deadly effect.

According to yet another opinion, ghosts and poltergeists are 'recordings'. When there is a powerful emotion, sometimes at death and sometimes not, a recording is believed to be embedded into the fabric of time, and this recording will continue to play over and over again until the energy embedded disperses.

Projections

For those who do not believe in ghosts, hauntings are all in our minds. According to Freud, ghosts are a projection of our subconscious mind manifested by our fear of death and the unknown. Ghosts are psychological phenomena: we see them because we expect or want to see them. A grieving widow sees her dead husband because she needs to; she needs the comfort of knowing that he is all right and happy in the next world. Her mind produces the experience to help itself cope with the stress of the loss.

Since we know so little about the power and capacity of our own minds, it's possible that they can even produce physical manifestations, such as apparitions and noises – projections that even others may be able to see and hear. But they are not 'real' in any sense, just the conjurings of powerful imaginations.

Portals

The idea of a 'portal' or a 'doorway' to another dimension is not a new one. Many researchers believe that there are places all over the world that serve as 'doorways' from our world to another. These portals are thought to provide access for entities to enter our world. They may be the spirits of people who have lived before, or they could be something else altogether. Some researchers even believe that they could be otherworldly beings from another dimension.

One of the most common locations for these portals seems to be in cemeteries. As a rule, most cemeteries are not haunted, but recently ghost hunters have collected dozens of anomalous photographs taken in graveyards. An explanation offered for this is that cemeteries become haunted because they provide access for spirits, or entities, to pass from one world to the next.

Ghosts are actual beings living in one or more parallel dimensions

The concept of a parallel universe is a fairly complex one. To put it simply, this theory suggests that there are one or more (perhaps an infinite number) of complete universes co-existing with us on a plane we are generally not aware of. Picture a lot of soap bubbles all floating around in a room. Each soap bubble contains an entire unique universe, and although there are hundreds of bubbles in the air, each is independent of all the others. Occasionally, two bubbles will collide and stick together, creating a passageway between the two universes.

Any type of spectral appearance, sight, sound or anomaly can fit into the theory of parallel dimensions. Thus, when we see an apparition, especially one seemingly from another time and place, it could be that we getting a rare glimpse into another dimension or reality and we are seeing events develop in that plane of existence.

Another theory with a sci-fi theme suggests that ghosts might also be the result of time anomalies, if time is non-linear. An event that happened in the past might be seen briefly in our time because of fluctuations in time/space.

Inaccuracy and distortion of the truth
Those who do not believe in ghosts claim that ghost stories are nothing more than inaccurate distortions of the truth, and offer the following reasons:

• A legend that has been told so many times that it is accepted as truth. Urban legends such as the Vanishing Hitchhiker can fall into this category
• Deliberate distortion – because often the ghost story is more interesting (and more profitable if you're selling your story to the papers) than the truth

- The mind playing tricks on a person. Innocent objects and events are misinterpreted as ghostly phenomena
- Honest error due to illusion. For example, a shadow on the wall becomes a bogeyman, a white curtain fluttering in the moonlight becomes a ghost . . .
- A hoax or deliberate fraud. For example: the Cottingley Fairies (1917) and the Amityville Horror (1975–6)

Ghosts exist only as figments of our imaginations
This theory can be made to apply to every kind of paranormal manifestation there is, and in some cases it is probably at least partly correct. Medical studies have proved that when certain parts of the brain are stimulated, various perceptions are disturbed, such as visual, auditory and tactile functions. Various external stimuli such as very low-frequency sound waves and high fields of electricity can cause hallucinatory experiences that for the subject are indistinguishable from reality.

Indeed, schizophrenics often relate seeing, hearing and even talking to very real entities that nobody else can see or hear, but medical science has not thus far found the cause for this. Are they really seeing things that nobody else can see or hear? The consensus seems to be no – that it is 'all in their heads', owing to an unknown short circuit in the make-up of their brains – but nobody really knows for sure. Further study in this particular type of mental health disorder may eventually shed light on some areas of the paranormal. However, applying this theory to haunting experiences still leaves a lot of questions unanswered, such as how to explain it when more than one person sees the same phenomena. Sceptics use the term 'mass hysteria' for situations like this, but nobody has offered an explanation for the core catalyst causing many brains to suddenly go haywire.

Obviously, this theory needs a lot of work, but it will probably be among the first to be proved or disproved by science. Time will tell . . .

GHOSTS ARE HERE TO STAY

Although there have been plenty of theories for and against (some of which are more outlandish than the possibility that there is life after death!) we still can't give a categorical answer to the question – do ghosts exist?

The thousands upon thousands of documented experiences that people around the world have had since the beginning of recorded history bear witness to the fact that hauntings are a relatively common part of the human experience. Whether they exist or not, one could say, ghosts are here to stay, and ghost hunters will continue to investigate hauntings as long as they are reported. We've seen that in the overwhelming majority of cases a natural cause or a logical explanation can be found, but what about those rare cases that raise more questions than answers?

In the next three chapters we'll reopen the case files of three important and well reported hauntings which have never been satisfactorily explained. Sighs and whispers, footsteps, strange writing on the wall, missing objects, flying objects, unusual apparitions, stone throwing, levitations and possession – the three investigations that follow have it all.

Do you need proof? Read on. Maybe one of the case studies will make you change your mind.

2

THE ENFIELD POLTERGEIST

'Stones fall on to your kitchen floor, as if they had come through the ceiling. Somebody, or something, starts banging on the wall. Things disappear, and reappear somewhere else. Before long, you realise it can't be an earthquake, or Concorde, or mice. It must be something else – something entirely inexplicable and very frightening indeed.'

GUY LYON PLAYFAIR: THIS HOUSE IS HAUNTED (1980)

The case of the Enfield poltergeist – which ran from August 1977 to September 1978 – is regarded as one of the most amazing poltergeist cases ever investigated. It got massive press coverage at the time and was captured in detail by a writer we both know and admire, Guy Lyon Playfair, in the fascinating book entitled *This House is Haunted.*

If you were around at the time you may remember something of the case. For those of you who don't know the details of the story, and even for those who are familiar with it, let's reopen the Enfield files.

30 AUGUST 1977

In a semi-detached three-bedroom council house in Enfield, North London, Peggy Hodgson, a divorcee in her mid forties, puts two of her four children to bed. Peggy has two boys and two girls aged from seven to thirteen: Janet, Pete, Margaret and Billy.

A few hours later, Janet Hodgson (age eleven) and her younger brother Pete (age ten), who shares a bedroom with her, complain that their beds are 'jolting up and down and going all funny'. Mrs Hodgson goes into Janet and Pete's bedroom and sees no movement – as far as she is concerned her kids are messing about. She tells them to go to sleep and goes back downstairs.

31 AUGUST 1977

At 9.30 p.m. Janet and Pete tell their mum they can hear shuffling noises in their bedroom. Janet thinks it sounds like a chair being dragged along the floor. Mrs Hodgson takes the chair out of the bedroom, says goodnight to her kids and turns off the light; but as she does she too hears something shuffling across the floor. She immediately turns the light on to see the children in bed under their covers and the furniture as normal. Convinced she is imagining things, Peggy turns the light off once more. The shuffling noise starts up again.

Peggy, Janet and Peter hear four loud knocks on the partitioning wall of the house. Mrs Hodgson turns the light on and sees a heavy chest moving about eighteen inches across the floor, well beyond the children's reach.

When it stops she pushes it back against the wall, but as she turns away it moves once more to its former position. This time she finds she can't move the chest at all.

Shaking with fear, Mrs Hodgson tells her children to get out of bed and go downstairs with her. The neighbours' lights are on, so the Hodgsons, still in their night clothes, run next door for help. The neighbours, seeing the Hodgsons in obvious distress, search the house and garden but find nothing. Then they too hear inexplicable knocks on the walls. The neighbours are now scared and call the police.

At 11 p.m. the police arrive and hear the knocks too. One officer sees a chair moving across the floor. Later she confirms what she saw in writing:

Statement by Policewoman

Mr Grosse
Society for Psychical Research
1, Adam and Eve Mews
Kensington

On Thursday 1st September 1977 at approximately 1 am, I was on duty in my capacity as a policewoman, when I received a radio message to XXX, Green St, Enfield.

I went to this address where I found a number of people standing in the living room. I was told by the occupier of this house that strange things had been happening during the last few nights and that they believed that the house was haunted. Myself and another PC entered the living room of the house and the occupier switched off the lights.

Almost immediately I heard the sound of knocking on the wall that backs onto the next door neighbour's house. There were four distinct taps on the wall and then silence. About two minutes later I heard more tapping, but this time it was coming from a different wall, again it was a distinctive peal of four taps. The PC and the neighbours checked the walls, attic and pipes, but could find nothing to explain the knockings.

The PC and the neighbours all went into the kitchen to check the refrigerator pipes, etc., leaving the family and myself in the living room. The lights in the living room were switched off again and within a few minutes the eldest son pointed to a chair which was standing next to the sofa. I looked at the chair and noticed that it was wobbling slightly from side to side, I then saw the chair slide across the floor towards the kitchen wall. It moved approximately 3-4 feet and then came to rest.

At no time did it appear to leave the floor. I checked the chair but could find nothing to explain how it had moved. The lights were switched back on. Nothing else happened that night although we have later reports of disturbances at this address.

Carolyn Heeps

THE NEXT FIVE DAYS AND NIGHTS

The strange events continue. Small plastic bricks and marbles fly around the house, and when picked up they are hot to touch. The police, a local vicar and a local medium get involved but no one can stop it.

The Hodgsons decide to contact the *Daily Mirror*, who send a reporter, Douglas Bence, and a photographer, Graham Morris, to visit the house. Nothing happens when the reporters arrive, but just as they are about to drive off, the 'flying bricks' promptly resume.

Bence and Morris rush back in and a toy Lego brick flies across the room, hitting Morris on the forehead as he takes a picture. (Later, when Morris develops the negative, he notices an inexplicable hole in it and the flying brick is nowhere to be seen.)

Statement by Graham Morris (Photographer)

I saw the 'Lego' pieces flying about, and I was hit on the head by a piece while I was attempting to photograph it in flight. I had a bump on my forehead after the incident.

Statement by Douglas Bence: I was hit by a 'flying piece of Lego'.

Statement by David Thorpe and Douglas Bence (newspaper photographer and reporter) on the events at 2.10 am Wednesday 7 Sept. Statement taken at 2.55 am.

We were standing back from the door on the landing
and were looking into the bedroom at the books on
the mantelpiece. There were three books and the
middle book had been found twice before on the
floor. The girl Janet became restless in bed and
the restlessness seemed to preface the
manifestation we were trying to witness. While
looking at the book we heard a bang and David saw
the chair in a toppling movement and it moved
about 4 feet from its original position. Mrs.
Hodgson in the next room was also restless at this
time. Mr. Grosse immediately examined the girl
and said he found her in a deep sleep. We then all
went downstairs.

5 SEPTEMBER 1977

Senior reporter George Fallows is so impressed by his
colleagues' experience that he follows up the story himself. He suggests that the Hodgsons call in the SPR
(Society for Psychical Research) which in turn contacts
Maurice Grosse, a member and resident of North London. Grosse arrives at the house, a week after the
disturbances began. For the next few days nothing out
of the ordinary occurs.

8 SEPTEMBER 1977

Around 2 a.m. Grosse and Morris hear a crash in Janet's
bedroom. They rush in and find her bedside chair lying on

its side about four feet from where it should be. Janet says she was asleep and didn't see the chair move.

At around 3 a.m. the chair moves again, but this time Morris is ready and captures the event on film. Grosse sees doors open and close by themselves and feels a sudden breeze move up from his feet to his head.

Thursday 8th September (Wednesday night)

1.15 am:
Janet was sleeping in room on her own. Myself (M.
Grosse), G. Fallows, D. Bence, D. Thorpe were
downstairs in the living room. I had been keeping
watch in Janet's room for about an hour with no
results and we had all withdrawn downstairs.
There was a bang and I quickly ran upstairs
followed by the others. Janet was in bed
distressed and crying. She had used the pail at
the end of the bed and as she got back in bed the
book flew off the mantelpiece and landed on the
floor by the door. The book was replaced, and Mr.
Grosse sat with her until she went to sleep and
went downstairs.

1.45 am:
There was another bang – I rushed upstairs
immediately and found the same book in
approximately the same position – about four feet
from the mantelpiece. I examined Janet and
considered her to be fast asleep. She was
securely tucked up in bed. As at that time I

considered that I may be inhibiting the phenomena
by staying in the room, I told Douglas Bence and
David Thorpe to stay at the door of the bedroom
and try to get a photograph of any action. I went
downstairs and sat with G. Fallows.

2.10 am:
There was a loud bang and I rushed upstairs
followed by Fallows. Messrs Bence and Thorpe were
standing at the door of Janet's bedroom. Mr.
Thorpe had just managed to photograph the
movement of a chair. The chair between the beds
had been thrown forwards 4 feet onto its face.
Messrs Bence and Thorpe reported that before the
incident both Mrs. Hodgson in the next room and
Janet had been restless. (Mrs. Hodgson said the
next day that she had heard the bang. At the time
she had a very bad headache, and this went almost
immediately after the bang). I again examined
Janet and considered her to be in a deep sleep. I
replaced the chair. The reporters went
downstairs and I stayed in the room for about
another 15 minutes and then went downstairs.

2.45 am:
There was another loud bang. I again rushed up the
stairs and found the chair again about four feet
from where I had placed it. This time I noticed
that the front right leg had been bent. I called
Mr. Fallows who went over to examine Janet whilst
I watched them. He found her to be in deep sleep

(he used the word 'unconscious'). He lifted her
hand, then let it go (it appeared to 'flop' – his
words), and he gently pushed her head to one side
and found no resistance whatsoever. From her
sleeping position and posture I felt that she
could have been in a trance-like state (her mouth
was open and her breathing very shallow). She was
securely tucked up in bed.

10 SEPTEMBER 1977

The Enfield case makes the front page of the *Daily Mirror*.
Grosse, Mrs Hodgson and her neighbour take part in a two
and a half hour *NightLine* programme for LBC radio.

THE FOLLOWING DAYS, WEEKS AND MONTHS

Statement by Graham Morris, photographer

On the night of September 13th, 1977, while
setting up my camera equipment in XXX Green
Street, Enfield, in the hope of recording the
movement of objects in the back bedroom, three of
my electronic flashguns developed faults
simultaneously, after being switched on and
charging in the normal manner elsewhere in the
house. As soon as they were set up in the bedroom,
they started to drain themselves of power, thus
deadening the cells and rendering them
unserviceable.

The equipment, two VIVITAR 292 and one ROLLEI E
36 RE units, had been in my possession for more
than two years and none had ever given trouble.
They are generally considered to be foolproof,
the Rollei (costing £130) being one of finest
flashguns available. After leaving the house,
all three resumed normal functioning. I am unable
to explain this episode.

Date: 27/11/77
Signed: Graham Morris

The strange phenomena continue. Electrical systems in the house don't seem to operate: as soon as camera flashes are recharged they are quickly drained of power, infra-red television cameras set to do remote monitoring of the bedroom fail to operate. BBC Radio reporters' tapes are damaged, with the recordings erased or the metal inside some of the machines bent.

Grosse is joined in the investigation by writer Guy Lyon Playfair, who is a highly experienced observer of poltergeist activities in Brazil.

In the days, weeks and months that follow, the knocking on walls and floors becomes an almost nightly occurrence. In addition, furniture slides across the floor and is thrown down the stairs, drawers are wrenched out of dressing tables, toys and other objects fly across the room, bedclothes are pulled off, water is found in mysterious puddles on the floors, there are outbreaks of fire followed by inexplicable extinguishing, and curtains blow and twist as if in the wind when all windows and doors are closed.

There are even accounts of human levitation – Janet says she is picked up and flung about her room by an unseen entity (and her levitation is witnessed by neighbours passing by who look up into the girls' bedroom). She says that sometimes the curtain beside her bed twists several times in a tight spiral and attempts to wrap itself around her neck as if trying to strangle her. This is backed up by her mother, who says she has seen it happen.

A harsh male voice is heard – coming from Janet's throat. Janet says she has no control over the voice, and is often in a 'trance-like' state when the voice occurs. The voice claims to be several different people, and often uses obscene language. There is one character, however, who keeps reappearing. This is 'Bill', who says he died in the house.

Grosse suggests that the source of the poltergeist activity may have intelligence of some kind, since it can rap out answers to simple questions – one rap for no, and three for yes. During one session, Grosse asks how many years ago the supposed entity had lived in the house – and 53 raps follow.

The following are inexplicable events personally experienced by me (Maurice Grosse).
All experiences have taken place in good lighting conditions.

1) I have clearly seen glass marbles and plastic pieces in high speed transit with unusual

trajectory. These objects appear to emanate from walls and windows at heights varying from five to seven feet. They always fell to the floor without bouncing.

2) While I was sitting in the kitchen one evening writing up my notes, an aluminium teapot standing on the kitchen top near the gas stove started to vibrate violently and jump up and down on the kitchen top. I was alone in the room at the time.

3) A table lamp placed on the floor at the foot of a bed completely out of reach of any person and clearly in my sight tilted its shade at an angle of 45 degrees and a few seconds later moved back again to the vertical position.

4) The toilet door opened and closed on its own a number of times. Each time nobody else has been in the vicinity and no draughts have been apparent.

5) A cardboard box 2 ft x 1 ft x 1 ft 6 in with cushions and a soft toy inside it was thrown at me whilst I was communicating with the 'entity' by knocking. This happened in the bedroom and the family were in bed at the time and under observation.

6) I was standing in the bedroom, holding the door open and facing into the room. A slipper flew at me from the far side of the room and hit the door by my head.

7) A certificate in a plastic frame was pulled off the wall directly behind my head. The family were in bed at the time, and the nearest member of the family was eight feet away from the wall. There was nobody else in the room at the time.

8) The carpet in the bedroom was continuously pulled up at the edge to form an identical shape each time. I have been unable to repeat this pattern myself.

9) I was standing in the living room in front of the settee about one foot away from it. There were eight or nine people in the room at the time, most of them standing. Nobody was sitting on the settee. Suddenly the settee flew up vertically to a height of about four feet and turned over backwards, falling to the floor upside down.

10) I saw Janet levitated out of an armchair and deposited in the middle of the room complete with the cushion she was sitting on. She levitated up in a sitting position and moved forward in that position approximately four feet. I was sitting facing her across the room at the time, and was just about to talk to her when it happened.

11) I saw Mr. Burcombe – the uncle – pulled out of his chair and whirled around 180 degrees before falling to the floor. The whirling motion was remarkably fast and this episode happened in the house.

12) The doors on the kitchen wall units have been seen to slide back and forth on their own.

13) Tubular door chimes fixed on the living room wall were seen to swing from side to side. This happened many times.

14) A paper handkerchief settled on top of my head when I was standing in the bedroom. It settled very slowly and gently on my head.

15) Many times while sitting either in the kitchen or the living room I have heard distinct sounds resembling footsteps walking across the bedroom floors. Nobody was upstairs at the time.

16) Mrs. Nottingham (Mrs N was the next door neighbour involved since the first night) and myself were unable to pull Margaret down the stairs while she claimed she was being held fast by the ankle with one leg in the air. She was standing on one leg at the time and she was not holding on to anything. Only after we twisted her around was she released.

17) Penny and twopenny pieces have dropped on to the floor next to me, both in Mrs. Hodgson's house and in Mr. Burcombe's house. They appeared to drop straight down. There was no bounce. They were not thrown.

In addition to these events, I have experienced a considerable amount of 'knocking phenomena' which has been accompanied by very strong vibrations on the walls and floors. I have also heard very loud bangs coming from the radiators not explicable in terms of the usual water system noises.

I have been present when a number of events have happened behind my back or not directly in my view that in my opinion were not physically caused by any person present. This includes water and fire episodes.

THE INVESTIGATION CONTINUES

Janet spends six weeks in Maudsley Hospital, in South London, where she is tested for any signs of physical or mental abnormality. None are found, and during her hospital stay the poltergeist activity ceases at Enfield, only to resume on her return.

Professor Hasted, head of physics at Birkbeck College, University of London, conducts experiments on Janet to determine any changes in body weight that might occur during levitation. The results are inconclusive: 'The J.H. data show two sudden five-second weight-increase signals of about one kg and a minute gradual weight increase which eventually returns to normal. We can find no explanation of these data in physical terms.'

The SPR sends in two more researchers: Anita Gregory and John Beloff. Gregory is highly sceptical and convinced that the voices are the muffled voices of Janet and her thirteen-year-old sister, Margaret, covering their mouths with their bedsheets or averting their faces while producing this 'phenomenon'.

During her visit, Gregory 'catches' Janet cheating – a video camera is set up in a room next door to Janet's and it records her bending spoons and bouncing up and down on her bed. Janet admits to having done this, claiming, according to Gregory, that 'she wanted to see if the investigators would catch her – they always did.'

Janet's uncle, John Burcombe, talks to Gregory about Janet. He is convinced that Janet has taught herself to talk in a deep voice, as he knows her to be a mischievous child, who enjoys misleading strangers. He also tells Gregory that Janet is an athletic girl who could easily jump from her bed to the floor to make it seem as if she is being 'thrown' by the 'entity'.

Gregory declares that she has seen no genuine paranormal activity during her investigation. When it does occur she says she is always made to face the door and can hear the children giggling when objects were thrown. In contrast to Grosse, who believes paranormal activity is present, Gregory is convinced that all the activity is due to Janet's trickery, possibly with the assistance of her mother.

After sixteen months, the events finally subside and the Hodgson family continue living their normal lives.

WERE THESE GENUINE PHENOMENA?

The case was thoroughly researched by the Society for Psychical Research, in particular by Maurice Grosse, who gathered much evidence in support of paranormal activity over those months. By contrast the two other reporters from the SPR, Gregory and Beloff, declared it all to be trickery. Since the event, however, in personal communication with Maurice Grosse, Beloff has stated that following his detailed re-examination of the case he has changed his mind about his earlier conclusions.

SO WHO ARE WE TO BELIEVE?

The video evidence produced by Gregory clearly suggests fraud, but what about the numerous witness reports from a number of different people with different backgrounds and different religious beliefs, including sceptics? Police officers, politicians, psychologists, psychiatrists, journalists and social workers all reported the poltergeist activities. Could these people have been so easily deceived?

Oct. 23rd events sworn by 10 witnesses

This statement was prepared by Mr. Maurice Grosse, investigator in charge of enquiries into the events taking place at Green St, Enfield. The enquiry has been designated 'The Green Street Poltergeist Investigation'.

We, the undersigned, declare that the following statement on the events that took place at Green Street, Enfield on the night of Sunday October 23rd 1977 is true, and if required to do so are prepared to swear to this statement under oath.

STATEMENT

The family Hodgson retired to bed at approximately 9.30 pm in the front bedroom. Mrs. M. Hodgson, Margaret and Janet were together in the double bed, with Mrs. Hodgson on the right, Janet on the left, and Margaret in the middle. Billy was in the single camp bed on the right of the double bed.

After a series of events involving the throwing of plimsolls, a slipper and the front of a dolls house, together with the pulling of a plug attached to the bedside lamp from the power socket, knocking was heard coming from the front bedroom. It appeared to come from the floor.

Mr. Grosse said he would try and communicate with 'whatever was causing the knocking' by a code, one knock for 'No' and two for 'Yes'. He knelt on the floor by the top of the camp bed, and in answer to his verbal questions distinct knocks, both loud and soft, were heard in this code, although some knocks exceeded two in number. We were unable to give any physical explanation whatsoever to the knocking. A strong vibration in the floor and walls could be distinctly felt during the knocking.

Mr. Nottingham and Mr. Burcombe examined the house thoroughly while some of the knocking was taking place but they could find no agency to serve as an explanation. Most of the knocking could be distinctly heard in the vicinity of the

double bed although it often came from different
positions on the floor.

Mr. J. Burcombe - Mr. V. Nottingham - Mrs. S.
Burcombe - Mrs. P. Nottingham - Denise Burcombe -
Mrs. M. Hodgson - Paul Burcombe - Margaret
Hodgson - Mr. M. Grosse - Janet Hodgson

Sceptics argue that all these people could have been deceived and, because the Hodgsons went to the newspapers in the very beginning, the whole thing was without doubt a money-spinning hoax. This is an accusation the Hodgsons vigorously denied and have continued to deny to this day.

It was also claimed that Mrs Hodgson was trying to get to the top of the housing queue, as it was not uncommon for council tenants to create 'haunted houses' if they were unhappy with their accommodation. This could well be true for some, but is not the case with the Hodgson family as the mother was still living at the same address over 25 years later. If her motivation was to effect a move, it was spectacularly unsuccessful. (According to Playfair, one of the first questions Mrs Hodgson was asked was if she wanted to move and she said 'No way'.)

Another theory is that Maurice Grosse, who had lost his young daughter in a car accident only a year earlier, was too willing to believe in the paranormal. Again this is unlikely, as Grosse is a highly experienced paranormal researcher who was and is fully aware of the theory that the mind may be able to trick a person into belief in the paranormal. In his own words the projection theory 'fails to account for all the allied phenomena that surrounds the physical activity'. It also doesn't explain how other people can witness the same events.

If this was indeed a case of the mind's ability to conjure up images and hallucinations, then it was an example of hallucination on a massive scale which in itself is remark-able. Either that or young Janet was a veritable magician producing special effects and psychological trickery to rival Derren Brown!

And none of this explains why the phenomena suddenly stopped.

THE POLTERGEIST FACTOR

What other reason can be put forward for the Hodgsons putting up with having their lives disrupted for over a year, their household invaded by investigators, psychiatrists and mediums?
We mentioned poltergeists in Chapter One, and Enfield is considered to be a classic example of poltergeist activity. It fits three significant criteria for this kind of phenomenon:

1. a family group that includes a child entering or in puberty
2. a family suffering poverty and disharmony at the time: Mrs Hodgson was recently divorced and funds were limited
3. a council house: statistically these are more likely to experience poltergeist activity

For paranormal researchers this case is a rare find, and we only wish we had been around to investigate it ourselves. All we can do now is look at the evidence nearly thirty years on and see how it stands up under the scrutiny of present-day methods of investigation.

The record taking and witness statements taken are detailed and thorough. There were also about six hundred pages of tape transcripts from about two hundred tapes. Every attempt has been made by the investigators to remain objective and calm and to report the facts.

One of several pictures of Janet flying through the air. Here Janet looks elated rather than frightened. Janet's bedroom was made famous by these photographs and others showing objects being thrown around in the air. The pictures on her wall are easy to date as there is a large picture of the then teenage heart throb David Soul on the wall in his role in the 70s series Starsky and Hutch.

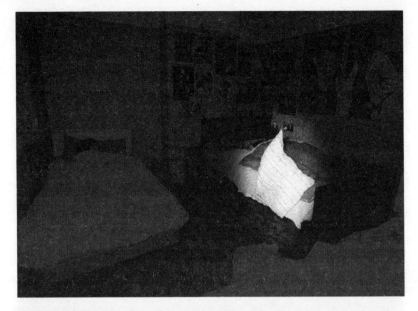

Here we have an interesting sequence of shots. In the first photo the pillow is facing towards the camera. In the next photo the pillow has doubled up and is going in the opposite direction.

*In the third photo the pillow has again reversed direction, and
in the last it is on the floor. So in fact the pillow is doing
a zig-zag motion, and that's physically impossible.*

The photographic evidence remains compelling. During the investigation two automatic cameras were set up in the room, and were controlled by a button outside the room, so if the investigators heard anything happening in the bedroom they could start the cameras going. The cameras were set to flash at half-second intervals and some very interesting episodes were captured.

The voice recordings are just as extraordinary. Without a doubt the tapes of the interviews with 'Bill' through Janet – who was just eleven at the time – are among the scariest things we have ever heard. But are they genuine?

During the investigation psychiatrists and local doctors were brought in to see whether 'Bill' was Janet being mischievous, or whether a second personality was developing, or whether perhaps there was indeed a paranormal 'entity'. Speech therapists suspected that the voice was not coming from Janet's usual vocal chord equipment but was made by the second set of vocal chords that all people have. Actors can be trained to speak using these 'false chords' to produce a deep, gravelly voice, but it can be a painful process. Their theory was backed up by a recording of 'the voice' on a laryngograph (which registers patterns made by frequency waves as they pass through the larynx). However, to keep up this 'gravelly' voice for hours on end would naturally have had consequences on Janet's normal voice. Yet for some unknown reason Janet's voice did not seem to be affected.

What about the video? Isn't that proof positive that Janet was a fraud? Yes and no. Some of the activity reported would be very hard, if not impossible to fake, and it's been suggested that the case most likely began with genuine phenomena, but soon began to include trickery. Why? As the media demanded paranormal activity, eleven-year-old Janet and thirteen-year-old Margaret were not going to allow them to go away disappointed, and revelled in the attention. All children enjoy play-acting and it would have highly unusual if the girls hadn't played a few tricks now and again.

ALL ABOUT JANET

Those who aren't convinced have consistently argued for one of two explanations for the Enfield poltergeist. One is fraud, and the other is the psychic force of the medium – the agent at the centre of the disturbance, which in this case was Janet.

Professor William Roll (b. 1926), a director of the Psychical Research Foundation in Durham, North Carolina, has suggested that poltergeist activity is due not to a disturbed entity in the afterlife but to the extreme sexual frustration and anger of a teenager during the years around puberty. And it is this suppressed energy which 'externalises' all the poltergeist phenomena. This theory is interesting but it cannot explain:

- the voices of older persons being heard
- very heavy furniture being lifted
- poltergeist stone throwing, objects flying or levitation
- verbal or code responses by the poltergeist to questions and commands

- some poltergeist utterings being disgustingly filthy and obscene
- no poltergeist activity occurring in the overwhelming majority of houses inhabited by adolescents reaching puberty
- poltergeist activity occurring where no adolescents reside.

It's been suggested that the girls in the Hodgson family, in particular Janet, had excess energy associated with puberty which caused the poltergeist problem. But this does not explain the specific incidents as explained above and numerous other cases of poltergeist activity all over the world that don't involve teenagers. And if the energy by young girls at puberty is the cause of poltergeist activity, then wouldn't households the world over where early teenagers reside be pestered by poltergeist activity?

Reviewing the evidence thirty years on and the arguments put forward by sceptics, we have yet to find a satisfying explanation. Those who deny the existence of poltergeists (or who claim that the disturbances are caused by an unknown force or by fraud) have so far been unable to give a logical, rational and scientifically objective alternative explanation for the phenomena.

THE HUTCHISON EFFECT

We couldn't conclude this chapter without mentioning one intriguing explanation that has been put forward to explain the Enfield enigma: the Hutchison effect.

In the early 1980s a Canadian physicist called Hutchison created from a range of equipment in his workshop a machine that generated large opposing electrical and magnetic fields. When the machine was up and running it amazed the Canadian by exerting strange effects over a random selection of objects placed nearby. Cups were seen to levitate, logs of wood stood on end by themselves, and yogurt slurped out of a pot. Even fairly large metal objects were able to move or were bent by a seemingly invisible force.

All this seems very sci-fi but it has been captured for all to see on video. Spontaneous fires break out and extinguish themselves, and sparks and flashes of light appear and disappear. What Hutchison seems to have achieved with his machine was the recreation of many aspects of poltergeist activity simply by using the forces of electricity and magnetism in a previously uncombined form.

Some studies suggest that the hidden environmental hazards of electricity pylons, microwaves, televisions, mobiles and computers may have a negative effect on a person's health, causing problems such as migraines, thyroid disorders and even cancer. Some who subscribe to Hutchison's theory take this one step further by suggesting that certain people can become hypersensitive to the constant bombardment and this exerts a peculiar effect on their body and on the electrical goods around them. Somehow their body stores up electricity like a human battery and then at times of stress discharges it all in a flash. This overloads the electrical appliance, computer or television and causes it to explode.

Could the Hutchison effect have played a part in the events of 1977 to 1978? Mrs Hodgson continued to live in the house but until her death a few years ago her life was plagued by illness. She also lost a son to cancer. Despite Janet being the focus of the investigation it's Mrs Hodgson who seems to have suffered the most from the public ordeal played out in front of the world's press. Photographs of her taken at the time show someone who looks exhausted, strained and bemused by it all.

Could all this hint at possible environmental factors operating in the house and the vicinity? It could be anything from high local electromagnetic fields to chemical or gas pollution or even seismic activity. Such environmental factors have been implicated in hauntings and as a cause of long-term disease and poor health. It's important to point out here that no such trouble was ever reported in the house next door (they were semi-detached) which there should have been if environmental factors were involved. But did Mrs Hodgson or Janet become hypersensitive?

Of course, all of this has not been scientifically proved, but as paranormal researchers we find the theory that certain hypersensitive people can create poltergeist activity almost as intriguing as the possibility of poltergeist activity. Although it doesn't explain why the phenomenon stopped so suddenly, it seems that the Hutchinson effect might suggest a whole new approach to the investigation of the Enfield enigma.

OUR CONCLUSIONS

'As far as I'm personally concerned the aim was to produce the facts about the case and I think that's what I've done over the last 30 years. I'm not a theoretical man, I'm not putting forward theory about the case. What is certain is that the facts are what makes this most interesting. I present the facts, people read them and they can make up their own minds.'

'Another vivid memory – the fact that all the time I was there they all slept in the same room with the light on at night. This is not consistent with any kind of trickery.'

MAURICE GROSSE, 2005

Whatever way you look at the Enfield enigma, it's both unique and remarkable. If the case is judged as an example of the power of the human mind to conjure up images, it is an amazing example of hallucination on a grand scale that fooled a remarkable number of people. If Janet and her family were frauds, they produced special effects the like of which has not been seen before or since. And their motivation certainly wasn't money. Two newspapers tried to bribe confessions of fraud out of the girls but failed despite offering huge sums of money.

From the point of view of the paranormal investigator the case is spectacular because it exhibits the whole gamut of reported poltergeist activity. Also, because the activity took place over at least a sixteen-month period, it offered investigators the unprecedented opportunity to test it rigorously at their leisure.

From a historical perspective Enfield represents a true

milestone in the history of hauntings and paranormal investigation. The case captured the world's attention, and the subsequent investigation was carried out in the unprecedented glare of the media spotlight. Everybody was talking or thinking about it! And some of us have hardly stopped talking or thinking about it since!

It also highlighted a fact (often forgotten by writers and movie makers) that hauntings are just as common to council houses and just as likely to happen to ordinary people as they are to stately homes, ancient castles and lords and ladies.

Despite the nay-sayers and Janet's little sideshow, can we be really certain that nothing paranormal happened in the Hodgson household? The impartial photos, the detailed statements, witness statements and remarkable evidence still stand and make this 1977 case one of the best demonstrations of paranormal influence in a normal family's life.

3

THE CARDIFF POLTERGEIST

'Ideas, like ghosts, must be spoken to a little before they will explain themselves.'

CHARLES DICKENS

Why and how (and if) poltergeist activity occurs has been debated by experts and scientists for decades.

As we've mentioned earlier poltergeists are so-called 'noisy spirits' believed to haunt individuals or families, not the houses they live in. Usually, the activity that accompanies a poltergeist haunting focuses on the presence of one particular individual, who is always around when the haunting takes place. Reports indicate that poltergeists seem to enjoy causing mischief, and even causing harm. They make loud noises and move objects. They may hurl vases from mantels or move heavy pieces of furniture in front of astonished observers. They may throw dirt or stones or create foul smells. Unexplained lights may been seen and footsteps heard.

Hundreds of independent studies have been done on poltergeists. A majority of the cases revolve around an individual or 'agent', as they are called. The phenomenon seems to be linked to a type of subconscious psychokinesis

(PK) on the part of the agent. (Psychokinesis, as you may recall, is the process of consciously or unconsciously moving or otherwise affecting physical objects by the mind only, without making any physical contact – think Uri Geller and spoons.) The studies have discovered that most of the poltergeist agents are girls under the age of twenty who are totally unaware that they are involuntarily directing the poltergeist energy.

While still not much is known about the power of mind over matter, the investigations have uncovered a link between the agents and states of poor mental or physical health. Emotional problems associated with agent personalities often include anxiety, hysteria, anger, obsessions, phobias and schizophrenia. In some cases with psychological help to relieve the emotional tensions the poltergeist energies diminish and disappear.

It should be pointed out, however, that while a majority of poltergeist cases revolve around unstable human agents, typically female children or adolescents, there are cases where all of the people involved are psychologically stable. There are cases where there are no young people and no obvious adult mischief-makers. There are cases when the poltergeist doesn't injure or hurt or terrify. These cases remain a mystery.

In this chapter we'll travel back in time, to June 1979, to take a look at one such mystery. As you'll see the Cardiff Poltergeist case is untypical in almost every aspect. It's not as famous as Enfield but it's just as remarkable and makes for an interesting comparison.

JUNE, 1979

John Matthews, the proprietor of a lawn mower repair workshop and adjoining garden accessories shop, contacts the Society of Psychical Research (SPR) with reports of inexplicable disturbances. Matthews tells the SPR he is genuinely concerned that these disturbances, which involve stone throwing and the inexplicable movement of objects, could not only frighten away potential customers but actually cause an injury.

Matthews asks for advice and help as the activity had been going on for several months now and he is anxious about it. He explains that he has no knowledge or experience of this kind of thing and that it was his local priest who suggested that a poltergeist might be responsible.

The SPR appoints paranormal investigator David Fontana to investigate the workshop and make a report.

Fontana phones Matthews, who invites him to visit the workshop. Matthews instructs Fontana to enter via the garden accessories shop (which is directly in front of the workshop with two connecting doors between the two rooms) or to go round the building to the workshops door that opens on to the yard at the back. Matthews arranges to visit on an afternoon when the shop will be closed but gives no indication of the time he will arrive.

On the scheduled day Fontana walks round the side of the premises (which is a small end-of-terrace building dating back to the end of the nineteenth century) to the workshop. He knows his approach can't be seen by anyone in the workshop as there are no windows between him and the workshop. As Fontana enters the workshop – where John Matthews and a visiting salesman are seated opposite each other on low boxes with their hands on their knees – a small stone hits the machinery on the floor near Matthews' feet with a loud 'pinging' sound.

Matthews isn't in the least surprised by the missile and says calmly to Fontana, 'There you are, he's welcoming you.'

WE'D LIKE YOU TO MEET PETE!

The two men tell Fontana that although they were initially sceptical they have seen enough happen in the workshop to convince them that some force or other, inexplicable by normal means, is behind it all. They have nicknamed this force 'Pete'.

According to Matthews some months previously Pete first made his presence felt by throwing large stones on to the roof of a shed at the back in which John and one of his workmen were watching a rugby match on television on a quiet Saturday afternoon. Since then the stone throwing has become so frequent and so persistent that the police have even been called in to catch suspected young culprits, but at no time have they found anyone who might be responsible.

Matthews goes on to tell Fontana that strange things have also occurred inside the workshop. Coins, bolts and small stones have been thrown against the walls or found littering the floor of the workshop when he arrives in the morning. Objects of unknown origin such as pens, keys, old pennies dating from 1912 seem to fall from the ceiling or appear mysteriously on the work surfaces. Tools on racks swing with no apparent cause, a blue case has been thrown violently around the room, and planks of wood, far too heavy to be thrown by hand, have been hurled through the open door of the workshop. Matthews' wife, Pat, has had stones thrown at the door while she was in the toilet at the back of the workshop, dust has been thrown down Matthews' collar, and loud knocks on the windows have often been heard when no one has been visible outside. And most frequent of all is the movement of small floats used in the carburettors of the lawnmowers under repair.

Sometimes these events occur when Matthews is alone in the workshop, but they also occur when he and others are present or when he is absent. Matthews believes Pete has tried to be helpful on some occasions by laying cutlery on the table for breakfast in the morning.

Inexplicable events have also begun to occur in the home of two other people closely involved in the case: Paul and Yvonne, the brother and sister-in-law of John's wife Pat.

MEET THE WITNESSES

In the days that follow Fontana interviews John, Pat, Paul (Pat's brother) Yvonne (Paul's wife) and Michael (a business associate of John's who works with him in the workshop). Paul has recently taken early retirement from his plumbing business, and Yvonne often helps out at the workshop and retail shop. All five say they have witnessed many of the events described by Matthews, and their accounts tally. All five strike Fontana as respectable, responsible, practical, honest and unpretentious, middle-aged people. With the exception of Paul, who had one inexplicable encounter in an apparently haunted house, none has had any previous paranormal encounters. All seem mystified by what they have seen and eager for an explanation.

Fontana also interviews Matthews' daughter, a psychiatric nurse, who has witnessed some of the events and who, after initial doubt, is now fully convinced of their genuineness.

LET THE CHALLENGE BEGIN

One of the most persistent occurrences reported to Fontana by the above witnesses concerns the small carburettor floats. The floats measure about two centimetres long and two centimetres across and have a sharp needle end. Time and time again these floats are discovered out of position when John unlocks the workshop in the morning. John tells Fontana that on one occasion he left a float on the top of an unlit gas heater and challenged it to be moved. On his way home Paul felt something prick his palm and on opening it discovered it to be the float. John and Paul returned to the workshop to find no float on the top of the heater.

John is emphatic that Paul did not pick up the float on leaving. Unfortunately there is no way for Fontana to prove that this happened. If it had been an isolated incident he might have been inclined to suspect that Paul had unwittingly picked it up or that John had somehow slipped it into his pocket, but in the light of all the other strange events and the integrity of the witnesses he is less sure.

John also tells Fontana that on another occasion after a day of apparent stone throwing he lost patience. Convinced that some of his employees were fooling around, he asked them to join him in the retail shop after closing time and sit with their hands flat on the counter while they checked to see whether the sounds of stone throwing would continue. The sounds did continue, and one of the employees suggested that they ask whatever was responsible for the disturbances to bring 'named tools' from the workshop into the retail shop. According to John, every time they challenged Pete to bring a tool it arrived, seemingly falling from the ceiling and materialising on the way down. So swiftly were the tools produced that John was finally convinced of the genuineness of the phenomena.

In the months that follow Fontana also witnesses some of the strange happenings that Matthews and other family members have described to him.

One day John tells Fontana that, irritated by the stone throwing, he picked up a small stone and threw it some twenty feet away into the far corner of the workshop where most of the phenomena seemed to originate. In seconds the stone appeared to return from the same corner and strike the wall near him. He repeated the action – with the same result. The next day Fontana has a go:

```
I tried my own hand at stone throwing, again from
twenty feet away and aiming into the same corner
of the workshop, and to my surprise a stone was
returned, hitting the wall behind me. I tried
```

```
again with the same result. Over the following
days and weeks John, Pat and I spent much time in
the stone throwing game. Sometimes we got
results, sometimes we were ignored. Nothing
happened if we threw stones elsewhere in the
workshop. Only one corner, which we named the
active corner, prompted a response.
```

According to Fontana and the other witnesses the stone in flight is never seen but can be heard striking the wall with a ping and clattering to the floor. (The invisibility of objects in flight has been often reported in poltergeist cases.)

The stone throwing with an unseen partner convinces Fontana that he is witnessing paranormal phenomena. It seems clear to him that Pete is aware of the stone throwing and willing to join in. Pete also seems to show that he's aware of expressions of anger towards him by initiating a more active stone throwing when the person throwing the stones is upset or angry.

FONTANA SUSPENDS HIS DISBELIEF

Although Fontana eventually came to believe that Pete was genuine, he was not easily convinced. In his book *Is there an Afterlife?* (O Books, 2005) he describes his struggle with what he calls 'morning after scepticism'.

According to Fontana, when investigating at Cardiff he would witness the phenomena and leave that day convinced of its genuineness, but overnight his rational mind would try to convince him that such things simply couldn't happen. Over the next few days his doubts would multiply as he convinced himself again and again that there must be some kind of rational explanation. However, once Fontana had ensured that reasonable precautions had been taken against fraud, poor observation, mistaken inference or other natural explanations, he gradually learned to lay his morning after scepticism to rest.

For the most part the stones returned by Pete did not appear to be the same ones that had been thrown, lessening the possibility that the stones were simply bouncing back. Fontana also conducted experiments on days when no stone throwing occurred, to see if he could make them bounce back, but this proved to be impossible. He also always observed the hands of John and other witnesses present to ensure that they were not faking matters.

Final confirmation that John and Pat were not frauds came to Fontana when they went on holiday. During their absence Fontana called unannounced at the workshop and spoke to Michael, who told him that no poltergeist activity had taken place that day. Michael believed that it required the energies of two people to enable anything paranormal to occur, and sure enough when Fontana started throwing stones, returned stones appeared straight away. This seemed to confirm Michael's theory, but when Michael left the room Fontana experimented by himself and found that the activity continued while he was alone in the workshop.

Another startling event that Fontana witnessed personally concerned a brass 25-pounder shell case from the

Second World War that was kept in the workshop as a souvenir. John placed the shell at the far end of the workshop and asked Pete to hit it. At once a stone ricocheted off the surface with a loud ping. Fontana tried and failed to hit the shell and then asked Pete to help – whereupon his throw hit it. Nobody was ever hurt during Fontana's investigation, although there were some near misses. According to Fontana only someone or something with a 'superhuman sense of timing' could have prevented injury.

Although contact with Pete was never made via the raps and bangings frequently reported in poltergeist cases, a further indication, apart from the stone throwing, that contact was established came when John and other members of his family playfully asked Pete if he would bring them money. Three old pennies, all dated 1912, and crumpled £5 notes were found both in the workshop and the retail shop the next morning.

FAKING IT?

Throughout his investigation Fontana was keen to eliminate the possibility of fraud. There were in total effectively four people who were present when the phenomena took place and might have engaged in faking. They were John, Pat, Paul and Yvonne. An unknown accomplice would have been needed to account for the stone throwing when John and Pat were on holiday and when Fontana was alone in the workshop.

Although it was impossible to obtain conclusive proof,

Fontana observed the witnesses carefully and nothing ever gave him the slightest reason to suspect fraud might be the case. He made extensive searches of the workshop to check for mechanical devices or tricks such as sticking stones to walls or ceilings, in order to discount every possible explanation. In addition Fontana discovered no places in the workshop where an accomplice could hide. The floors and ceilings did not conceal secret cupboards. In short there was no hiding place.

Nor was there any motive for fraud. On the contrary, Fontana observed that the family was more concerned about the adverse affect this would all have on business, and there were indications that it did frighten customers away. All in all Fontana believed his witnesses to be reliable, honest and decent people who disliked publicity and were simply mystified by what was happening.

Furthermore Fontana brought along a research assistant on one occasion and she too observed the stone throwing. The possibility of it all being a practical joke with Michael responsible was also considered, but Michael was not present when many of the phenomena were witnessed and he took no part in the stone throwing experiments.

All this led Fontana to the conclusion that he had indeed witnessed an intriguing example of poltergeist phenomena. He writes: 'In sum, I am in no doubt that it would be very difficult for even the most determined critic to fall back on the argument of fraud at any point during my period of investigation. I was extremely fortunate in witnessing so many phenomena myself and in the company of individuals of whose integrity I had plenty of time and opportunity to satisfy myself.'

COULD ANYTHING ELSE EXPLAIN IT?

Is it possible that all the phenomena were simply a consequence of some environmental factors causing local physical disturbances, such as passing traffic or geophysical activity?

As the premises were near a busy street, vibrations from passing traffic might have been a possible candidate for some of the phenomena, such as the tools swinging. Fontana investigated this possibility by observing the workshop when big trucks passed by and confirming that there were no signs of vibrations. Furthermore the workshop was at the back of the premises and unlikely to be affected by the passing traffic.

Fontana also dismissed geophysical effects. There were no records of seismic disturbances during the period of haunting, and even if minor disturbances that were too small to register occurred, this couldn't explain why the phenomena didn't appear to be random but seemed to have a purpose. The action of ground water seemed equally unlikely, according to Fontana. Not only did this too fail to address the seemingly purposeful activity witnessed in the Cardiff case, but the relevant area was not subject to flooding or affected by the sea.

If a normal explanation isn't possible, could Pete somehow be a projection from the minds of one of the people involved? Was Pete an example of paranormal power or externalised emotional frustration on the part of someone living? Was this a case of unconscious psychokinesis (PK)?

In cases of unconscious PK an adolescent is typically involved, but here there were no adolescents, all five witnesses being middle-aged. Nor was there evidence of intense emotional frustration in any of them. In addition, no laboratory evidence has so far suggested conclusively that objects can be thrown or moved by will-power alone. Evidence for super ESP remains inconclusive. On balance, concludes Fontana, 'it seems we can dismiss the idea that Pete was not more than a living person venting his or her internal turmoil paranormally on the premises and on those working there.'

What then of the possibility that Pete was a ghost or a surviving personality? In their wide-ranging and scholarly assessment of poltergeist phenomena *Poltergeists* (1979) Gauld and Cornell set down a number of requirements that need to be met for a particular case to be attributed to a surviving personality. These include the activity not being strictly tied to the comings and goings of a particular person, evidence of intelligent behaviour, evidence of behaviour that appears contrary to the wishes of the witnesses (remember that they feared an adverse affect on business), and paranormal phenomena which are beyond the capabilities of living agents. The Cardiff Poltergeist satisfied all these conditions and one more besides, which we haven't mentioned yet but will do later: the appearance of an apparition.

Apparitions are not typical of poltergeist cases, but towards the end of this one Paul reported seeing the apparition of a young boy. It's also important to add at this point that over the months Pete demonstrated qualities associated with a separate personality. For example, he would respond to anger, he attempted to be helpful by laying out cutlery and co-operated by leaving out money or hitting the shell on request. He also didn't allow anyone to get hurt. All the witnesses admitted that over time they grew almost fond of him. Paul even went so far as to tell Fontana that he felt 'privileged' by his involvement in the case.

Having experienced and witnessed the events at Cardiff, Fontana could not eliminate the theory that Pete was a surviving personality. Much of his behaviour seemed to suggest a young boy keen to draw attention to himself and to establish a rapport, rather than an adult. A large rubber ball and a teddy bear disappeared from the workshop and were later found in a hiding place, but more telling evidence was provided by Paul, who on three occasions saw an apparition of a young boy. He described him as about twelve years old. On the first and second occasions Paul called out to him, and Pete responded by throwing a stone or a float, but on the third occasion the figure seemed to be waving, as if in farewell. Paul had previously had an apparent paranormal experience in the house and it is likely that he had certain psychic gifts.

Taking this argument further, if Pete had been a young boy, were there any clues to his identity? Fontana believes that there were. He discovered from local rumour that a small boy had been killed in a traffic accident some years previously. This was confirmed when the boy's elder brother, now an adult, read the poltergeist story in the local newspaper and contacted Fontana.

THE CASE CLOSES

Fontana devoted two years to the Cardiff poltergeist investigation, but it came to an end shortly after the third sighting of the apparition by Paul, at a time when the premises were being reorganised and redecorated. A few months later John and Pat moved to a new and larger workshop, where no disturbances took place. The old workshop has passed into other hands and has been converted to a restaurant. Again no further hauntings have been reported.

Since Fontana was so heavily involved in the case it's only fitting that we conclude with his words: 'Is it possible that Pete was the young boy killed on the road outside the premises and that he was attracted by the kindness, respectability and compassion of John and Pat? Did Paul's psychic abilities play a part? Probably we shall never know. Yet the impression made upon all of us involved in this case remains a strong one. For John and Pat in particular it seems as if for a short period the veil between the worlds was lifted.'

OUR CONCLUSIONS

This case stands out because it contains a number of features unusual in your typical poltergeist haunting. Let's remind ourselves of them:

- There were no adolescent children involved
- There were no obvious emotional problems among those involved
- There were no apparent motives for fraud
- Pete's behaviour, particularly in the stone throwing, suggested responsive and intelligent behaviour
- Attempts were made to be helpful, as in the cutlery incidents in the kitchen
- The incidents were not associated with any one person as an agent
- A clear impression of a distinct personality who wanted to communicate or be acknowledged was given

As we've seen during his investigation Fontana considered, investigated and eliminated the other possible alternative explanations in his investigation. There remains, of course, the matter of his own credibility. We only have his investigation and his evidence to rely on. No videos or photographs were produced during the investigation, so we haven't even got these to dissect. All we have is his word. Is that enough?

All those who know and work with Fontana believe that it is. He doesn't seem to be a man who would be easily convinced or deluded, and his impressive achievements speak volumes for his credibility as a paranormal investigator. A long-standing and respected member of the SPR, Fontana has a PhD in psychology and is currently Distinguished Visiting Fellow at Cardiff University, in South Wales, and Professor of Transpersonal Psychology at Liverpool John Moores University.

Having reviewed the case and Fontana's impeccable credentials it is impossible to escape the possibility – and we stress that vital word possibility – that Pete might have been a surviving personality.

4

BORLEY RECTORY

'If, for example, you broach the subject of Poltergeists to them (scientists) they will murmur something about an "outrage to common sense" and "gross superstition" – forgetting that all scientific progress is from the "outrageous" to the common-place, and that often the "superstition" of to-day is the science of to-morrow.'

HARRY PRICE: POLTERGEIST OVER ENGLAND:

THREE CENTURIES OF MISCHIEVOUS GHOSTS

(LONDON: COUNTRY LIFE LTD, 1945)

The haunting of the Borley Rectory is undoubtedly one of the most famous and written about in Britain, as well as one of the most controversial. The investigation was conducted between 1929 and 1948 by Harry Price, founder and director of the National Laboratory of Psychical Research in London and renowned ghost hunter. According to Price, Borley was 'the best authenticated case in the annals of psychical research'.

Price's findings have been heavily criticised over the years, and many people believe that the Rectory was never haunted at all: they put all the phenomena down to trickery, misinterpreted natural phenomena, and Price's intense desire to investigate a haunting. The sheer volume of sightings and experiences, however, by independent witnesses, suggests that although many of the phenomena were not paranormal, a percentage remains which, even today, can still be seen as inexplicable.

Borley Rectory in 1937

THE 'HISTORY' OF BORLEY RECTORY

The tiny parish of Borley is located in a desolate, sparsely populated area of rural Essex about sixty miles northeast of London. It's a lonely place and would be largely forgotten were it not for the fact that it was once the location of a rectory that became known as 'the most haunted house in England'.

The Rectory, a gloomy and unattractive three-storey red brick building, was built in 1863 for the Revd H.D.E. Bull and his large family. According to legend, for which there is no historical documentation, the Rectory was built on part of the site once occupied by a medieval monastery, where a tragedy had taken place.

There are a number of versions of the story. One was that a thirteenth-century nun from a nearby convent tried to elope with a lay monk from Borley. With the help of another lay monk they made their tragic escape one night by horse and coach. They were captured. The nun was interred alive in one of the monastery walls and her lover was hanged. The fate of the accomplice was unknown. According to another version the nun was interred and both men were hanged. A different, less romantic version has it that the nun and her lover did escape, but they argued and he strangled her in the monastery grounds. He was later hanged. Yet another version replaces the monks with grooms, but they had the same unlucky fates. There was also the 'screaming girl theory', not widely believed or supported by any evidence, that shortly after the Rectory was built, a young girl was seen one night clinging to the windowsill of the Blue Room on the second floor. She fell to her death.

In 1892 the Revd Bull died in the Blue Room. Harry Bull then took over from his father until 1927, when he too passed away in the Blue Room, now with a reputation as the most haunted room of the house. According to local lore, the entire building was haunted and villagers avoided it after dark.

After a year in which the house stood empty, the Revd Eric Smith and his wife, both professed sceptics of the paranormal, moved in. Previously twelve clergymen had turned down the post. The Smiths lived there for three years, after which, in October 1930, the Revd L.A. Foyster and his wife Marianne moved in, and stayed for five years. In 1937 (after the Foysters had moved out and the Rectory had been empty for two years) the property was leased to Harry Price for a whole year, and the results of his investigation were published in his book *The Most Haunted House in England*.

The Rectory was gutted by fire in 1939 and damaged beyond repair. The ruin was finally demolished in 1944.

LET THE HAUNTINGS BEGIN!

Borley first attracted the attention of ghost hunter Harry Price in June 1929, when an article in the *Daily Mirror* mentioned ghost sightings there and revived legends attached to the place. According to local lore from around 1885 a phantom nun had been seen drifting about the grounds, especially along a path dubbed 'the nun's walk'. The nun was seen both by day and at night, but most often at dusk; on one occasion she was allegedly seen by all four daughters of Harry Bull. There were also sightings of a phantom coach and horses; Harry Bull had seen the coach driven by headless coachmen. The editor of the *Daily Mirror* invited Price to join his reporter Mr V.C. Wall at Borley.

It was generally believed that the ghostly nun was the

spirit of the thirteenth-century nun who had tried un-successfully to elope with the monk from the local mon-astery. It's difficult to know whether this story had been around for a long time, or was a result of sightings during the Revd Bull's tenancy. It is also possible that Henry Bull's daughters created some of the stories about the eloping nun, but at this distance in time it is impossible to know for sure. What is certain is that there were reports of sightings when Bull and his son Harry were in residence. In 1886 a nurse was said to have left because of strange phenomena, possibly phantom footsteps. Around 1900, the four sisters of Harry Bull saw the ghostly nun in the garden during the daytime.

The Bulls must have got used to the strange phenom-enon, as they remained there until the death of Harry Bull in the Blue Room in 1927. (By all accounts Harry Bull seems to have been a vibrant and jovial man, as he once said that he would return after his death, and make his presence known by throwing mothballs.)

Many local people were also witness to the phantom nun. A Mr and Mrs Edward Cooper, who lived in a cottage near to the Rectory, claimed to have seen the ghost, and also witnessed a phantom coach and horses. In the year after Bull's death, when Borley was unoccupied, the ghostly nun was seen numerous other times by local witnesses.

The next cluster of reports came from the previously sceptical Eric Smith and his wife. During their short stay at the Rectory they apparently complained of mysterious footsteps, doorbells ringing of their own accord, and phantom stone throwing. They were so unsettled by the activity that they contacted the *Daily Mirror*, who sent along a reporter to write a feature for the paper. Harry Price got involved and so began his long and controversial association with the Rectory.

PRICE INVESTIGATES

Price and his secretary, Lucie Kaye, arrived at Borley Rectory on 12 June 1929. According to Price's account given in *The Most Haunted House in England* (1940) the Smiths told him the haunting had begun almost as soon as they moved in. There were strange mutterings, a woman's voice that moaned and exclaimed, 'Don't, Carlos, don't,' phantom footsteps and, of course, sightings of the phantom nun. There were also sightings of a strange light which appeared inexplicably in the windows of the unused wing, odd black shapes and the ghost of Harry Bull in the Blue Room.

Price's instant response was to ask permission to stay at the Rectory for a few days. While staying there, he thoroughly investigated the premises. He interviewed the staff and others and compiled a long list of everything that had gone on in the house in the past fifty years. The list was an incredibly long one and mentioned displacement of objects, smashed pottery, footsteps, voices, banging of doors, unexplained bell rings, sudden temperature changes, singing, music, strange lights, coach-like rumblings outside the house, the sound of galloping horses, smells both horrible and pleasant, and footsteps in the snow.

On his first evening Price said he heard bells and saw strange rains of objects tumbling down stairs. A candle was hurled and a window pane smashed. In all he witnessed a remarkable sequence of poltergeist phenomena and later wrote: 'Although I have investigated many haunted houses before and since, never have such phenomena so impressed me as they did on this historic day. Sixteen hours of thrills.'

Price later held a séance in the Blue Room, where he and others allegedly heard a faint tapping in response to questions. The spirit identified itself as Harry Bull and said it wished to attract attention.

Shortly after Price's first visit the Smiths left Borley, complaining that the Rectory had no piped water, no gas or electricity and was uncomfortable and difficult to run. (The Rectory had 23 rooms on its ground and first floors, plus some cupboards off the ground-floor stairwell. The cellars were also quite extensive, as were the attics.) Price went again on several occasions but had nothing to report comparable to his first visit. This comparative calm was shattered, however, with the arrival of a new rector in October 1930. According to Price an astonishing series of phenomena began, reaching their height of violence in June 1931. Their focus appeared to be Marianne Foyster, the rector's wife. Numerous witnesses and invited guests confirmed many of them.

The Foysters were purportedly witness to poltergeist phenomena, ranging from smashed glasses and stone throwing, to mysterious writing on the walls and on slips of paper that mysteriously appeared out of nowhere.

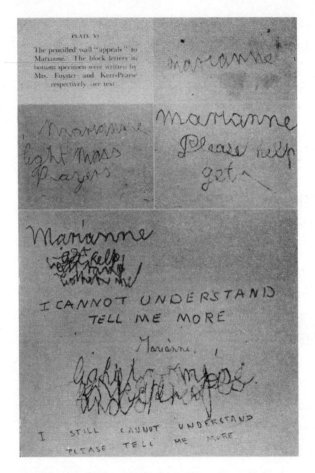

The mysterious 'writings on the wall'.

Marianne, who had a heart condition, is also said to have been thrown from her bed by a strange force (although some doubt whether Marianne did indeed have a heart condition and suggest that her fainting fits were designed to add drama to the proceedings). The strange writing is the most curious part of the phenomena, defying mistaken identification of natural events, although a rational explanation cannot be ruled out in any circumstance. (Paranormal investigator Peter Underwood submitted the Borley wall writings to a professional graphologist, whose opinion was that they were all produced by Marianne Foyster with the exception of one piece, the word 'Edwin'.)

Price paid another visit to the Rectory while the Foysters were there, in October 1931. Once again a variety of violent phenomena greeted him. From October 1929 to January 1932 Price declared that over two thousand paranormal incidents took place. They included: voices, footsteps, apparitions, strange odours, the production, disappearance, and transference of objects, bell ringing, the throwing and dropping of bottles, stones and other missiles, booby traps, the overturning of furniture, outbreaks of fire, the locking and unlocking of doors and personal injuries of a mild nature. And, of course, the famous messages to Marianne. During this time Marianne admitted to Price that she hated the Rectory and wanted to leave. Since the poltergeist activity almost always occurred when Marianne was around, Price suspected that she was the agent of poltergeist activity. In fact Price allegedly told Lionel Foyster to his face that he was of the opinion that his wife had produced the 'phenomena' they had witnessed during their visit. Price was very dismissive of Borley at this time. (He was more interested in a young lady called Mollie Goldney, with whom he was having an affair, and wanted to get back to their hotel in Cambridge rather than spend more time at the Rectory.)

After the Foysters left in October 1935, the house stood empty for a couple of years, but the phenomena continued. Although the presence of Marianne seemed to precipitate the most paranormal activity, unexplained events occurred at Borley both before and after the Foyster residency. In the words of Price, 'Every person who has resided in the rectory since it was built in 1863, and virtually every person who has investigated the alleged miracles, has sworn to incidents that can only be described as paranormal.'

Price was given the opportunity to study the haunting further when no one could be found to live in the Rectory. He leased the house for a year, and advertised in *The Times* for 'responsible persons of leisure and intelligence, intrepid, critical and unbiased', to form a team of 48 investigators who would spend several nights in the abandoned building. He drew up a blue book of protocols for carrying out observation periods and reporting phenomena, and supplied ghost-hunting equipment that included a remote-controlled movie camera, still cameras, fingerprinting paraphernalia, felt overshoes for quiet movement and steel tape measures to check the thickness of walls. The assistants were dispatched all over the house and told to draw chalk rings around every movable object, note markings and messages on walls and record all strange occurrences. The lease began in May of 1937 and little, if any, poltergeist activity was witnessed during this year-long study. The most common occurrence was the movement of objects out of their documented locations, and the sounds of footsteps. A mysterious coat appeared, but no sightings of the nun were observed. Some witnesses felt a sudden chill outside the Blue Room, and certain parts of the house were consistently colder than others. There was, however, one important new development.

The daughter of S.H. Glanville, Price's leading investigator, allegedly obtained information about the supposed murdered nun by means of a planchette – a device for registering automatic writing. Her name was Marie Lairre. At the age of nineteen she came to Borley from a convent at Le Havre and was murdered and buried in the vicinity of the Rectory by a member of the Waldegrave family – the local landowners – on 17 May 1667. She now wanted mass and proper burial to be put to rest.

Price left the Rectory in May 1938. He concluded that no single theory could explain all the phenomena. He believed a poltergeist was present, but a poltergeist could not explain the apparitions of the nun. He claimed there were at least a hundred witnesses to various phenomena, of which the Marianne messages were the most striking.

Although it was established that there had never been a monastery at Borley, eminent cleric Canon Phythian Adams read Price's *The Most Haunted House in England* and advanced a theory. He interpreted one of the cryptic wall writings and suggested that the bones of the murdered nun might be found under the ruins of the Rectory. Sensationally, in 1943, Price dug up the floor of one of the cellars. Portions of the skull of a young person were discovered. Two years later these remains were buried in a nearby churchyard and masses said for the repose of Marie Lairre, even though the identity of the skull was impossible to establish. There are some who believe that what was dug up in the Rectory cellar was in fact old sow's bones which Price then with a sleight of hand turned into the bones of the nun in order to create publicity for a second Borley

The Rectory in 1943, destroyed by fire.

book. This was why they were buried at Liston rather than Borley, as Jackson, the labourer who assisted with the digging, had told the Borley villagers that he was sure they only found pig's remains in the cellar.

On 27 February 1939, the Rectory burned down. The owner at the time, Captain Gregson, who told Price he had experienced unaccountable happenings during the short time he lived there, was sorting books in the hall when a stack fell over and upset a paraffin lamp. (This may very well have been an insurance scam – Gregson bought the Rectory with the intention of profiting from its haunted reputation. Even before he moved in he had sought Price's advice on how best to get visitors to look round the building.) The first part of the house to burn was the Blue Room upstairs over the hall.

Although Price never said that he accepted any of the theories advanced about the nun or claimed that the bones he dug up were hers, he did insist that his whole investigation was scientific. When he died in 1948, Price believed he had presented a case for one of the best ghost stories of all time. In his second book on Borley, *The End of Borley Rectory* (1946), he wrote: 'If, six years ago, I came to the conclusion that I could find no other explanation for some of the Borley phenomena than the popular theory of survival after death, I unhesitatingly declare I am still of that same opinion . . . I would go so far as to state that the Borley case presents a better argument for "survival" than any case with which I am familiar.'

He went on to say: 'The Borley phenomena occurred in the way they were said to occur. They were of paranormal origin. They have been scientifically proved . . . Fraud, mal-observation, exaggeration, natural causes and trickery, conscious, unconscious or subconscious could not have accounted for them.'

And Price cited the testimony of over a hundred witnesses and amateur investigators in support of this claim.

THE EVIDENCE IS RE-EXAMINED

After Price's death his research was re-examined by psychical researchers Eric Dingwall, Kathleen M. Goldney and Trevor H. Hall, all of whom were critics of Price. Dingwall and Goldney, both psychical researchers, had known Price for thirty years, and Hall was sceptical about the paranormal in general.

The investigators worked for several years on the case, studying the documentary evidence, interviewing witnesses, checking stories presented by Price as accurate. They had two main questions to answer: One – could Price's account be relied on? Two – apart from Price, was there any evidence to show that the Rectory ever was haunted?

The first question was much the easier to answer, and their final report shows only too clearly that Price probably did manipulate, sub-edit and occasionally heighten the evidence, which had been not nearly so impressive in its original form.

Charles Sutton, a reporter from the *Daily Mail*, said he had on many occasions suspected Price of perpetrating fraud – and had even caught him at it. On one particular evening when he was with Price at the Rectory a large pebble hit him on the hat. After more noisy phenomena Sutton seized Price and found his pocket to be full of pebbles and stones. Sutton telephoned his newspaper, but after a conference with a lawyer the story was killed. The editor said it was Sutton's word against Price's, and everyone would believe Price.

Perhaps the best evidence for fraud, however, came from Mrs Smith, who in 1949 signed a statement that Price himself had caused the phenomena. She stated that, contrary to Price's accounts, nothing had occurred in the house that she considered paranormal, despite the minor happenings that had earlier been reported. The alleged strange lights in the windows of the unused wing could have been the reflection of passing trains, although this is unlikely, and 'Don't, Carlos, don't' could have been the voices of passers-by.

The Smiths also believed tricks were being played on them by residents of Borley who did not want a new rector. The Smiths knew the locals thought the house was haunted, and they had contacted the media to help dispel fears – not, as Price had suggested in his books, to investigate the phenomena. The unfortunate and un-wanted result was the revival of ghost legends and the publicity that followed Price.

Mrs Smith further stated that after Price arrived she and her husband and others were astonished at the swift onset of the phenomena. They immediately suspected Price as the perpetrator.

S.H. Glanville, the first assistant to be enrolled by Price in 1937, also told Dingwall, Goldney and Hall that he 'deplored the laxity' of Price's observations. There was no common log-book, each investigator was unaware of the work of others, and most were not qualified investigators. Glanville had no faith in the planchette material either, believing it to be produced by the subconscious of the operators. He did not believe in the existence of Marie Lairre and thought the auditory phenomena could be explained by acoustics in the courtyard.

All in all, Dingwall, Goldney and Hall agreed that there were too many examples of dubious research to be ex-plained away by carelessness or haste. Price's investigation in their eyes all seemed part of a careful attempt to build up a 'good story' and throw out reports that might cast doubt. They also left little doubt that, in their view, Price himself was responsible for some of the 'phenomena' he reported – particularly on the occasion of his first visit in 1929.

The investigators answered their second question – apart from Price's, was there evidence to show that the Rectory was haunted? – by pointing out that the poltergeist phenomena did not begin until Price appeared on the scene, and accounts before or after Price could be explained psychologically. The authors concluded in their book, *The Haunting of Borley Rectory* (1956), that Borley Rectory was 'absolutely ideal' for these psychological mechanisms to take hold and operate. They argued that: 'The influence of suggestion on the investigation of haunted houses cannot be exaggerated. In every ordinary house sounds are heard and trivial incidents occur which are unexplained or treated as of no importance. But once the suggestion of the abnormal is put forward – and tentatively accepted – then these incidents become imbued with sinister significance: in fact they become part of the "haunt".'

According to the authors, after the burning of the Rectory, the publication of *The Most Haunted House in England* and the astonishing newspaper publicity which followed, it is not surprising that visitors to the ruins and amateur investigators hired by Price reported further phenomena. So influenced were people by the legends and stories about the place that the simplest events, such as losing a pencil, the failure of a motor cycle to start or getting a twig attached to one's clothing, were hailed as examples of supernatural forces still active at Borley.

The case put forward by Dingwall, Goldney and Hall to discredit Price's work was a powerful one. The possibility, however, that at least some of the phenomena may have been paranormal can't be entirely discounted.

A SHADOW OF DOUBT

Many sceptics have pulled apart Price's work at the Rectory, explaining all recorded phenomena as misinterpreted natural occurrences, hoaxing and hearsay. But did Price deserve this criticism?

There is no question that Harry Price was one of the most influential figures in the formative years of ghost research. He was a highly charismatic personality whose energy and enthusiasm for the paranormal made him the first celebrity ghost hunter. He was instrumental in bringing ghost research to the general public, realising that only by making the research entertaining could he attract the attention of the masses. Given his popularity and controversial approach it's not surprising that his work and his motives would be attacked.

Although Price was a colourful character it must not be forgotten that many who witnessed him work never doubted either his sincerity or the fact that experiences inexplicable to them had occurred while they were on duty. One such witness, Ellic Howe, speaks for many of them.

'Suppose for a moment that Price was quite aware that he was setting the stage for a colossal hoax. If he had that sort of thing in mind he never gave the game away – or at least not to me. His acting must have been consummate. But I don't think he was acting. Why, if the Borley haunt was phoney, did he take the trouble to spend a tedious hour before dawn standing with me in the notorious Blue Room? Was it just to impress me? I don't think so.'

Many witnesses also stood by their belief that the Rectory was haunted and that the phenomenon they saw was genuine. Mrs Henning, the widow of the rector of Lyston-cum-Borley from 1936 to 1955, for example, believes from personal experience that the Rectory was haunted.

'I lived at Borley near the Rectory and the church from March to December 1936 and in the adjacent village for nineteen years. I maintain there is a great deal of evidence that the Rectory was haunted before Mr Price ever visited it and certainly after Mrs Foyster had left.'

For some the main impact of Harry Price's book about the haunting of Borley Rectory comes from the testimony of the rector, Lionel Foyster. It is difficult to read the diary of events, recorded in great detail and printed in the famous book, and fail to be impressed by the sheer weight of evidence. Harry Price wrote:

'Mr Foyster very assiduously kept a record of all these strange events, and his diary finally assumed gigantic proportions. I believe that he has more than 180 typed quarto sheets of notes recording the day-to-day activities of the Poltergeist. When I informed Mr Foyster that I was compiling a monograph on the haunting of Borley Rectory, he very generously permitted me to reprint verbatim selected portions of his diary. These extracts he kindly selected himself and wrote them out in his own hand.'

It's hard to believe that Foyster's diary is all fiction or hallucination.

Although Price's methods are still considered dubious, opinion among paranormal investigators has recently swung back in favour of possible paranormal activity at Borley Rectory. English investigator of ghosts and president of the Ghost Club Society, Peter Underwood, has collected a mass of material which he claims offers positive proof – Harry Price regardless – of the haunt. Voices, footsteps, curious odours, loud and distinct thumps, crashing crockery, a phantom cat, are all vouched for, he says, by reliable witnesses. So are the Borley Phantoms.

WHAT ABOUT THE PHOTOGRAPHS?

Many dozens of mysterious photographs were taken throughout the years, some of them showing what appeared to be strange dark figures and apparitions in the grounds around the Rectory. The mysterious photos show a floating brick, an unknown floating ribbon-like thing and other ghostly figures.

In 1957 it was suggested that a photograph published in *Life* magazine years earlier, purportedly showing a mysterious 'floating brick' at the Borley ruins, may have been a photographer's trick. The photograph was taken in 1944 when workers were clearing away the rubble from the fire. The photograph allegedly captures a brick floating, but it could have been a trick of the camera lens

The supposed 'floating brick' captured on film at Borley Rectory (the photo on the left is a detail of the one above).

angle. Interviewed in 1957, the photographer said the brick was probably tossed down from an upper-storey window by a workman, and the photo was shot at such an angle that the workman could not be seen. The photograph had originally been a joke to suggest that this is the sort of thing poltergeists might do, and Price, unlike the photographer, reportedly was in on the joke, but he still passed off the photo as evidence of poltergeists.

Although the great majority of the photographs taken at Borley can undoubtedly be explained logically, not all of them can. To this day anomalous images that defy rational explanation continue to appear on photos taken in the Rectory grounds. The question remains: are these pictures nothing more than fakes, or something of a much more spiritual nature?

BORLEY TODAY

Reports of paranormal activity continued after the fire. In 1954 newspaper accounts reported ghosts still appearing at the site. Even the burning of a Borley village chicken house was also somehow connected to the Rectory's haunted history. Over the decades the reports have not stopped.

As recently as 2002 two workmen required the use of electric drills and a heavy-duty extension lead to bring power from the church to the churchyard. For no apparent reason when the men went to use their drills they found there was no power. Returning to the extension lead power point in the church to ascertain why, they continually found the plugs disconnected from the supply.

In 2003 the residents of one of the properties built on the site of the Rectory garden reported poltergeist activity in their kitchen. In 2005 another resident of a property close to where the Rectory once stood allegedly heard the sound of heavy breathing follow her whilst she walked in her garden at dusk.

It's important to state at this point that Borley Rectory no longer exists. After the fire the ruins suffered further damage from high winds before finally being demolished in 1944. The site was subsequently split up and sold off as individual plots on which were built several private bungalows. The only original building remaining on the site is the former Rectory Cottage (a building itself older than the Revd H.D.E. Bull's rectory), much extended and altered to the rear, which today is also a private residence.

It must be borne in mind by visitors today that the only part of the village to which the public has the right of admittance is the churchyard and Borley Church itself, although this is kept locked at all times when not in use and access is only available through one of the village key-holders. The notoriety which the haunting of Borley Rectory has given the village has resulted in much un-welcome and unwanted attention and abuse of the loca-tion and its inhabitants over the years. Not surprisingly many Borley residents today are deeply suspicious of visitors.

THE JURY'S STILL OUT!

'As for Borley Rectory I think I would have to say that it never was "the most haunted house in England". That was created by the human drama of its inhabitants over the years and the people that it seemed to either attract or who came in contact with it. The complex personal and psychological relationships of particularly the Foysters, Frank Peerless, Edwin Whitehouse fuelled something which had been smouldering for many years, albeit at a local level, with the addition of Harry Price who acted as a kind of latent catalyst setting things in motion. [*Sir George and Lady White-house, with their nephew Edwin Whitehouse (later Dom Richard, O.S.B.), were neighbours who constantly visited the Foysters and testified to witnessing the phenomena. Marianne Foyster was having an affair with the lodger, Frank Peerless, aka Lawless*]. However, that being said, I do feel that certain aspects of the case do point to paranormal activity having taken place, with particular reference to the auditory phenomena of footsteps inside the building, the window lights seen and the appearance of an apparition resembling a nun. These thread through all the other events and on these happenings the whole "most haunted house" edifice was allowed to grow. Now at this distance in time from the main events and with all the players having left the stage it becomes increasingly difficult to separate the legend from the reality.'

> Paul Adams, one of the UK's leading experts
> on Harry Price and Borley Rectory, developer
> and owner of www.harryprice.co.uk

The controversy over Borley shows no signs of going away. In 1992, Robert Wood published *The Widow of Borley*, a critical look at both Marianne Foyster and Price. In 1996 Ivan Banks wrote *The Enigma of Borley*, a book that revives the uncertainty surrounding the case. Edward Babbs's 2003 *Borley Rectory: the Final Analysis* offers a detailed and intriguing assessment of the case.

In 1998 Vincent O'Neil, the adopted son of Marianne Foyster and her second husband Robert O'Neil, created the Borley Ghost Society as a source of information about the case. The O'Neil family moved to the United States in 1946. Marianne told Vincent nothing about the case – he learned of it in 1994, two years after her death. Vincent, who claims to be psychic, is of the opinion that some authentic phenomena happened at Borley and that his mother, being young and sensitive at the time, became a focus for them. (In November 2004 the Borley Ghost Society was dissolved by Vincent O'Neil, who now states that he wishes to have nothing more to do with publicising the Borley case. He cites the disturbance caused to the Borley villagers and the memory of his mother as his reasons for pulling the plug on his website.)

Price certainly believed that Marianne was a focus for poltergeist activity, but recently Marianne's unusual marriage and personality have attracted almost as much attention as the ghosts themselves. Her admission to Price that she hated Borley has led some to suggest that she used the situation as a way of spicing up the boring routine of country life. Living with an elderly man in the middle of nowhere, she had no prospect of excitement and a house that was ugly and hard to run without an army of servants and money for its upkeep. Sadly there's no way of finding out for sure now, as Marianne passed away in 1992, taking the truth with her.

Others have suggested that the building lent itself well to paranormal activity. The natural acoustics of the place may have played a part. The Rectory was situated in a remote and melancholy spot, had a succession of eccentric owners and was never loved by its inhabitants. The whole place was a recipe for a haunting. This argument is taken one step further by those who believe buildings absorb emotions and a part of the personalities of those who live there, creating a record of the inhabitants not just in the furnishings but in every brick. This, of course, can't be proved and does not explain reports of haunting after Borley was demolished.

Another theory is that natural forces were at work. Perhaps the Rectory was on a ley line?

Ley lines are alignments of a number of places of geographical interest, such as ancient megaliths. Their existence was first suggested in 1921 by the amateur archaeologist Alfred Watkins, whose book *The Old Straight Track* brought the phenomenon to the attention of the wider public.

The existence of apparently remarkable alignments between sites is easily demonstrated. Some believe the early inhabitants of Britain determined the placement of Stonehenge and various other megalith structures, buildings, monuments or mounds according to a system of these lines, which often pass through, or near, several such structures. The leys may have had some astronomical significance, or to relate to traditional religious beliefs associated with these sites. Others believe ley lines are invisible lines of energy that can enable images and sounds to be stored and played back even today. Although this might explain the phenomenon at Borley, the existence of ley energy has yet to be proven conclusively. Many researchers have studied leys and consider them to trigger sightings of ghosts such as the Borley nun.

Sceptics argue that ley lines can be explained completely by chance alignments of random points, but some are investigating the possibility of these points having electrical or magnetic forces associated with them.

Theories continue to be put forward, and the Borley controversy rages on with no sign of abatement. In all, the case has generated more attention than any other haunting on record: hundreds of articles, books, lectures, movies and even a play have been written, produced, presented and published. Yet despite the wealth of documentation and literature, and all the interest from believers, scientists and sceptics, we still don't know for sure if Borley was or is haunted.

OUR CONCLUSIONS

It's clear that the whole Borley story is worthy of investigation – and of its reputation as the most haunted house in England. It's equally clear that Harry Price's version of it, however consciously or unconsciously misleading, leaves much to be desired. Indeed, to some people, its unreliability is in itself sufficient to discredit everything connected with Borley. To others, Dingwall, Goldney and Hall's report is just as misleading, as it shows a bias against the haunting of the Rectory as strong as Price's bias in favour of it, and that they were more interested in attacking Price than in anything else.

It must always be borne in mind that Price was a first-rate journalist and not a scientist trying patiently to ascertain what the facts were and how best to interpret them. He was content to tell the tale in the most interesting and convincing way he could and leave others to pick holes in it if they felt so inclined.

In essence, Price wanted quick and sensational results which he could easily publicise and so earn fame and an enviable notoriety. It always astonished me that anyone really took him seriously. Yet there were many who believed in him and his work, and he even got support for some of his more spectacular stunts such as those with Joanna Southcott's box and the mysterious Brocken manuscript, both of which 1 believed at the time to be fakes. The Borley story was merely another of Price's sensational cases, and it was certainly the most successful and attracted more attention than any of the others. I think that it deserved it. It is one of the best of all ghost stories and few people could have told it more convincingly than Harry Price.

Dr Eric Dingwall

Whether or not Borley Rectory was haunted during Price's investigation is now virtually impossible for us to determine. If you want to believe it was, there is nothing to stop you. Many believe the place still is. On the other hand you may want to dismiss the whole affair with contempt or amusement or surrender belief with reluctance – whichever course you decide on you'll find plenty to support you.

There is no doubt that during its lifetime a series of highly unusual characters inhabited the Rectory or were in one way or another connected with it. Was the combination of local reputation and eccentric behaviour too good an opportunity for a lover of publicity such as Harry Price to miss? Does Price's evidence depend not on scientific fact and hard logic but on those sincere but fallibile human skills of observation, supposition, lively imagination and self-persuasion? Could all of the reports be faked, hallucination or just rational happenings perceived by those who want to believe in ghosts as genuine paranormal activity? Was Borley ever haunted? Is Borley still haunted?

In our opinion to suggest that every single paranormal incident reported at Borley can be explained logically or as hallucination is unscientific and narrow-minded. The frequency and longevity of the phenomena, along with the integrity of certain witnesses, suggests that the possibility – and once again we stress the word possibility – of paranormal activity should not be discounted.

It has been suggested that every student of the paranormal should visit Borley at least once. We don't recommend it, but if you do decide to visit Borley to soak up its atmosphere, remember to respect the privacy of its residents and the peace of this mysterious and magical place. The chances are you won't, but should you see, hear, feel, sense or come across anything which you think is strange, or which you think can't be explained rationally, please let us or the Ghost Club (see Appendix) know. It can then be added to the ever expanding and yet to be closed case file devoted to this most famous of hauntings.

5

EXTRAORDINARY PROOF

'Sir, I make a distinction between what a man may experience
by the mere strength of his imagination, and what imagination
cannot possibly produce.'

BOSWELL: LIFE OF JOHNSON

For millennia there have been countless reports from
people who say they have seen, heard, felt or even smelt
ghosts; but despite this we still can't prove whether ghosts
exist or not. It isn't hard to see why doubt lingers and why
sceptics remain to be convinced, as there is a lack of solid,
tangible evidence: all we often have to rely on is eyewitness
accounts. Having said this, there are tantalising pieces of
evidence that some believe do provide proof of an afterlife.
Others disagree and find alternative explanations for
them. In this chapter we'll take a look at some of the
best-known extraordinary pieces of evidence for the existence of ghosts, so you can make up your own mind.

In recent years, the development of EVPs – electronic voice
phenomena – in which a voice from an unknown source is
captured by a recording device, has become one of the most
intriguing and compelling areas of ghost research. The
emergence of video and television as a medium for recording

paranormal activity is also an expanding and exciting new avenue of research, but let's begin with photographs.

We know from experience how much people love ghost photographs. Not only are cameras affordable and portable, but there's also just something extraordinarily compelling about photographic proof. Have a look and see.

PHOTOGRAPHIC EVIDENCE

Convincing ghost photos are extremely rare, so let's take a look at a few that we think are very, very good.

Faking ghost photos through double exposure and other kinds of trickery has been around as long as photography itself; and today, digital image manipulation and computer graphics can easily recreate ghostly images that look really genuine. But the photographs below are considered by many to be untouched, genuine photographs of ghosts.

The Brown Lady

This photograph is perhaps the most famous and well-regarded ghost photograph ever taken. The ghost is thought to be that of Lady Dorothy Townshend, who, with her husband, Charles Townshend, 2nd Viscount of Raynham, resided at Raynham Hall in Norfolk in the early 1700s.

Raynham Hall mansion was owned by the Townshend family for over three hundred years. Dorothy was the sister of Sir Robert Walpole and before her marriage to Charles it was rumoured that she had been the mistress of Lord Wharton, 'whose character was so infamous, and his lady's complaisant subservience so notorious, that no young woman could be four and twenty hours under their roof with safety to her reputation', according to a source quoted on http://paranormal.about.com.

No one knows for sure, but it was thought that Charles suspected Dorothy of infidelity. According to legal records Dorothy died and was buried in 1726, but it was suspected that the funeral was a sham and that Charles had imprisoned his wife in a remote corner of the house, where she remained until her death, from the pox or a broken heart, many years later.

Dorothy's ghost is believed to haunt the oak staircase and other areas of Raynham Hall. In the early 1800s, King George IV, while staying at Raynham, saw the figure of a woman in a brown dress standing beside his bed, and noted that her face was pale. He was said to be so terrified that he refused to stay another hour in the house.

She was seen again standing in the hall in 1835 by a Colonel Loftus, who was visiting for the Christmas holidays. He saw her again a week later and described her as pale skinned and wearing a brown satin dress. It also seemed to him that her eyes had been gouged out.

A few years later, Captain Frederick Marryat and two friends saw 'the brown lady' gliding along an upstairs hallway, carrying a lantern. As she passed, Marryat said, she grinned at the men in a 'diabolical manner'. Marryat fired a pistol at the apparition, but the bullet simply passed through.

Until 1904, when it was sold, a portrait identified as being of Lady Dorothy hung in the hall. In the portrait the woman is dressed in brown and has large shining eyes. It was said that the portrait looked normal by day but at night the face took on an evil appearance.

In 1926 the ghost was seen again by the young Marquis Townshend. In September 1936 Lady Townshend hired photographers Indra Shira and Captain Provand to take photographs of the house for *Country Life* magazine. While taking the photographs Shira noticed what looked like a shadowy figure dressed in white moving down the stairs. He asked his assistant to take a photograph and although the assistant could not see anything he aimed his camera in the direction indicated by Shira.

'Captain Provand took one photograph while I flashed the light. He was focusing for another exposure; I was standing by his side just behind the camera with the flashlight pistol in my hand, looking directly up the staircase. All at once I detected an ethereal veiled form coming slowly down the stairs. Rather excitedly, I called out sharply: "Quick, quick, there's something there." I pressed the trigger of the flashlight pistol. After the flash and on closing the shutter, Captain Provand removed the focusing cloth from his head and turning to me said: "What's all the excitement about?" '

When the photograph was developed the brown lady appeared as an outline wearing what looked like a wedding gown and veil. The photograph was published in *Country Life* magazine in December 1936 and became an overnight sensation. Experts past and present have examined it and no evidence of fraud has ever been found.

The Staircase Ghost

This photograph was taken by the Revd Ralph Hardy, a retired clergyman from White Rock, British Columbia. He intended merely to photograph the elegant spiral staircase (known as the 'Tulip Staircase') in the Queen's House section of the National Maritime Museum in Greenwich.

Much to his surprise, when he developed the photograph there emerged a shrouded figure climbing the stairs, seeming to hold the railing with both hands. Experts who have examined the original negative, including some from Kodak, have concluded that there is no sign of it having been tampered with.

This photo isn't the only evidence of ghostly activity at the Queen's House. The 400-year-old building is credited with several other apparitions and phantom footsteps even today. Reports include unexplained sounds of footsteps in the vicinity of the staircase, the mysterious chanting of children's voices, the figure of a pale woman frantically mopping blood at the bottom of the Tulip Staircase (it's said that three hundred years ago a maid was thrown from the highest banister, plunging fifty feet to her death), slamming doors, and even tourists being pinched by unseen fingers.

The Ghost in the Burning Building

On 19 November 1995, the Town Hall at Wem, a quiet market town in northern Shropshire, was burned to the ground. Many witnesses gathered around to watch as the old building (it was built in 1905) was destroyed by the flames. A local resident, Tony O'Rahilly, was among those spectators, and he took photographs of the fire with a 200mm telephoto lens from across the street. One of his photos shows what looks like a small, partially transparent girl standing in the doorway. Neither O'Rahilly nor any of the other onlookers or the fire-fighters remembered seeing the girl there.

O'Rahilly sent the photo to the Association for the Scientific Study of Anomalous Phenomena which, in turn, presented it for analysis to Dr Vernon Harrison, a photographic expert and former president of the Royal Photographic Society. Harrison studied carefully both the print and the original negative, and concluded that it was genuine. 'The negative is a straightforward piece of black-and-white work and shows no sign of having been tampered with,' Harrison said.

No one knows for certain who the little girl might have been, but there is a possible clue in Wem's history. According to local records, in 1677 the town suffered a huge fire which destroyed many of its old timber houses. The story goes that a young girl named Jane Churm started it by accidentally setting fire to a thatched roof with a candle. Many believe her ghost haunts the area and was present on the night of the Town Hall fire.

The Madonna of Bachelor's Grove

This now famous photo was taken during an investigation of Bachelor's Grove cemetery near Chicago by the Ghost Research Society (GRS). On 10 August 1991, several members of the GRS were at the cemetery, an abandoned one-acre graveyard on the edge of the Rubio Woods Forest Preserve, near the suburb of Midlothian, Illinois. Reputed to be one of the most haunted cemeteries in the US, Bachelor's Grove has over the years been the site of well over a hundred different reports of strange phenomena, including apparitions, unexplained sights and sounds, and even glowing balls of light.

GRS member Mari Huff was taking black-and-white photos with a high-speed, infra-red camera in an area where the group had experienced some anomalies with their ghost-hunting equipment. The cemetery was empty, except for the GRS members. When one photo was developed, this image emerged: what appears to be a lonely looking, semi-transparent young woman, dressed in old-fashioned white clothing, sitting on a tombstone.

Sceptics have called the photo a double exposure. Among those who believe the photo shows a genuine anomaly, however, are Dale Kaczmarek, founder and president of the GRS, and Troy Taylor, co-founder and president of the American Ghost Society. Taylor showed the photo to several professional photographers, who ruled out double exposure.

The Spectre of Newby Church

The Revd K. F. Lord took this photo in 1963 at Newby Church in North Yorkshire. Newby Church was built in 1870 and, as far we know, does not have a tradition of ghosts and hauntings or other peculiar phenomena. Those who have carefully analysed the proportions of the objects in the photo calculated that the spectre is about nine feet tall!

This is a controversial photo because it is just too good. The shrouded face and the way it is looking directly into the camera makes it look as if it was posed – a clever double exposure. Yet supposedly this photo too has been scrutinised by photo experts who say the image is not the result of a double exposure.

The Revd Lord has stated that nothing was visible to the naked eye when he took the snapshot of his altar. Yet when the film was developed, standing there was this strange hooded figure.

Freddy Jackson

This photo, dating from 1919, is part of a group photograph taken of the Maintenance Group of HMS *Daedalus* on the runway at Cranwell in Lincolnshire. The ghostly face pictured here is positioned on the top row, fourth from left, and is said to be that of Freddy Jackson, an air mechanic who had been killed on the very same airstrip a few days earlier, stumbling into an aeroplane propeller.

The photo is an official RAF photo, and the photographer came from outside the base, which eliminates any chance of there being any tampering with the photograph. How could he know who the man was? Members of the squadron, on the other hand, easily recognised the face as Jackson's. It has been suggested that Jackson's spirit, unaware of his death, decided to show up for the group photo.

SO WHAT MAKES A CONVINCING GHOST PHOTOGRAPH?

First it needs to be examined by experts in photography to eliminate the possibility of fraud. Natural explanations also need to be ruled out. If it passes those two tough tests (and, believe us, the majority of so-called ghost photographs don't!), then the key factors for us are clarity, recognition, honesty and intention.

The very best ghost photos capture what is clearly a human form – a body or face that is instantly recognisable as such. Although they may not always look as solid as a flesh-and-blood living person, the form is clearly discernible. This kind of clarity in a photograph is extremely rare. It's so rare, in fact, that when this kind of clarity shows up in a photo today, it is immediately suspected of being a hoax. With today's digital cameras and computers, fakes are easy to create.

If this kind of clarity isn't present – which it usually isn't

– snapshot takers and ghost hunters alike search for ghostly evidence of other kinds in their photos. Nowadays, ghost photos tend to depict 'orbs', 'ectoplasm' (a kind of strange mist) and 'vortexes'. (We'll explore these kinds of photos and how useful they are when it comes to searching for evidence in our next chapter, on typical captured evidence.)

Another convincing clue to suggest that a ghost photo may possibly be genuine is that the figure is recognisable as a known person who is no longer living and therefore, like Freddy Jackson above, has no business showing up there.

Because ghost photos are easily faked in any number of ways, we also have to rely on the honesty of the photographer.

Intention is another factor. Most of the best ghost photos were taken unintentionally. In other words, they weren't taken by people who were out to get a ghost on film (or chip in the case of digital cameras). The accidental nature of these photos lends them credibility because the photographers didn't have an agenda – it wasn't their intention to capture a ghost image, it just happened, and they are just as surprised as anyone else to discover it.

The famous photos above all seem to meet the above criteria, and that's what makes them seem convincing.

HOW DO APPARITIONS SHOW UP ON FILM?

So far there is no explanation for how or why apparitions show up on film, if indeed they do. In most cases nothing is seen by the naked eye, but the camera captures anomalies such as balls or streaks of light or patches of fog. In rare cases filmy human shapes appear.

The Ghost Research Society (GRS) of Illinois maintains one of the finest collections of spirit photographs from around the world. Each photograph is analysed by being scanned through a computer and digitalised, which produces images of high resolution. Minute details can then be scrutinised. Negatives are carefully examined and photographic experts and scientists are consulted.

GRS president Dale Kaczmarek suggests that about ninety per cent of all alleged spirit or ghost photographs can be explained naturally. What appears as paranormal anomaly can be caused by flaws in the film or developing, fog or specks on the camera lens or light reflected from the lens. It can also be caused by simulacra, which is when odd shapes are created by random patterns in natural settings or shadows. Digital cameras are particularly problematic as they often show fuzzy areas and can easily be manipulated on a computer. (We'll talk more about the use of cameras in our chapter on investigative techniques.)

Of the ten per cent of spirit photographs that cannot be explained naturally about eight per cent are photographs of shadows, streaks and blotches of light that have no apparent reason for being. These photographs are considered to be paranormal, but not necessarily of a ghost or a spirit. The remaining two per cent are the extremely rare photographs, like those mentioned above, that appear to be free of fraud and which also defy natural explanation.

VIDEO FOOTAGE

Video footage of ghosts is even rarer than photographic evidence. In these days of high technology the potential for fraud is huge here, and most parapsychologists dismiss or are highly critical of video footage for this very reason.

A good example of the kind of video footage likely to be taken a little more seriously is that captured by CCTV camera at Hampton Court on 7 October 2003. Here the footage wasn't taken on a ghost investigation but entirely by accident; its legitimacy has been attested to by the security camera operators (and we have no reason to disbelieve them); and thus far, after careful examination, no reasonable, natural explanation (including fraud) had been given for its existence.

Hampton Court Palace
On 7 October 2003 closed-circuit security cameras at Hampton Court Palace, the huge Tudor castle outside London, captured an image of a man in a robe-like garment stepping from a shadowy doorway, one arm reaching for the door handle. The area around the man appears somewhat blurred, and his face appears unnaturally white compared with his outstretched arm. Was this a ghost or a practical joke?

'We're baffled too – it's not a joke, we haven't manufactured it,' said Vikki Wood, a Hampton Court spokeswoman, when asked at the time if the photo the palace released was a Christmas hoax. 'We genuinely don't know who it is or what it is.' Wood said security guards had seen the figure in closed-circuit television footage after checking it to see who kept leaving open one of the palace's fire doors.

'It was incredibly spooky because the face just didn't look human,' said James Faukes, one of the palace security guards. 'My first reaction was that someone was having a laugh, so I asked my colleagues to take a look. We spoke to our costumed guides, but they don't own a costume like that worn by the figure. It is actually quite unnerving,' Faukes said.

Belgrave Museum

Another piece of video footage that captured the public's attention was filmed in December 1998 in Leicester, England. Security cameras captured a strange apparition-like figure at the city's historic Belgrave Museum. We've included this example because it is well known and because it shows just how sceptical paranormal investigators can be when it comes to ghosts on film.

Belgrave Hall has a reputation for hauntings, and the staff immediately and somewhat prematurely jumped to the conclusion that they had perhaps caught one of the spooky residents on video. The media were alerted and it was soon world news that a ghost had been caught on video. The image of the apparition-like figure lasts for a mere second or two, while a ghostly apparition-like fog can be seen appearing and moving in the background behind a brick wall.

Curator Stuart Warburton commented: 'The security cameras at the back of the hall triggered off one night at about 4.50 a.m., and then suddenly . . . two figures appear on the film. The camera freezes for about five seconds and then the figures disappear. And then we have a mist that swirls along the top of the wall, which we cannot explain . . . The hall is haunted, there is no question about that.'

ISPR (International Society for Paranormal Research) field investigators were invited in to explore the hall to see if it really was haunted, and also to help shed some light on the video image that was captured. The field investigators consisted of parapsychologists, psychics and other ISPR paranormal investigators who all were highly experienced with haunted houses.

Although the psychics in the team came to the conclusion that there were ghosts inhabiting the Hall, after extensive investigation the ISPR team found no evidence or trace of paranormal activity or energies from the place where the figure was spotted on video.

After examining the security video footage that was thought to possibly contain a ghost, the ISPR concluded that the footage and the strange image were 'environmental' and not paranormal in nature. Here's what the ISPR interim report concluded, in their own words:

1. The images on the CCTV film are natural phenomena created by atmospheric discharge.
2. The CCTV film containing the images, displayed certain electronic anomalies that could have caused the video film within the CCTV system to create the

illusion of drifting mist, forming into seemingly solid shapes.

3. During paranormal activity, electronic equipment, such as video and audio recorders, are often known to malfunction. The reason for this is the subject of continuing investigation by Dr Montz and the ISPR.

4. On the night of 26th March, the full ISPR Investigative Team headed by Dr. Montz, found Belgrave Hall to contain a number of active entities. These were identified by their full names and verified by reference to the historical records kept by Belgrave Hall Museum Curator, Stuart Warburton. These records were previously unseen by the ISPR Team.

At the time of the ISPR report Ciarán was doing his investigative psychology MSc and had access to some hi-tech video equipment. He came up with the same conclusion as other sceptics have since: that it's a leaf travelling across the lens and going in and out of focus.

QUESTIONS ABOUT GHOSTS ON FILM

It is easy to see why critics of this field have had so many problems with ghosts on film. It has a long history of fraud.

Some supposed Spiritualists first abused the public by constantly creating one fake photograph after another. In early spirit photographs ghostly faces would float above or alongside portraits of living subjects. In some photographs full-form spirits appear. In order not to disappoint clients, unscrupulous photographers doctored their work, super-imposing extras or creating ghostly effects through double exposure. The frequency of fraud in spirit photography eventually led to its decline in popularity, but along the way it claimed some famous victims, including the eminent Sir Arthur Conan Doyle, who was fooled by amateurish fake photographs of the fairies in the Cottingley fairies case.

Photography of ghosts is a very different story in contemporary ghost investigation, in which the camera is one of the most important tools. Photographs of haunted sites are shot with a variety of still and video cameras, including high technology equipment, in an effort to capture anomalies on film. Regular and infra-red film is used. Cameras are connected to various detection sites and are triggered whenever a device is activated by phenomena. In some investigations, two different cameras with two different types of film are used to shoot the same areas at the same time. The results of the two are then compared. Infra-red film may show invisible sources of light and heat, indicating the possible presence of ghosts.

Unfortunately, despite the sophistication of these techniques, the potential for fraud since the heady days of spiritualism hasn't decreased but increased. The same high technology that ghost hunters have to rely on in their investigations is the same equipment that is being used by frauds to fake ghost sightings. Frauds are now capable of creating fakes that appear so convincing they can even fool top experts in photography and video analysis. Unfortunately the advent of new technology brings with it new problems with exposure, lighting and developing. When there is no way to determine which sources are fakes and which are legitimate, then most sceptics are inclined to take the view that everything must be considered suspect.

DO YOU HEAR VOICES?

The process of recording a spirit's voice on audiotape is referred to as EVP, or electronic voice phenomena. It's an incredibly popular concept with paranormal investigators but an incredibly controversial one too. EVP researchers believe they capture on tape voices of the dead, but sceptics contend that the voices, which are typically faint and difficult to understand, come from radio or TV or are imagined from static and white sound.

EVP is the first high technology attempt to communicate with the dead. One of the world's most respected scientists, Thomas Alva Edison (inventor of the phonograph and developer of the modern light bulb), believed that it would one day be possible to build a machine that would help humans communicate with the dead. He once said: 'If our personality survives, then it is strictly logical or scientific to assume that it retains memory, intellect, other faculties, and knowledge that we acquire on this Earth. Therefore . . . if we can evolve an instrument so delicate as to be affected by our personality as it survives in the next life, such an instrument, when made available, ought to record something.' Unfortunately, Edison did not live to see his invention take shape.

Although attempts were made to record voices on tape in the years that followed, EVP remained in obscurity until the unexpected discovery of a Swedish opera singer, painter and film producer named Friedrich Jurgenson. His interest in electronic voice phenomena was sparked one day in 1959, when he recorded the sounds of birds singing in a forest. When he played the tape back, he heard a female voice say, 'Friedrich, you are being watched. Friedel, my little Friedel, can you hear me?' It was the voice of his dead mother. Jurgenson went on to record many other voices over the next four years, and he published two books: *Voices from the Universe* and *Radio Contact with the Dead.*

Dr Konstantin Raudive, a Latvian psychologist, heard of Jurgenson's experiments several years later. At first he was sceptical, but then he tried the experiments himself and wound up recording many voices, including that of his deceased mother. Over the years Raudive recorded more than 100,000 voices, an achievement which led to EVP voices also being known as 'Raudive voices'.

In the 1960s and 1970s, EVP became a legitimate, if controversial, arm of paranormal research. American researchers George and Jeanette Meek and psychic William O'Neil recorded hundreds of hours of EVP with radio oscillators. They claim to have worked closely with another scientist, Dr George Jeffries Mueller. The only 'catch' was that Mueller was deceased.

Sarah Estep, one of the most outspoken EVP researchers, started the American Association of Electronic Voice Phenomenon (AAEVP) in 1982. She claims to have communicated with thousands of ghosts, as well as with aliens. Perhaps the most famous and best funded device in the 1980s was the spiricom invented by George Meek, a retired engineer, with the alleged help of a discarnate scientist who communicated with him during a séance. Unfortunately the success rate of spiricom was poor, but this did not stop Meek pursuing increasingly sophisticated ways to reach the other side.

Allegedly EVP voices are never heard on recording, only on playback. They are said to be either faint or clear and can speak or sing in a variety of languages. They are identifiable as men, women and children and according to reports the voices suggest that they can communicate through central transmitting agencies on the other side. To anyone keen to listen to a sample we can suggest the following websites:

http://www.electronic-voice-phenomena.net/index.php
http://aaevp.com/

EVP has many enthusiastic supporters who believe the voices heard are evidence of paranormal activity, but it also has many critics who doubt whether the voices are genuine. Between 1970 and 1972 the Society for Psychical Research (SPR) commissioned psychical researcher D. J. Ellis to investigate EVP, and he concluded that the sounds were susceptible to imagination and most likely a natural phenomenon. The Rorschach sound test confirms that a person can listen to sounds and interpret them subjectively. Other sceptics believe that the voices are caused by psychokinesis when sounds are imprinted on the tape by the experimenter.

Despite poor experimental records, EVP researchers continue to devote time and energy to finding a way to capture something on tape that proves life after death. In the last few decades EVP has moved into other media, including TV, video and film cameras and computers. Researchers all over the world have reported seeing images and hearing voices produced by their TVs for which there is no known cause, as well as spontaneous printouts from computers.

WHERE DO THE VOICES COME FROM?

Sceptics assert that there is nothing to EVP at all – that the 'voices' are either hoaxed, random noise interpreted as voices, real voices already on the tape, or voices picked up from radio, cell phones and other such sources.

It has been suggested that the voices are simply sub-jective interpretations – that we tend to hear voices in random patterns of sound, rather in the way that we often see faces in random visual patterns. The argument is that because of the significance to humans of speech and facial recognition, the human brain has an in-built tendency to create these perceptions even when there is no 'objective' basis for the experience. It's also been suggested that they come from the researchers' own subconscious, that some-how the researchers' thoughts are projected on to the tape.

For others the Raudive voices are genuinely mysterious, even paranormal. Some really believe they open up the possibility of communication with the dead. This is why many researchers go to cemeteries seeking EVPs. (In this context, the phenomenon is sometimes called instrumental transcommunication, or ITC.)

There are exceptions, but most parapsychologists today aren't focusing on EVP research, and modern reports by sceptics in parapsychological literature find no evidence of anything paranormal in such recordings. That does not deter the devoted, of course: it is claimed that there are more than fifty thousand sites on the internet devoted to EVP!

OUR CONCLUSIONS

Ghosts have fascinated us for millennia, for there have been sightings for that long. If you've seen or sensed a ghost yourself, that will be proof enough for you, but if you are like the majority of people who have not experienced the phenomenon, proof will always be wanted. It wasn't until the invention of photography and recording devices (both audio and video) that tangible proof was actually possible. But do they provide definitive proof?

The answer of course is no, since photos and recordings can be hoaxed, and many are open to interpretation. But as we've seen there may be a few exceptions: the photos and recordings in this chapter are for the most part considered genuine – that is, not deliberately hoaxed or fabricated.

Although famous captured evidence has not yet yielded concrete, scientific proof of ghosts or the afterlife, we believe that it has provided enough unexplained evidence to serve as proof for believers and give pause to sceptics.

6

TYPICAL EVIDENCE

'Matters of fact well proved ought not to be denied because we cannot conceive how they can be performed. Nor is it a reasonable method of inference first to presume the thing impossible and then to conclude that the fact cannot be proved. On the contrary, we should judge of the action by the evidence and not of the evidence by the measures of our fancies about the action.'

JOSEPH GLANVILLE: SODUCISMUS TRIUMPHATUS (1681)

It's important to stress again that the evidence discussed in the previous chapter which seems to defy all natural explanation is extremely rare. The majority of investigators don't uncover this kind of clarity. In this chapter we'll take a look at the kind of evidence that is typically presented as 'proof' that ghosts do exist.

PHOTOGRAPHIC ANOMALIES

These types of photos are the most commonly reported and you will probably see more photos on the Internet of supposedly mysterious balls of light, called orbs, than of anything else. They are thought by many to be an indication of a ghostly manifestation, so it is no wonder that the appearance of an orb on a photograph generates much excitement. Those hazy light circles which, unseen to the human eye, suddenly appear on a photograph taken in an allegedly haunted location are often hard to explain.

To appreciate how much interest there now is in orbs, type 'ghost orbs' into an internet search engine. Google conjures up thousands and thousands of webpages. Sites from New York and Sydney to Dallas and Brighton are peppered with theories, witness testimonies and photographs, some of them incredible. These mysterious lights can, it seems, be photographed anywhere – in homes, garages and gardens, even at parties – but particularly in cemeteries and allegedly haunted locations. A classification system according to size has been devised and the anatomy – the inner and outer layers of the entities – named and analysed. Also shown on these sites are other sub-categories of the phenomena: rods, light slugs, mists and vortexes. In the USA, courses are offered in the techniques of orb photography and the International Ghost Hunters Society presents a 'Floating Orb Award' for the most convincing.

WHAT IS AN ORB?

An orb, in the context of paranormal photography, is a light anomaly that is captured on a photograph. It is not necessarily round in shape. Many L-shaped and crescent shaped orbs have been identified, for example. Some orbs even have the appearance of feathers or threads. There are also sub-categories of orbs, for example vortexes (more swirling motion) and mists (more hazy). Traditionally it is circular balls of light that paranormal investigators refer to as orbs. Other light shapes are generally referred to as light anomalies.

As far as we know it all seems to have begun in 1974 when parapsychologists Kerry Gaynor and Barry Taff were studying the well-known Entity Case of Carlotta Moran in Culver City, California, and saw strange lights. According to Gaynor: 'We were seeing little pops of light. They would happen quickly. We would try to shoot the camera, but they were happening too quickly and we just couldn't catch them. We were shooting with a Polaroid and with a 35mm camera.' Taff described the lights as 'three-dimensional, greenish-yellow to white balls of light'. Gaynor also said: 'But I was very concerned that somebody was faking it by projecting light on to the wall. So I said to it, "If you're really here, come off the wall." I didn't think anything would happen. But then the light pulled right out of the wall and floated into the middle of the room. It started spinning and twisting and expanding in different directions simultaneously. I had nine professional photographers shooting every angle of that room. It was extraordinary because it was floating in the middle of the room and the light was dimensional. It is very difficult to fake something like that. If you project light, you have to project it on to a flat surface. You can't project light into empty space unless you have some kind of very sophisticated laser system. This was not likely a sophisticated hoax because this house had twice been condemned by the city, and the investigators had sealed off the entire bedroom. Nobody could go in or out during the photo session.'

Unlike in this case, orbs are mostly unseen at the time the photos are shot, and are discovered only after the film is developed. The prevailing theory is that paranormal investigators are able to capture spirits on film due to the wider spectrum of light that film is sensitive to, as compared to the human eye. Common film is responsive to both the low end of the spectrum and the high end of the ultraviolet spectrum, both invisible to the naked eye. Sceptics counter these claims with theories that include tricks of light, flaws in the film, errors in development (and judgement), lens flare, water spots, and simple deliberate fraud.

THE HISTORY OF UNEXPLAINED LIGHTS

Even though photographic anomalies are currently hot topics on the internet, they are nothing new: unexplained lights have been reported for centuries. The term 'earth lights' comes from a scientific explanation put forward by Paul Devereux in 1982 that the lights are produced by the earth itself. Also known as 'spooklights' or 'ghost lights', these can be almost any colour, of varying intensity, shape and size, and can on occasion give off sounds. They may appear as luminous vapours, have glowing tails, pulse, move erratically and sometimes even explode. Experiences of them are varied and they may have a number of causes.

Will-o'-the-wisps are small sources of light, usually blue in colour, seen moving around marshes and woodland, keeping fairly close to the ground. Also known as 'fairy lights', 'corpse candles' and 'fox fire', they were feared in medieval times as a menace to travellers – who could be led astray, or 'pixie-led', by mischievous fairies and pixies. The cause of the phenomenon is not understood. It was originally believed to be ignited marsh gases, but this has been discounted in recent experiments and the latest theories suggest some kind of chemical reaction.

St Elmo's fire is an electrical luminescence often seen around high masts or poles. Other forms of associated luminescence are high-altitude energy discharges and lightning effects. These include ball lightning and lightning associated with volcanoes. Earthquake lights are observed during earthquake activity, close to fault lines in the earth's crust. Some theories of 'earth lights' say that they usually occur near the sites of major and minor faults, but they do not need an earthquake to make themselves evident.

Lab experiments have demonstrated piezoelectric effects with certain rocks such as quartz, and sparks or small balls of light can be produced if enough stress is applied to them. Other theories for the occurrence of earth lights include electrical charges in the upper atmosphere and the natural electrical charge of the earth itself.

Today strange lights captured on photograph are, without doubt, one of the most popular but contentious subjects within the field of paranormal investigating.

Serious scientific explanations like those offered above have divided paranormal investigators and caused them to take strongly differing views, ranging from total conviction that the lights are genuine paranormal phenomena, to an equally strong conviction that the vast majority can be explained by science or misjudgement or error on the part of the photographer.

ARE ORBS REAL?

In our opinion a very high percentage of so-called orb photographs are simply misidentification of conventional 'flaws'. We've discussed the phenomena with a number of professional photographers, some of whom work exclusively in digital. One particular photographer was particularly scornful when we mentioned that some people thought that orbs were paranormal. She believed that orbs are generally down to the quality of camera as they are often due to pixel fall-out and the camera trying to compensate. Also, if you use a flash the camera will focus on the largest object (i.e. the tree, wall or person etc.) and anything like dust will be very out of focus, and when the light from the flash hits this it creates a large 'flare' in the picture. Digital cameras can also 'see' infra-red wavelengths, and so infra-red light could reflect off particles in front of the lens and create the impression of an orb.

Orbs have also appeared, though less commonly, on video footage, but here too they could be explained to some extent by the theory of infra-red radiation.

It's also possible that some light anomalies occur which

do not have the appearance of the classic orb, i.e. a hazy, grey object. Instead they appear as a light. These could be reflections from quartz, insects or metal. Alternatively they could be the result of accidental photographic capture of stars or aircraft, or, as mentioned above, caused by film or processing faults. Even air-carried moisture from breathing and the flash reflection that results could be responsible for light anomalies.

The theories above are convincing and certainly apply to the great majority of photographic anomalies, but there may be a few exceptions. Ciarán doesn't think orbs are genuine representations of ghosts, but Yvette believes there are a number of reasons why a tiny percentage may be genuine. Firstly, there seems to be a strong association between haunted locations and the appearance of orbs. We don't just use digital cameras on ghost investigations, we use them at parties, on holiday and so on, but for some reason the orb phenomenon is very rarely captured under these circumstances.

Secondly, if all orb anomalies are simply explainable as flaws, then given the huge volume of orb photos posted on the internet there are a lot of cameras out there that have inherent faults. Most of the major manufacturers have carried out their own analysis of these anomalies, and most have admitted that of the examples they have examined, in particular orbs that are not grey, not all can be explained.

WHAT IS AN ORB, IF IT IS PARANORMAL?

The most popular theory is that an orb is an indication of a paranormal manifestation, or, to put it more simply, the early stages of a ghost formation. It is said that a ghost will draw energy from its surroundings as it is about to manifest itself. Energy can be present in three forms: heat, light and sound – and reported hauntings often feature one or more of these forms. For example, 'cold spots' have often been reported during hauntings. This could be the ghost drawing heat from the surroundings as an energy source. The energy continues to be drawn from the environment to a point where it expresses itself as a light. Whether the light is constant, flashing, or a hazy faint glow, this is what is known as an orb.

Another theory is that an orb is a spirit moving between different dimensions or 'planes of existence'. Yet another explanation is that an orb is in itself an actual manifestation of psychoactive energy which 'empowers' paranormal phenomena.

Whilst all of these theories are possibilities, and none can be entirely proved or dismissed, it is impossible to make any real judgement on the matter. For us not only is the jury still out on the existence of orbs, it is also out on the nature of orbs.

ORBS ON PHOTOGRAPHS: A CHECK-LIST

Until unusual images on film that appear to defy rational explanation are adequately explained by science, paranormal researchers will continue to examine them with great interest and wonder. When a photograph of an orb is examined, it is crucial to consider the following before jumping to conclusions:

- Was the photograph taken in dusty conditions? e.g. in a building that had not been visited for some time. Were there any reflective surfaces close by when the photograph was taken?

- Was any person using a torch nearby?

- Was the camera lens clean?

- Were there any draughts or pockets of warm air present when the photograph was taken?

- Have the negatives from conventional film been retained for closer scrutiny?

In the case of a photograph being taken in a dusty location, an orb may be nothing more mysterious than particles of dust being raised. Nearby reflective surfaces could have 'bounced' flash from the camera back on to the lens, causing strange light effects. This could also be the case with a torch being used nearby.

If the camera lens was dirty then particles on the lens would appear as anomalies on the photograph. Also, dust and pollen can be carried on draughts and warm air which, when photographed, causes orbs to appear.

157

If an anomaly occurs then it is good practice to obtain a duplicate picture to see if it can be recreated. Failure for the anomaly to reappear suggests a fault in the development process. With digital pictures, a second picture should be taken instantly after the first, under exactly the same conditions. This second picture acts as a control, and aids identification of the anomaly. For example, if a grey, hazy ball appears in exactly the same place on both pictures than it may be a speck of dirt on the lens.

This process of elimination should continue until all possible explanations are exhausted. Objective investigators should never jump to conclusions, as it is partly their genuine attempt and failure to provide a rational explanation which will make their evidence more compelling. When we investigate a picture which appears to show an orb, we take into account all the considerations above. We would never say that it is an orb, we suggest the possibility. We only really take note of apparent orbs that seem to be producing light, or glowing. We also look for streaking behind it, much like a comet, as this could possibly suggest that the 'object' is moving very rapidly, far too fast to be an insect or falling dust.

VOICES IN THE WIND

'Then away out in the woods I heard that kind of a sound that a ghost makes when it wants to tell about something that's on its mind and can't make itself understood, and so can't rest easy in its grave, and has to go about that way every night grieving.'

MARK TWAIN

In the previous chapter we mentioned EVP recordings, which have become a popular method for amateur enthusiasts to provide evidence of a haunting. During the 1970s and early '80s, EVP was tremendously popular among paranormal researchers and it has caught on again in recent years. Even Hollywood has caught on to EVP with the 2004 suspense thriller *White Noise*, starring Michael Keaton as a husband who becomes obsessed with trying to contact his dead wife. When he finally succeeds and hears her voice on tape, he opens up a portal to another world.

In the late 1960s, EVP began to be accepted as a legitimate form of paranormal research, but like orbs it has remained extremely controversial. The problems arise because of the way in which messages are normally recorded. They are rarely simple messages but often are fragments and sounds that require hours of listening to understand. This often leaves the research open to criticism, but by using detailed, restricted and well-monitored techniques to achieve EVP recordings, much of the room for error can be eliminated from your experiments.

We have heard dozens of recordings of what might be voices and the sounds of ghosts on tape. But we often have to ask ourselves just what we are hearing. Are they accidental recordings of the researchers themselves? Sounds that have no meaning? Or real ghosts?

Many researchers make the valid point that there is a natural human inclination to project meaning on to otherwise innocent or random sounds. 'Humans are exceptionally wonderful at finding patterns in noise,' says Edwin C. May, Ph.D., president of the Laboratories for Fundamental Research. 'The hardware in our sensory system is designed to see changes in things.' So when we hear repeated sounds, our brain picks out and pieces together what sound to us like spoken words. If you listen to thousands of pieces of audio, Dr May contends, you will eventually find one that sounds like a voice. 'It's the monkey on the typewriter issue.'

EVP researchers counter that the highly interactive communication they have engaged in would be impossible to discount as interference or brain tricks. Unfortunately the authenticity of an EVP recording is at present impossible to prove, as all that we really have is the word of the researcher that it is not a hoax or caused by a natural phenomenon.

QUALITY CONTROL

EVPs are mostly captured on audiotape. The mysterious voices are not heard at the time of recording, but only when the tape is played back. Sometimes amplification and noise filtering are required to hear the voices.

Some EVPs are more easily heard and understood than others. And they vary in gender (men and women), age (adults and children), tone and emotion. They usually speak in single words, phrases and short sentences. Sometimes they are just grunts, groans, growling and other vocal noises. EVP has been recorded speaking in various languages. The most fascinating aspect of EVP is that the voices sometimes respond directly to the people making the recording. The researchers will ask a question, for example, and the voice will answer or comment. Again, this response is not heard until later when the tape is played back.

It is true that the quality of EVP recordings varies widely. The great majority are of such low quality that we are left to guess what the voice is saying. There are a few, however, and these include the Raudive recordings mentioned in the last chapter, that are quite clear and are usually categorised as Class A recordings. These EVPs represent the best evidence for a phenomenon yet to be fully understood.

Where do these voices come from? This is the big question. Do they come from our own subconscious? Are they angelic or demonic in nature? Do they cross over from other dimensions of reality? Are they the voices of dead people? Are they a misinterpretation of random noise? What are they?

A FATE WORSE THAN DEATH?

For now let us temporarily consider the controversial theory that they are the voices of dead people. The ghost phenomenon has always raised unsettling questions about what happens to some of us when we die, and EVPs seem to be direct communication from these spirits. They offer us the holy grail of ghost investigation: hard evidence. The voices are right there on the recordings. They respond, answer questions, and even ask questions of their own. There are hundreds of these voices documented – maybe even thousands.

There are EVPs reflecting the full range of human personalities and emotions. These voices are not only self-aware, but their interaction with researchers indicates that they are aware of the living. They can hear us and see us. Do they know they are dead? Do they know we are alive? Do they know the difference?

The great majority of these voices seem to be stuck in a kind of limbo, and there is a kind of confusion and uncertainty in many of the things they say. If EVPs are evidence of an afterlife, perhaps the question we should be asking ourselves is not what they are, but what does this imply for us? We too might get stuck struggling to make contact with strange beings walking around with tape recorders. We're not ones to think negatively about death and its aftermath, but EVPs seem to suggest that life after death might not be as clear-cut or as peaceful as it is often thought to be.

OUR THOUGHTS ON IT ALL

Some researchers automatically dismiss all orb photos and refuse to accept them in their research. Others feel that every orb photograph they obtain is proof positive that they have captured a ghost or spirit on film. Not everyone believes that the voices EVP researchers hear are other-worldly spirits. Some sceptics say that EVP is nothing more than radio interference. Others say that people who claim to have heard these voices are either imagining them or else their minds are creating meaning out of insignificant sound, projecting what the person wants or expects to hear on to the recording. To date neither sceptic nor believer has been proved one hundred per cent right or wrong.

There is no doubt that much of the evidence currently being brought forward to prove the existence of ghosts is highly controversial. Does this mean then that orb photos and EVP recordings are useless when it comes to paranormal investigating? If such photos are presented as 'proof' of a location hauntings or an EVP recording is used as 'evidence' of the existence of a ghost, then as far as we are concerned, the answer is yes. We look for evidence that will withstand the most hardened critics out there, and with the overwhelming evidence stacked against orbs and EVP, it is unwise and unscientific to use them as hard evidence. We do make exceptions to this rule though: if evidence of outstanding quality and integrity is presented that defies natural explanation, it would be equally unscientific and unwise for us to reject the paranormal as a possible explanation.

Hopefully, with paranormal investigators all over the world showing ever greater interest and dedication, some significant advances in our understanding of orbs, EVP and the like will one day be achieved. Until then, as far as we are concerned, the jury is still out.

We find typical captured evidence and the amount of it produced utterly compelling and definitely worthy of investigation. But one thing we have learned over the years is that as far as investigation of the paranormal is concerned there is nothing wrong with not reaching an absolute conclusion and therefore leaving a case open.

7

THE DARK SIDE: 'EVIL' CASES

'Especially important is the warning to avoid conversations with the demon. We may ask what is relevant but anything beyond that is dangerous. He is a liar. The demon is a liar. He will lie to confuse us. But he will also mix lies with the truth to attack us. The attack is psychological, Damien, and powerful. So don't listen to him. Remember that – do not listen.'

FATHER MERRIN IN *THE EXORCIST* (1973)

In folklore and mythology all over the world evil spirits, also known as demons, are supernatural and malevolent beings that can be conjured and insecurely controlled.

The notion of evil spirits is as old as human kind itself. Demons are found in many religions, and many cultures have developed a rich mythology of demons as a result. The study of demons is called demonology, while the worship of demons is known as demonolatry.

In Hinduism there are three kinds of beings, the devas (gods), the manushyas (human beings) and the asuras (demons). In Buddhism the word demon can refer to a sentient being in either Hell realm or Asura realm, depending on the tradition. In Islam tradition attributes to Muhammad the statement that every man has an angel and a demon appointed to attend him. The former guides him toward goodness, while the latter leads him to evil ('Mishkat', i., ch. 3).

In St Mark's Gospel, Jesus casts out many demons, or evil spirits, from those who are afflicted with various ailments (such as epileptic seizures). The imagery is clear: Jesus is far superior to the power of demons over the human beings that they inhabit, and He is able to free these human victims by commanding and casting out the demons, by binding them, and forbidding them to return. These events occur throughout the gospel accounts, and are associated with miraculous healing, and are consequently part of the 'good news', along with the announcement that 'the kingdom of God is at hand'.

In some present-day cultures, evil spirits and demons are still feared in popular superstition, largely due to their alleged power to 'possess' humans, and they are an important concept in many modern occultist traditions.

Because of this strong association with religion, theologians, philosophers, practitioners, clergy and psychical researchers have debated the existence of 'evil spirits' for centuries. Few subjects have sparked more passion, more tension and more controversy. But is any of it real? Do evil spirits exist?

EVIL SPIRITS

From the earliest recorded times evil spirits, or demons, have been accused of perpetuating every imaginable crime against humanity, including that which is considered most heinous, possession. From physical attack to lustful and murderous temptations, to panic and causing nightmares, evil spirits, or the idea of them, have terrified us for centuries.

Some scholars explain evil spirits psychologically: they are hideous creatures of our own making that serve to torment us as just punishment for some wrongdoing. Others feel that in order to validate the existence of God, we must have a Devil, and if God has Angels, then surely the Devil has his own followers, demons. Others believe demons to be the spiritual and, sometimes, physical manifestation of an evil or malevolent force. Yet others describe them as vengeful, malevolent spirits of the dead, intent on causing harm to the living.

But demons weren't always considered evil. To the ancient Greeks daemons, from the Greek word diamon meaning 'divine power', 'fate' or 'god', were intermediary spirits between god and humankind, rather like guardian spirits. They could be either good or evil, depending on circumstances and the individual they attached themselves to. Good daemons were supportive and encouraging, but evil daemons could lead people astray with bad counsel. The Christian church labelled all such pagan spirits as evil, which is why today demons are traditionally associated with evil.

For centuries evil spirits have been blamed for a host of ills and misfortunes, but the best known perhaps are cases of possession, which we'll discuss later in this chapter, and cases of demonic sexual molestation, where an evil entity masquerades as a man or woman to molest, some say sexually, its victim.

In Western demonology, an incubus is a male spirit or demon that disturbs the sleep of a woman, often subjecting her to nightmares or unwanted sexual intercourse. During the Middle Ages incubi (from the Latin incubare, 'to lie upon') were thought to be particularly fond of seducing nuns and other women committed to the celibate life. The female equivalent of the incubus is the succubus (from the Latin succubare, 'to lie under'), a female demon or spirit who is said to disturb the sleep of a man and initiate sexual intercourse with him.

Victims of what is called 'Old Hag syndrome' claim that they awake abruptly to find that they cannot move, even though they can see, hear, feel and smell. There is sometimes the feeling of a great weight on the chest and the sense that there is a sinister or evil presence in the room. Sceptics argue that rather than witches, ghosts or demons there is probably a medical or scientific explanation for Old Hag Syndrome, such as indigestion, sleep disorders or repressed tension.

Sexual repression is thought to be the most likely explanation for cases of demonic sexual molestation. Others believe that tales of encounters with night demons might be easily explained by a phenomenon known as sleep paralysis. Sleep paralysis is a condition that occurs in the state just before dropping off to sleep or just before fully awakening from sleep. The condition is characterised by being unable to move or speak. It is often typically associated with a feeling that there is some sort of menacing presence, a feeling which often arouses fear but is also accompanied by an inability to cry out.

The paralysis may last only a few seconds, but it leaves a lasting impression.

Sleep paralysis, along with medical problems and sexual tension, can probably explain the great majority of cases but, as is so often the case with paranormal investigation, can we be sure they explain them all?

FEEDING ON FEAR

'Evil spirits are negative attitudes, destructive emotions rooted in fear. Some of the more common evil spirits are resentment, anger, shame, guilt, anxiety, hatred, greed, revenge, jealousy. All thinly disguised forms of fear, their presence in a human system gives harmful physical agents something to attach themselves to.'

KEN CAREY: VISION

When it comes to evil spirits our imagination tends to run wild. Fiery monsters from some hellish abyss are liable to fill the minds of those who have seen their supposed likeness in modern media-based depictions. However, if you take a look at eyewitness accounts and reports of encounters with evil entities, such terrifying visions are extremely rare. Typically when an evil spirit 'attacks' it tends to be in complete invisibility. Think about it: if you wanted to scare the living daylights out of someone isn't the best way to lash out undetected and without warning?

By causing uncertainty and confusion, evil spirits start to take hold of their victims. In many ways this early stage of 'attack' is said to be very similar to the phenomena caused by hauntings and poltergeists: strange noises, whispers, footsteps, objects moved and so on. Minor but sustained scare tactics establish a fuel source for the entity: the victim's fear of what they do not understand.

Next, if the 'attack' continues, a mental barrage of temptation, terrible dreams and fear may consume the person. Constant sleep deprivation may occur and the victim's mental and emotional weaknesses will be exploited. Physical phenomena will increase in both duration and intensity: larger, heavier objects will move and harder poundings will occur. There may also be actual biting and scratching as part of the debasing physical assaults on the intended victim.

This struggle, this stalking of the essence of an individual, may take weeks, months, or even years. The aim is to slowly dominate and conquer the will of that person and set the stage for the ultimate demonic goal and desire: possession.

POSSESSION

'All that spirits desire, spirits attain.'

KAHLIL GIBRAN

Unwanted possessions have been recognised since ancient times and have been blamed for a number of problems and ills. Possession is a condition in which a person feels they have been taken over, or 'possessed', mentally, physically and emotionally by an outside spirit entity or separate personality. This entity then controls all aspects of their personality. It has essentially taken over. Temporary possessions that take place during a séance are considered harmless, as are voluntary possessions by gods or spirits that take place during religious and healing rituals; but when an evil spirit attempts to take over permanently the personality and life of an unwilling subject it is thought to be extremely dangerous.

Possession hasn't always been viewed as demonic in the West. There are some who believe that possessing spirits are souls or the dead who simply don't realise they are dead and try to return to a body, or they are spirits who have a message they want to communicate to someone. In either case the victim experiences mood disorders, strange noises and lights, voices, poltergeist phenomena and sometimes perhaps temporary insanity.

The belief that mental illness may be caused by possessing spirits is an ancient one. Spiritism, a European off-shoot of spiritualism founded by Allan Kardec in the nineteenth century, holds that certain mental illnesses have a spiritual cause and can be treated through communication with spirit guides. Kardec's theories caught on in France but not in the rest of Europe. They have, however, found an enthusiastic response in Latin America, particularly Brazil, where many still practise spiritist healing.

In the early part of the twentieth century James Hyslop, president of the American Society for Psychical Research (ASPR), put forward the controversial theory that many of those who suffer from mental problems such as multiple personality disorder could be showing signs of possession. Another alternative theory on possession was put forward by American psychologist Carl Wickland, who believed that spirits were not evil but simply confused and trying to finish their worldly business in a living person. This could cause any number of mental problems. In his controversial book *Thirty Years among the Dead* (1924) Wickland recommended using mild electric shock to help the spirits leave. This view still has a number of supporters, among them psychiatrist Dr Ralph Allison, who wrote in his book *Minds in Many Pieces* (1980) that various of his patients exhibited signs of demonic possession and required exorcism as well as conventional treatment.

Such alternative theories have the support of some psychiatrists and adherents but, understandably, they are not endorsed by the medical or scientific community or by the majority of parapsychologists.

EXORCISM

According to tradition there seems to be only one cure for an unwanted possession and that is exorcism. In many cultures and religions all over the world demons have been exorcised. In Catholic Christianity demonic possession – in which demons battle for a person's soul – are dealt with by formal exorcism rites that date back to 1614. Except for possession by the Holy Spirit, Christianity regards possession as the work of the devil, and formal exorcisms continue to be reported to this day. These exorcisms are highly controversial, yet despite opposition from learned circles, some churches continue to practise this so-called demon purge. It's interesting to note that many other religions have similar ceremonies for ridding people of these mysterious entities.

As with most controversial subjects, demons have made their way to Hollywood. *The Amityville Horror* (1979, remade in 2005) was a movie supposedly constructed around a true story, but was later exposed as a hoax and spawned a host of lawsuits. *Poltergeist* (1982) was another movie offering, playing on the theme of the demonic entity preying on a young child. *The Haunted* (1995) portrayed the so-called true events that took place in the home of Jack and Janet Smurl in West Pittston, Pennsylvania, from 1985 to 1987. This particular case received wide attention in the media. Although the house went through three exorcisms and investigations by demonologists Ed and Lorraine Warren, the demon apparently refused to leave.

Perhaps the most famous of all demon movies, however, is *The Exorcist* (1973), which chronicles the demonic possession of a young girl and the ensuing efforts of the clergy to exorcise this foul creature. What is less well known but, we believe, even more compelling than the movie itself, is that a decade after the making of the film, a priest from the New York diocese came forward to support the facts presented in the story. He said he had been directly involved in the 1949 exorcism in St Louis on which it was based.

Shortly afterwards, for reasons unknown, he was 'transferred' by the Bishop to 'parts unknown' . . .

THE ST LOUIS EXORCISM

The St Louis exorcism was the real 1949 case of alleged demonic possession that inspired *The Exorcist* – both William Peter Blatty's 1971 best-selling book version and William Friedkin's hugely successful 1973 film.

The story began in Cottage Hills, Maryland, St Louis, and involved a young boy called Robbie Doe rather than a teenage girl as depicted in the book and the movie. Robbie was the product of a dysfunctional family and a troubled childhood.

In January 1949, the family of thirteen-year-old Robbie heard scratching sounds coming from inside the walls and ceilings of the house. They thought mice might be to blame but an exterminator could find no sign of mice. This was nothing, however, compared to the alleged physical assaults on Robbie. His bed shook so hard that he couldn't sleep at night. His blankets and sheets were torn off the bed, and when he tried to hold on to them, he was reportedly pulled off the bed and on to the floor with the sheets still gripped in his hands.

THE DIARY

William Peter Blatty, a student at Georgetown University at the time, first became interested in the story after reading about it in a newspaper. Scanning the papers for information, he discovered that one of them actually listed the name of the priest involved. His name was the Revd William S. Bowdern. However, priests who perform exorcisms are said to be sworn to secrecy, and Bowdern refused to comment on the case. Later, when writing his book, Blatty changed the identity of the possession victim to a young girl, but the exorcist of the novel remains an apparently thinly veiled portrait of Bowdern.

Father Bowdern never publicly acknowledged the fact that he was involved in the St Louis case. Before his death in 1983, however, he did discuss it with other Jesuits, and eventually these stories reached Thomas Allen, an author and contributing editor to *National Geographic*. It was Allen who managed to find one of the participants in the case, Walter Halloran, who was then living in a small town in Minnesota. Halloran was reluctant to talk but he did admit that there had been a diary.

Many of the early events in the St Louis case were believed to have been chronicled in a diary by the Jesuit priests who later performed the exorcism. It was thought to be a 16-page document that was entitled 'Case Study by Jesuit Priests'. It had apparently been intended to be used as a guide for future exorcisms. The diary was said to have been found in the old Alexian Brothers Hospital just before it was demolished. The only real evidence we have now about the case comes from this alleged diary and from witnesses who were present at the time. The Catholic Church has to this day never released details of the story.

THE 'ATTACK' INTENSIFIES

Family members witnessing the attacks on Robbie became desperate. They turned to the church for help and advice.

The Revd Luther Schulze, a Lutheran minister and the pastor from the family's own church, tried praying with Robbie and his parents in their home and then with Robbie alone. It didn't help. The weird noises continued to be heard in the house, and Robbie's bed went on shaking and rocking so violently that he was unable to get any sleep at night. Finally Schulze decided to question whether it was the house that was haunted, or the boy. He offered to let Robbie spend the night in his home and his parents quickly agreed.

That night, Mrs Schulze went to the guest room and Robbie and the minister retired to the twin beds located in the master bedroom. About ten minutes later, Schulze reported that he heard the sound of Robbie's bed creaking and shaking. He also heard strange scratching noises inside the walls, just like the ones that had been heard at Robbie's own house. Schulze quickly switched on the lights and clearly saw the vibrating bed. When he prayed for it to stop, the vibration grew even more violent. He stated that Robbie was wide awake but that he was completely still, certainly not moving in a way that would cause the bed to shake.

Schulze then suggested that Robbie try to sleep in a heavy armchair that was located across the room. While Schulze watched him closely, the chair began to move. First, it scooted backward several inches and its legs jolted forward and back. Moments later, it literally slammed against the wall and then it tipped over and deposited the boy unhurt on to the floor.

The Revd Schulze made a pallet of blankets on the floor

for Robbie to sleep on. As soon as the boy fell asleep, however, the pallet began to slide across the floor and under one of the beds. Robbie's hands were visible the entire time and his body was taut with tension. The blankets didn't even wrinkle at all!

According to some sources, Robbie's family then turned to the Catholic Church for help. His father went to the nearby St James Church in Mount Rainier, Maryland, where he met with a priest named Edward Albert Hughes. Hughes was sceptical and reluctant to get involved, but he did agree to go and see Robbie. During the visit, Robbie allegedly addressed the priest in Latin, a language that he did not know. Shaken by the experience, Hughes was said to have applied to his archbishop for permission to conduct an exorcism. The sources go on to say that the ritual was performed at Georgetown Hospital in February. Robbie seemed to go into a trance and he thrashed about and spoke in tongues. Hughes ordered the boy to be put into restraints but he somehow managed to work a piece of metal spring loose from the bed and he slashed the priest with it. The stories say that Hughes was worn down by the stress of it all and suffered a nervous breakdown.

Church records do not indicate that Father Hughes ever suffered a breakdown or that he ever even made an attempt to exorcise Robbie at Georgetown University Hospital. However, there are records that Robbie was checked into the hospital under his real name for several days during the period when the alleged exorcism attempt took place. The records say that he underwent extensive medical and psychological evaluations.

At about this same time, mysterious writing began to appear on Robbie's rib cage, back, wrists and thighs. When this skin branding occurred, Robbie's hands were allegedly always visible and his mother specifically notes that he could not have scratched the words himself. He had been under observation at the time and the words, according to witnesses, had simply appeared.

In early March, having been found normal and released from the hospital, Robbie went to St Louis with his parents. Unfortunately, he did not improve and various other relatives witnessed more of the skin brandings as well as the bed and mattress shaking on many occasions. On 8 March 1949, a stool that was sitting near the bed was seen flying across the room by Robbie's cousin. The boy was so concerned about Robbie that he even tried lying down on the bed beside him to stop the mattress from shaking. To his horror, it didn't work.

Finally, one of the relatives, who had attended St Louis University, went to see an old teacher there, the Revd Raymond J. Bishop. Although initially sceptical about the case, Bishop went to the house alone to give the boy a blessing. Again it didn't help and the bed still shook violently and the scratches still appeared all over the boy's body. Bishop then sprinkled holy water on the bed in the form of a cross. The movement suddenly ceased but, seconds later, Robbie was struck down with pain in his stomach. His mother pulled back the bed covers and lifted the boy's pyjama top to reveal red lines that zigzagged across the boy's abdomen. All the time Robbie was in clear view of at least six witnesses. At that point, it was decided to perform an exorcism and, surprisingly, the archdiocese agreed to the request.

The chronology throughout the remainder of the case is extremely confused. It is not clear how long Robbie stayed at his relative's house but it is known that he was taken to the Alexian Brothers Hospital in St Louis, possibly for as long as a month, and that parts of the exorcism were also carried out in the rectory of the St Francis Xavier Church. The rectory has since been demolished and replaced. It also isn't clear how many people were actually actively involved in the exorcism. The names of the exorcists given out in St Louis were Father Bowdern, Father Bishop and Father Lawrence Kenny. Father Charles O'Hara of Marquette University in Milwaukee was also present as a witness (he later passed on information about what he saw there to Father Eugene Gallagher at Georgetown), and in addition there were undoubtedly several hospital staff members and seminary students in attendance.

One of these students was Walter Halloran, the priest who knew about the diary. At that time, he was a strong and fit young man who had been asked along to hold Robbie down. For reasons unknown Halloran was removed from the exorcism about one week before it came to end, which leaves his account of it rather incomplete. And although efforts were made by the priests to bury the evidence, hospital staff members remembered the events with fear. One of the nurses involved stated that the priests had a terrifying time during Robbie's hospital stay and that what they saw was demonic in origin.

THE ORDEAL ITSELF

The exorcism itself apparently started at the home of Robbie's relatives. The priests came late in the evening, and after Robbie went to bed, the ritual began. The boy was said to go into a trance, his bed shook and welts and scratches appeared on his body. Bishop was said to have wiped away blood that welled up in the scratches while Halloran attempted to hold the boy down.

As the prayers commanding the departure of the evil spirit began, Robbie winced and rolled in a sudden seizure of pain. Over the next two hours, the boy was branded and scratched thirty times on his stomach, chest, throat, thighs, calves and back. When Bowdern demanded that the demon reveal itself, the words 'WELL' and 'SPITE' appeared on the boy's chest. Another time, the word 'HELL' appeared in red welts as the boy rocked back and forth, apparently in pain. All the while, he reportedly cursed and screamed foul language in a voice that 'ranged from deep bass to falsetto'. That night the ritual came to an end near dawn, but little progress had been made.

The ordeal continued in the weeks that followed, with many readings of the exorcism ritual. According to the witnesses, the boy's actions and words became more violent and repulsive as time went on. He was said to speak in Latin, in a variety of voices, in between bouts of screaming and cursing. He spat in the faces of the priests who knelt and stood by his bed, and his spittle and vomit struck them with uncanny accuracy and over great distances. He punched and slapped the priests and the witnesses. He constantly urinated and belched and passed gas that was said to have an unbelievable stench. He was even said to have taunted the priests and to have confronted them with information about themselves that he could not possibly have known. His body thrashed and contorted all night long, but strangely by morning he would appear quite normal and profess to have no memory of the events that had taken place after dark. He would spend the day reading quietly or playing board games with the student assistants.

The priests requested permission to instruct Robbie in the Catholic faith, hoping it would help strengthen their fight against the entity possessing the boy. His parents consented and he was prepared for his first communion. Robbie seemed to enjoy his instruction and was moved to the rectory, but when the time came for him to receive communion he broke out into a rage and had to be dragged into the church. The exorcism was clearly not working.

Father Bowdern, who had been working on the exorcism all this time, learned of an 1870 case that took place in Wisconsin, that seemed similar, and devised a new plan. On the night of 18 April, when the ritual resumed, Bowdern forced Robbie to wear a chain of religious medals and to hold a crucifix in his hands. Robbie became strangely contrite and attempted to engage Bowdern in conversation about the meaning of some Latin prayers. Bowdern ignored him and demanded to know the name of the demon and when it would depart.

Robbie then exploded with rage and five witnesses held

him down until he screamed that he was a fallen angel. Relentlessly Bowdern continued with the ritual, reciting it incessantly for hours until Robbie suddenly spoke in a loud, masculine voice. The voice, identifying itself as St Michael the archangel, ordered the demon to leave. Robbie went into violent contortions and spasms, but then he fell quiet and silent. Seconds later he sat up, smiled, and said in a normal voice. 'He's gone.' He then told the priests of a vision that he had of St Michael holding a flaming sword.

The exorcism was over at last.

THE AFTERMATH

Robbie left St Louis with his parents a week or so later and returned to Maryland. In May 1949 he wrote to Father Bowdern and told him that he was happy and had a new dog. He was, by last report, still living in Maryland and is a devout Catholic with three children. He has only very dim recollections of what happened in 1949.

Father Bowdern believed until the end of his life that he and his fellow priests had been battling a demonic entity. Those who believe him say there were many witnesses to the diabolical events that took place and that no other explanations existed for what was seen. A full report that was filed by the Catholic Church stated that the case of Robbie Doe was a 'genuine demonic possession'. According to Father John Nicola, who had the opportunity to review the report, 41 persons signed a document attesting to the fact that they had witnessed paranormal phenomena in the case.

For years after the exorcism, people who were involved in the case, or who worked at the hospital, shared stories of things they heard and saw during the ordeal. Nurses spoke of cleaning up pools of vomit and urine in the boy's room, and sounds of screaming and demonic laughter were heard coming from inside it. They also spoke of cold waves of air that seemed to emanate from the room. No matter how warm the rest of the hospital was, the area around the door to the boy's room always seemed ice cold!

Even after the exorcism, some believe that an evil presence lingered. For unknown reasons the room was locked and sealed off after the exorcism and was never reopened. According to witnesses, the lights refused to stay on in the room and the heating would not work. It was always cold and, on occasion, foul odours would drift from beneath the door. The entire section of the hospital was eventually closed, but whether or not this was because of the exorcism room is not known.

When the room was finally opened in 1978 to remove furniture before the hospital was demolished, it is said that the wrecking crew found the exorcism room had lain untouched since 1949. Inside a desk in the room was a copy of the exorcist's diary from the case, which was given to hospital administrators and later became the basis for the public's fascination with the story. And moments before the wrecking ball was about to demolish the room, some of the workman swore they saw something like a 'cat or a big rat or something' emerging. Whether this creature was paranormal or not we wouldn't like to say, but it has certainly added to the rumours, the mysteries and the fear surrounding the St Louis exorcism.

FACT OR FICTION?

There is still no explanation for what took place in 1949 and while the buildings directly involved in the exorcism have all gone, memories of them still linger, perhaps helped a little by the stunning and highly memorable depiction of the case in *The Exorcist*.

Many feel that Robbie was suffering not from demonic possession but from mental illness. He may have been hallucinating or suffering from some weird psychosomatic illness that caused him to behave strangely, curse and scream and to thrash about so violently. This explanation is possible, but it should be noted that those who suggest that this was nothing more than a hoax or a mental illness are all people who were in no way involved in the case. It also doesn't explain Robbie's instant recovery at the end of the exorcism and normal life afterwards with no hint of mental illness. Others suggest that Robbie was playing a prank and, either consciously or unconsciously, creating everything himself, but before his parents consulted a priest, they also had him examined by a psychiatrist who reported that the boy was quite normal, as did a medical doctor who gave him a complete physical examination.

Whether or not you believe in possession, the case remains an enigma that can't be explained away. The only way to dismiss every unusual thing that was reported in this case would be to say that everyone involved was a liar, drunk or insane. This is highly unlikely, considering that many of the priests involved were highly respected members of the community and many entered the case with a high degree of scepticism. As far as we are concerned we can't say that Robbie Doe was possessed, or not possessed, but what we can say is that this is one of the few cases of alleged 'possession' that has left us with many lingering questions. In spite of the sceptics there were, and are, many who believe the events were real.

THE OUIJA BOARD

The Ouija board is a device used to seek out answers to questions about the past, present and future and to receive messages from ghosts, spirits and other entities in spiritualism. The name is taken from the French *oui* and the German *ja* – both words for 'yes'. We've placed it in this chapter because, like possession, the Ouija is thought to be a controversial and dangerous method of interaction with the spirit world. In untrained hands it is believed to attract evil spirits.

Various forms of this method of divination have been used for centuries. In ancient Greece and Rome a small table on wheels was used to point out answers to questions, and we know that in China around 550BC similar devices were being used to communicate with the dead. In 1853 the planchette came into use in Europe. It consisted of a heart-shaped platform on three legs, one of which was a pencil, and the medium would move the device over the paper to spell out messages.

The modern Ouija, which is now marketed as a game, was invented by an American called Elijah J. Bond and sold to William Fuld in 1892, although the names of five other men keep cropping up in the various accounts of its history: Charles Kennard, Harry Welles Rusk, Colonel Washington Bowie, William Maupin, and E.C. Reiche. Reiche was a cabinet-maker, or coffin maker depending on the source, from Chestertown, Maryland, while Charles Kennard and some of the others were supposedly also connected to the area. (Curiously Ciarán did his undergraduate degree and embarked on his career in parapsychology in Washington College, Chestertown.) Fuld founded the Southern Novelty Company in Maryland, which later became the Baltimore Talking Board Company. They called the Ouija board 'Ouija, the Mystifying Oracle'. In 1996 the big toy manufacturers Parker Brothers brought the rights to the board and marketed it so effectively as a game that it sold more than their famous Monopoly game.

The Ouija board itself has a flat smooth surface marked with the letters of the alphabet, the numbers one to ten and the words yes and no. During a séance or other session each participant places a finger on the pointer, or planchette, and asks a question or for a message to be communicated. Although the fingers of the participants are on the planchette there is no conscious control of it and supposedly the planchette spells out the answer under the control of a spirit.

In parapsychology the Ouija board is believed to be a form of automatism: an unconscious activity that picks up information from the subconscious mind. Critics say that the Ouija is dangerous, not only because it can attract evil entities but also because users have no control over repressed material from the subconscious that might be released during a session. Edgar Cayce described it as a 'dangerous toy' and Ouiju boards have been known to fly out of control as though being directed by some unseen force. Advocates of the Ouija believe it to be a powerful and effective way to make contact with the spirit world, to divine the future and obtain daily guidance. Sceptics dismiss it all as nonsense, suggesting that the user is consciously or perhaps unconsciously controlling the movement of the planchette.

The Ouija has figured in many cases of mediumship. For example, the entity Sith initiated communication with medium Jane Roberts through a Ouija board in the 1960s and 1970s. And on 8 July 1913 a St Louis housewife called Pearl Curran was persuaded by her friend Emily Hutchinson to try the Ouija board. She did so and the name Patience Worth came through. This turned out to be the beginnings of an avalanche of information over a period of five years. Mrs Curran produced 2,500 poems, as well as short stories, plays and six full-length novels, all allegedly authored by Patience Worth, who claimed to be a seventeenth-century Englishwoman.

The Parker Brothers recommended way of using the board is for two people to sit opposite each other with the board resting on their knees between them. The planchette should be in the centre of the board and the two people should have their fingers lightly resting on it. One person should act as spokesperson and ask: 'Is anybody there?' This should be repeated until the planchette begins to move – hopefully to the yes and then to the centre. It is also possible to work with the board with a number of people sitting around a table, as the more people there are, the more energy is thought to be available to move the planchette. Also just one person can have success working alone with the Ouija board.

Those of us who have used the Ouija board say that when the planchette moves it feels as it someone is pushing it. This can soon be discounted if the information given out is not known to anyone present and needs to be researched to prove authenticity, but if the information is known it is possible that someone may have been pushing the planchette consciously or unconsciously.

This 'influence of suggestion in modifying and directing muscular movement, independently of volition' was given the label 'ideomotor effect' by the psychologist/physiologist William B. Carpenter in 1852. You may not know that you are moving the message indicator, but you are. Proponents of the ideomotor effect theory generally accept that it is possible to move the planchette unconsciously. They claim that the Ouija board opens a kind of shortcut from the conscious to the subconscious mind.

Advocates claim that the spirits are making use of the participants' muscles to produce the physical movement. However, it is often difficult to make sense of the communication at first, and words may run into one another or anagrams or codes may be used. In short, although some messages come through loud and clear it is often necessary to study messages carefully to make sense of them.

The Ouija board has been condemned by parents and religious groups who say it can cause emotional damage in the impressionable and sometimes even possession. Is this possible? Is the Ouija a potential link to the dark side, where you cannot control what can come through, or is it just a game?

Most psychics advise against the casual use of the Ouija board, suggesting that it can be a doorway to unknown dimensions or spirits on the lower astral plane who are often very confused and potentially dangerous. This, of course, can't be proved, but if the Ouija does not contact spirits could it access our own subconscious? Possibly, and for this reason if it is to be used for divinatory purposes it should be used with caution.

Since there are few accounts of positive, uplifting experiences with the Ouija, and many negative ones, we might assume that it is more attuned to, or more associated with, the negative aspects of our subconscious, and is therefore best avoided. However, if you are determined to use the Ouija anyway, it is highly recommended that you follow some rules of precaution:

• Begin by announcing that the session will only allow an experience that is positive or toward a higher good and that negative energies are not welcome.

- Don't ask for physical signs.
- When you're finished, close the board. This is an important step. When you're done with your session, slide the planchette to GOODBYE and remove your hands.

OUR CONCLUSION

There will always be controversy among people and organisations as to the existence and true nature of evil spirits. There are those who think that there are evil spirits out there who can attach themselves to the impressionable, and there are those who believe that evil spirits do not exist. We must always remember that where there is goodness, light and warmth, there is also likely to be evil, darkness and cold. Where there are miracles, there are possessions. If we close our eyes to the dark side of life, and refuse to consider it as a possibility, not only are we failing to be open-minded as paranormal investigators but we are also more likely to become vulnerable to its influence.

For us the most chilling thing about the issue of evil entities is the depth of the convictions of the believers. Personal accounts of demonic encounters are among the most harrowing stories we have ever heard. Do these encounters really happen? Who knows? True or not, it's evident that the people telling us these stories are utterly convinced that it is all real. As long as the concept of good and evil exists, could this mean that any phenomena experienced by humans will always have a good side and a bad one?

Do evil spirits exist? Every time we ask ourselves this question there is always another one that jumps straight in front of the queue: Does evil?

8

INVESTIGATIVE TECHNIQUES

'I have lost count of the number of times I have spent a night in "the most haunted room", of the hundreds of haunted houses that I have visited, of the thousands of cases of alleged haunting that have come to my attention; but still there is a definite excitement in learning about a fresh haunting, for there is always the possibility that this venture into the unknown may bring a never-to-be-forgotten experience, or better still, that this may be the spontaneous phenomenon that will prove for all time the objective reality of such activity.'

PETER UNDERWOOD: A HOST OF HAUNTINGS (1973)

We're often asked about the whats, wheres and hows of paranormal investigation. As you'll be 'working' with us on five new cases in Part Two, this chapter is designed to give you the basics of paranormal investigation. Even if you have been involved in an investigation before we hope you'll still find something of use here. Please bear in mind that these are guidelines we follow, but other paranormal investigators may use different approaches or methods. Paranormal investigation isn't an exact science and there will always be differences of opinion as to the best way to go about things.

A WORD ABOUT DEFINITION

Ghost hunting is the term for when you go to a place that is supposed to be haunted and try to capture some evidence on film (video and photos), or record sounds or interview eyewitness, etc. It's a popular term that is often confused with paranormal investigation, but paranormal investigation, although similar in some ways, is subtly different from ghost hunting.

Paranormal investigation means going to a place that has been clearly linked to paranormal phenomena and conducting experiments, gathering evidence, recording data (video, photos, audio, temperatures etc.), taking notes and interviewing witnesses. The aim of paranormal investigation is to prove or disprove a haunting – to, ultimately, investigate everything about the case. Assistance may be offered to the witnesses by educating them about what is going on and the options available to them. Psychics or mediums may sometimes be used to get a sense of the place and in some cases to try and establish contact with spirits.

We're a bit like detectives and forensic experts investigating a crime scene. We need to meticulously examine an area and carefully gather any evidence we can while not disturbing anyone or anything. We need to interview witnesses, take notes, research, take pictures and conduct a stake-out or in our case an all-night vigil. We need to be aware of all logical and natural explanations and do our best to find a reasonable conclusion. And like any good detective we need to be ready for anything!

GENERAL GUIDELINES

Generally we don't encourage people without training or experience to conduct a paranormal investigation. Before you head off camera in hand to that haunted cemetery it really is important that you have some idea of what you are doing, what you need and what you can expect. Reading this book is a great start. We also recommend that you contact an established organisation near to you for information and advice and join them on a workshop/hunt/investigation rather than going on your own. It's a good idea to get a feel for what you're getting yourself into! Bear in mind that not every investigation makes for an exciting, scary adventure. Sometimes it's difficult to keep your eyes open!

Here are some general guidelines for conducting a paranormal investigation for those who are simply interested in the process and for those who want to have a go for themselves:

- Find out all you can about the history of the place and or building. Newspapers, local historians, the internet and books can all be helpful in finding folklore or hard facts about the site.
- Gather as much evidence as you can about the haunting from local residents and witnesses. In many cases the most important aspects of an investigation are witness interviews, as the testimony of eyewitnesses often decides which direction the investigation will take.
- Prepare for every interview before conducting it. Be open-minded and considerate of the feelings and com-

fort of your witness at all times. Allow your witness to tell their story from beginning to end without interruption. Hold off questions until they have finished and make sure those questions aren't leading. For example: *Leading questions:* Did you see a ghost? Were you terrified?

Open questions: What did you see? How did you feel?

• As you gather information for your investigation please respect one very important consideration: the privacy of the residents in the area. Bear in mind that in some cases an overnight investigation may be the final course of action. Don't jump into it before you've done some preliminary research. A simple explanation for a reported haunting experience may be found early on in an investigation through interviews or researching the history of the location.

• If the place you want to investigate is a private property it is crucial that you get permission from the owners or residents. It's also wise to notify the police if you are going to be taking pictures in a public place, like a graveyard, in the small hours of the morning. If it's a public place like a hospital or school you also need to get permission from the site owners or caretakers. Always bring ID so that if you are questioned by anyone you can prove who you are.

• Never go alone. This just makes sense. If you fall over and hurt yourself or just get scared out of your wits you need someone there. And make sure you let someone know where you will be in case of emergency.

• The best times to investigate tend to be from 9 p.m. to 6 a.m. As we saw in Chapter One these are the hours most associated with haunting, but results can be produced during daylight too. If you plan to investigate at night always check the area out in daylight first so you are familiar with it. Look for dangerous places and obstacles that you may not be able to see in the dark.

- No smoking, alcohol or drugs at an investigation for obvious reasons.
- And don't wear perfume, cologne or anything else with a very noticeable scent. This is so that someone does not mistake the smell for a supernatural occurrence. Spirits are said to use scents and smells to get our attention. The no perfume rule applies to both indoor and outdoor investigations.

WHAT YOU NEED

We've divided the following into two categories: the basics and optional and advanced equipment. If you are going to treat yourself to some high-tech gadgets it's important that you properly understand their function and use first. Give yourself time to learn how to use them and practise using them until you feel comfortable. Are the high-tech gadgets essential? Although they can be helpful, we warn against becoming dependent on equipment. As long as you have the basics, have done your research and accumulated knowledge, and are open-minded, you really have all that you need.

THE BASICS

These items are essential for use in any investigation. They are easy to find, affordable and can fit into a small bag.

- Business card or ID with your name and contact information.
- Notebook and pens. A pocket tape recorder can be used also, but make sure you bring extra batteries (advisable given most overnights are conducted in the dark). Plans of the locations would be useful too, especially to pinpoint experiences.
- Two torches with extra batteries. It's also an excellent idea to tape a piece of red gel or cellophane over the lens to preserve your own and your fellow investigator's night vision. Also, some investigators prefer to use headset torches which free up their hands for note-taking and equipment carrying.
- Tape recorder with blank tapes: use a quality tape recorder and a separate external microphone. Good quality, branded type 1 – Normal position tapes are the best by far and are the only tape type that the majority of portable recorders will take. Avoid using micro-cassette dictation type recorders, as the quality of audio is poor! Always use brand new blank tapes, never record over old ones. A good quality digital audio recorder can also be used with great success, but avoid models that do not allow the user to connect an external microphone or only record in MP3 format, as this encoding removes a lot of the audio information at

the top and bottom of the frequency range. Models that record in .WAV or PCM format are much better.

- 35mm camera: nothing fancy, with at least four hundred speed film. Eight hundred speed film is also good at night but you will need to test your camera's flash strength to see which speed works best for you. For best results use black-and-white film. (It's almost impossible to buy infra-red film, or have it developed, so there's no need to worry about that.) Always buy good quality film. When you develop the photos let the processor know you want all the pictures developed, including those that they might think are bad ones.

- Digital camera. Many respected people in this field are adamantly against the use of digital cameras on ghost hunts or research. One reason is that there is no negative to look at to determine what an anomaly is, whereas 35mm negatives can be useful in analysing photos more closely. Another is that pictures can be easily tampered with using image editing software. We have always felt that digital cameras are useful and we use them in our research. Analysis of any interesting photos must only be done on image copies, with the original left untouched after their transfer to storage drive. Many regular digital cameras produced today are high quality and capable of taking photos on a par with 35mm cameras, and some can also take photos in a limited infra-red spectrum of light. Some even allow pictures to be taken using Nightshot IR in complete darkness. Additionally the ease with which you can store, analyse and delete uninteresting photos is an added bonus. Another advantage is the ability to follow an energy source or spirit on the move. Our first choice is still for the 35mm cameras, but we also recognise the advantages of digital cameras.

- Wristwatch: so you can log in times of arrival and departure and events.
- Thermometer: to detect changes in room temperature. Rapid temperature drops of ten degrees of more, with no discernible natural cause, are thought to suggest spirit presence. Some argue that the best to use are old-fashioned mercury thermometers, as they believe that digital ones can fail when electromagnetic fields are present, but mercury thermometers just don't react quickly enough to measure a rapid temperature drop. For accuracy we recommend an infra-red thermometer with laser pointer. Note: where the laser is pointed is where the temperature is measured – this style of thermometer is not appropriate for cold spots in mid-air.
- Compass: useful for navigation and also for picking up magnetic stimulus as a compass will react to magnetic or electrical stimuli that are often reported in haunted areas. Compasses can only respond to a magnetic stimulus, although magnetic fields can be generated from an electrical source.
- Chalk to mark areas.
- Labels to identify items.
- Talcum powder to put on the floor to detect movement. An alternative, and perhaps more accurate, method is to use motion detectors (see below).
- First aid kit in case of accident or injury.

- Tape measure, ball of string and a pair of scissors to mark and measure areas.
- Binoculars – can sometimes be useful.
- Motion detectors: to sense unseen movements. There are two main types of motion detector – the passive infra-red and the light beam barrier. Both types are best used to ensure that locations or trigger objects are not accidentally or intentionally tampered with.
- Jackets or weather appropriate clothes. It's just common sense, but if you are cold you are not at your best and your observation skill could suffer.
- Food and drinks (hot!) are also essential.

The above list is solely for those groups or investigators who wish to 'capture' evidence rather than discount every normal explanation. It's also for those who don't have the finances to purchase every gadget.

ADVANCED AND OPTIONAL

The following items can be extremely helpful but they are not essential. Remember, paranormal investigators were investigating hauntings and making great discoveries before most of these items were even invented. Before using any of these items in the field, make sure that you know how they work and what you are looking for. It is no use collecting readings or data if you cannot interpret them in a meaningful way. The inclusion of most of the environmental monitoring equipment is to ensure that a paranormal explanation is the most likely one. Think about it like this: If you have a checklist of normal explanations and at the bottom is a paranormal one, you need to tick off every normal one first before arriving at the conclusion that you have something paranormal. Ticking off those normal explanations (i.e. the equipment not capturing the data that supports them) strengthens your argument for paranormal evidence.

- Video camcorders (optional tripod): an important instrument for an investigation. Unlike still cameras they can give us constant visual and audio surveillance for review and observation after the investigation. The video cameras we use are equipped with infra-red capability. A video will show the length of time the phenomenon occurs, what is happening, the conditions surrounding the phenomenon, and possibly even the cause of the phenomenon. Most modern digital video recorders can be directly connected to a PC or laptop for transfer of footage or even use as a webcam with motion detection software.
- Night vision equipment: a light amplification system that takes in any available light including IR and amplifies it many times to make it visible. Night vision cannot work in total darkness hence the small IR illuminator that many have for locations with zero light.
- Spot lights: small, battery-powered spot lights can really help when it comes to setting up and taking down equipment. They can be used to get a better view and for safety reasons.
- Headset communicators: when you have a team of people investigating headset communicators are a good

idea for staying in contact if you separate or spread out. The hand-held walkie-talkies are fine, but the headset communicators free up your hands for recording notes and using cameras etc.

- Geiger counter: reads the amount of ionising radiation in the air and on an object. There are levels of ionising radiation around us all the time and you will be looking for anything abnormal. They are available for around £150 and are very simple to use. In fact they are not much different from an EMF meter.

- The EMF meter (the Electromagnetic Field meter): a valuable device for the modern paranormal investigator. With this instrument it is possible to measure and locate sources of electromagnetism. Common sources for household EM readings include such mundane objects as computer monitors, cellular telephones, bedside clock radios, and televisions. There are arguments both for and against using this type of meter. It has been suggested by some that spirits may disrupt the EMF within a location or emit their own EMF. Ciarán's view follows research being conducted in Canada and in the field in the UK by some researchers. This suggests that particular levels or miniscule fluctuations with the EMF can mildly stimulate a part of our brain which then, in turn, may evoke a physiological reaction and even a sensory hallucination in some individuals. Before using the EMF on an investigation, walk around the area and take initial readings around energy sources such as light poles or electrical outlets. Most units come with a manual describing most household and major appliances and their corresponding electromagnetic reading. When using EMF detection meters it is important to make a series of baseline measurements in order to highlight any unusual readings. A normal range of readings is between 0.1 and 10mG, though we hesitate to use the word 'normal' since some locations may have higher, man-made sources. If you are near a domestic appliance the reading can exceed 30mG as you get close to it. Most of the EMF meters on the market are hand-held, which is not ideal. When using them make sure you STAND STILL! Even moving around can affect the read-out slightly and unless you know this you may be incorrectly interpreting your data. In an ideal world you would purchase a tri-axial EMF meter (3-axis) as opposed to the 1-axis variety that flood the market. Both varieties have their uses in investigations, however, since a single-axis meter is generally a better tool for locating the source of an emission. Additionally, we use a 3-axis meter that can be left static and the data recorded on to its memory or fed directly into a computer – it takes out the possible human error in the whole thing!

MORE ABOUT EMFS

The sole reason many investigators and ghost hunters purchase an EMF detector is to help them locate ghosts, although it was originally designed to locate sources of electric and magnetic radiation and to offer a reading of the relative strength (and direction if you are a skilled and competent operator) of the EM field.

When an electrical current travels through the wiring or into an appliance, it produces an electromagnetic field, which consists of the electric field which is always present (even when the appliance is switched off) and the magnetic field which occurs when the power is switched on to the appliance. Certain medical conditions, including cancer, are suspected to be associated with prolonged electric field exposure – power line workers, for instance, have special suits to protect them as the electric field can be easily shielded.

However, in addition to the EMF present because of electrical wiring and appliances, EMF is found in nature as well. The earth produces EMFs, mainly in the form of DC (direct current, also called static fields). For instance, electric fields are produced by thunderstorm activity in the atmosphere. Magnetic fields are thought to be produced by electric (telluric) currents flowing deep within the earth's molten core. Factors as subtle as water running against certain geological strata of rock can also influence electromagnetic fields. All natural electrical events such as lightning produce both electrical *and* magnetic fields.

When we begin an investigation, we first of all obtain accurate 'background' readings of the location we are in to make notes of any source of EM radiation. The aim is to locate anomalies and highlight them for further examination. Once the background readings have been taken and the hunt/investigation is commenced in earnest, the EMF operator will continue to 'scan' the area for EM readings that are anomalous. That is, we are specifically looking for any EM reading that does not have an immediately plausible explanation or is not indicated on the background readings of the location. Many of the explanations for unusual EM measurements are not immediately obvious and yet are not indicative of anything paranormal.

The basic rule of thumb is that, when using highly accurate EMF meters, the field shows minuscule fluctuations, and it is these that are of particular interest to researchers.

- Infra-red thermal scanners: can pinpoint abnormal cold or hot spots on solid surfaces. This is another device that must be tested before use in the field. IR thermal scanners can only detect hot and cold spots on solid surfaces, not cold spots in the air. Currently they are only available from the USA, but they are not that expensive: a decent one starts at around $150.
- Air ion counter: measures positive and negative ions in the atmosphere. Again test before using and during an investigation look for abnormal readings. Air ion counters only quantify the numbers of air ions and indicate their charge – they are very difficult to use properly and require a great deal of care to avoid misleading information being obtained. We think that it may be best to drop the air ion counter in favour of the negative ion detector (NID), which simply indicates when the amounts of negative air ions exceed normal levels. Increased negative ion amounts have been linked to increased reports of paranormal activity within some locations.

THE INVESTIGATION

Have everyone meet at the location, then decide who will work each piece of equipment and divide into teams if necessary. Walk around the area to get a feel for the surroundings. You can also begin to set up any stationary equipment like cameras on tripods or motion detectors. Make a note of any areas that may cause you to get false readings or false positive pictures. If you are indoors take careful note of air vents, heater, electrical appliances, fuse boxes, computers, etc. Mark down the temperatures in the rooms and any EMF readings you get during this walk through.

When everything is in place and you're ready to begin, log in your start time and weather conditions and any other relevant information if you are outdoors. (If it's raining, snowing or foggy and you are scheduled to do an outdoor ghost hunt, reschedule it. You cannot conduct a proper investigation in these conditions unless the original eyewitness reported phenomena under such conditions.) Now you can start the investigation and take lots of pictures and recordings. You can either set up stationary recorders and just let them run or you can walk around with them. (Make sure afterwards that you view or listen to the whole tape.)

Every investigator or team should keep a log of events and times – everything needs to be logged, no matter how trivial. If you hiccup, log it in, as it may have sounded like something else to another member elsewhere in the building. Be sure to note anything unusual, especially meter and temperature readings, visual sightings and strange sounds. Also make notes of any feelings or emotions you experience that may be odd or out of place. You can compare notes after the hunt and look for similarities in readings and feelings in certain areas or at certain times.

During the investigation draw no conclusions. Share no ideas or opinions with the witnesses or owners until all the reports, photos and tapes are reviewed. You need to see the evidence and correlate it before you can give an educated opinion. Once these initial vigils have been conducted it may highlight areas or phenomena on which to focus more equipment.

GUIDELINES FOR TAKING PICTURES

You may have videos and tape recorders running, but cameras are still perhaps the most accessible, portable and immediate pieces of equipment for paranormal investigation. Your camera may provide that vital piece of evidence, but you need to ensure you use it correctly.

- Open your film and load your camera before entering a location, since you don't know when anything will happen.
- Use at least 400 speed 35mm film. 400 and 800 speeds work the best. Black-and-white film also works well.
- If you are an experienced photographer, you may want to try infra-red film, which also has had excellent results in the past.

- Make sure you note any other lights in the area, so when you view your developed pictures you won't mistake a street lamp for an orb.
- Clean the lens of your camera regularly.
- Watch for dust or dirt being stirred up in the area you are photographing. They can give false positive pictures.
- Remove or tie up any camera straps, which can look like a vortex when accidentally photographed. Long hair also needs to be tied back.
- Watch for reflective surfaces and make notes of them. The flash reflected off shiny surfaces such as windows, polished tombstones, etc. can look like an orb or other anomaly. Make a note of street lights and any other light source that may appear on the film.
- Let fellow investigators know when you are taking a photo so that you don't blind each other (we tend to shout out 'Flash!'). If you think you have a false positive, log the picture number so you can exclude that photo from the batch when they are developed.
- In cold weather or after consuming a hot drink, be conscious of your breath so you don't photograph that – it'll look like ectoplasm mist. If you think you may have done so, log that picture number and discard it when you develop the pictures.
- Take pictures anywhere and everywhere. If you feel something, or someone else does, take a picture. If you think you saw something, take a picture. Take photos whenever you get a positive reading on any piece of equipment.
- You may only get one or two interesting pictures for every hundred you take, so don't get discouraged. We've

been at sites where we didn't get any interesting photos at all and others where the results were more promising.

WORKING WITH PSYCHICS AND MEDIUMS

In general psychics are people with skills of telepathy and ESP who believe they can sense or pick up information from their environment and from other people. Sometimes, but not always, this information may come from another realm. Mediums on the other hand believe they can communicate with spirits of the dead. Many mediums are also psychic, but not all psychics are mediums.

Some paranormal investigators never work with psychics or mediums and never use techniques such as dowsing rods, Ouija boards or séances. They argue that, from a scientific viewpoint, the validity of these methods can be questioned. Some believe that evil spirits can be drawn to these types of activities. Others, and this includes us, prefer to explore all options and keep an open mind. We have found that involving psychics in an investigation can be incredibly helpful.

If you are open-minded to a psychic's impressions, and ask lots of questions about what they are sensing, whether what they're getting is correct or misinterpreted, etc., then they can be good to work with and can in some cases pick up a great deal of useful information, as well as offering an interesting insight into mediumship processes.

The downside of working with psychics is that all too often they are convinced they are right even if their perceptions are in direct contradiction to what the witnesses have perceived. They tend to have their set beliefs about ghosts and poltergeists, and nothing will get them to consider that alternative explanations may be possible. They also sometimes have trouble shifting their focus from the symbolic to the literal and you could end up with a lot of interesting but ultimately vague information you don't know what to do with.

The upside of working with open-minded psychics who have a sense of humour is that they have trained themselves to focus on the paranormal in a way few people involved in the investigation can. You can use their intuitive hunches to 'detect' more of what may be going on in a case. But remember that no psychic is one hundred per cent accurate in all cases, and a really good psychic is a rare find.

The best psychics and mediums we have worked with have the following qualities. They are confident without being egotistical. They have good people skills and a good sense of humour, especially about themselves and what they do. We have to consider how useful the information they provide is, how open they are to having their perceptions questioned and, last but by no means least, whether or not they have a good track record free of misperception and fraud. In addition, a psychic or medium who has extensive experience of visiting haunted locations may actually be susceptible to population stereotypes about where a ghost may have been seen – this is not a negative point, it's a useful one.

Finally, don't underestimate the importance of your

own perceptions. You may or may not be psychic, but all the equipment and all the séances in the world will not help if you neglect to develop your own keen intuition. Over the years we have learned to pay more and more attention to our own perceptions while on investigations. We have not yet seen an apparition or haunting, but we have certainly felt, heard, smelled and sensed things we simply can't explain.

WHAT IF I GET SCARED?

Paranormal phenomena can range from subtle things like knocks and cold draughts all the way up to the furniture being thrown about and full-blown apparitions. The chances are it won't but – you never know – anything can happen during an investigation.

Fear is the first reaction when something happens. It's a common, natural human expression. The key is to keep your fear from turning into panic and to try and verify what it is that you are hearing or seeing or sensing by taking notes. Even though a video recorder or tape machine may be recording it's still a good idea to take note of your feelings.

There have been many cases when paranormal investigators have run in fear from a location. There is no way of knowing how you will react in a situation until you are in it. We've lost count of the number of times we have felt the hairs raise on the backs of our necks, and on occasion we have halted an investigation prematurely because of some element of discomfort we could not explain. You've probably heard people say things like 'Ghosts can't harm you, they're dead' or 'There is nothing to be afraid of' many times but, however sceptical you are, you must be prepared to find yourself affected by the energy or atmosphere of a location in a way you might never have anticipated.

If you feel fear, try to stay calm so that your fear does not spread to the rest of the team and ruin the investigation. If you do panic, ask someone to take you home and separate yourself from the group and the investigation until the feeling passes.

WHERE TO LOOK

You can usually find haunted locations by word of mouth. These places don't always have to be old: a haunting can begin immediately after someone has died, or more typically on the anniversary of their death. Here are some suggestions, but you don't have to limit yourself to them, for as we pointed out earlier in the book, ghosts can be reported anywhere and by anyone.

Cemeteries

Tales of ghosts at cemeteries have been recorded in every culture far back into history. They are a good place to start an investigation. Check local records for the graveyards of people who have been murdered. Why cemeteries? Some believe they are portals to the other side or that some spirits are drawn to their former bodies.

Places of mysterious, violent or untimely death
This could be the site of a former battlefield where many lost their lives or where a murder was committed. It could also be the site of an accident. Some believe there is a connection between haunted locations and violent, untimely deaths.

Old buildings and hotels
The older a building is, the more likely it is to be haunted or to have stories of hauntings associated with it. Historic buildings, because of their age, have had more time in which to have spirits attach to them. These buildings are often open to the public and can give you an easy place to start. Many even have known histories of hauntings and you may be able to gain access to the building after hours by speaking with the caretakers.

Hospitals and nursing homes
The ghosts of dead patients and phantom workers have often been reported in both hospitals and nursing homes. What makes these cases stand out is that many of the witnesses are very credible people, usually doctors and nurses. However, strict administration policies can make it virtually impossible to get inside and conduct an investigation.

Schools
Schools, colleges and former sites of schools may have the build-up of psychic energies and imprints of all the highly emotional events that have transpired there.

Theatres and museums

There may be ghosts of past employees, actors or even people who came to the theatre or museum to watch a show or exhibit. Typically there is a room or balcony or area where no one goes because of strange happenings.

Churches

There is a long history of the faithful returning to the church they worshipped at. They may be looking for the salvation they were promised and cannot find.

Prisons and concentration camps

There is often said to be a connection between haunting and places where people were held together in pain and suffering.

WHAT ARE THE SIGNS OF A HAUNTING?

'A sensory experience in which there appears to be present a person or animal (deceased or living) who is in fact out of sensory range of the experient . . .'

BAKER, I. S.:*DO GHOSTS EXIST? A SUMMARY OF PARAPSYCHOLOGICAL RESEARCH INTO APPARITIONAL EXPERIENCES* IN J. NEWTON (ED.): *EARLY MODERN GHOSTS* (DURHAM, UK: UNIVERSITY OF DURHAM, 2002)

What are the signs of a haunting? We get this question a lot. There are many signs. Below is a list of some perceptual symptoms, for example what you can see, hear or feel as opposed to measurements taken with an EMF meter or IR thermometer.

Visual: Apparitions, hazes or mists, orbs (yes, they can be seen with the naked eye sometimes). Shadows and shapes, often seen out of the corner of the eye, but sometimes seen in the centre of your vision. Seeing someone you think you know, only to find out they were somewhere else entirely.

Audio: Names whispered or spoken out loud when no one is around, often mistaken for the voice of a friend or family member. A voice or voices heard where no one is present. These voices may be intelligible or unintelligible. Sounds heard may include children's laughter, babies' cries, animal sounds, footsteps etc. when no one is around, and sounds of items being moved or broken, after which everything is found to be in its proper place and intact. There may also be sounds of musical instruments, radios, records, or televisions playing when they are not.

Smell: Many people think that different smells represent different spirits, but others believe that spirits will emit a smell that was commonly associated with them in life, for example cigarette smoke or a favourite perfume.

Tactile: Cold spots with no explanation – some say the ghost is absorbing heat energy. Hot spots with no explanation – the ghost is expelling heat energy.

Textures: You may feel skin (usually damp) in the form of a hand grabbing you, or fur, as in an animal rubbing against your bare leg, etc.

Kinetic: We use the word kinetic to refer to those experiences where the activity involves a more obvious change to the physical world: some sort of movement. They can run the gamut of human possibility, but here is a short list:

- Items are moved or thrown across the room or slid across a surface, sometimes right off that surface.
- Items are hidden. About fifty per cent of the time these items will turn up some time later in very bizarre locations. For example a watch you wore yesterday and took off at night turns up in a cupboard that has been locked for the past year. An appearing object is an 'apport', a disappearing object an 'asport'.
- Mechanical equipment/fixtures activated without anyone being near them: toilets flushing, sinks/showers turning on and off, light switches flipping themselves on (see Electrical below), drawers and doors opening/ closing, locks engaging/disengaging.

Electrical: Some believe that almost any electrical appliance can be affected by a spirit. For example, the TV/radio/ stereo turns on and off without living influence. Fans and lights turn on and off without the switch being flipped. Perfectly healthy appliances short out or explode. Remotely operated toys, like RC cars, operate on their own.

This is by no means a comprehensive list, more like a generalised group of commonly reported experiences. Most of them have been experienced by our team.

PARANORMAL INVESTIGATION: A QUICK REVIEW

1. You hear about a possible haunting.
2. Do your research thoroughly. Get records, find news-paper articles, and dig up anything you can find. Where necessary get permission to visit the site or conduct interviews.
3. Conduct interviews with all the witnesses. Get all the facts and the stories.
4. Find people who are willing to help you or accompany you and visit the site without your equipment. Take notes and map out the area.
5. Conduct your first investigation. Use all the necessary equipment and record the event.
6. Review your investigation. Study everything. Did you make any mistakes?
7. Do more investigations to gather more evidence. Record anything.
8. Double check everything. Have you done all that you can? Conduct follow-up interviews with your wit-nesses to see if anything new has happened to them.
9. Write a final written report. Include stories, facts, photographs, theories, suggestions and anything rele-vant. If there is not enough evidence to make a con-clusion, don't. Leave the case open for future study.
10. If you are going to publish your results or circulate them on the internet, make sure you have full per-mission before using real names and stories.
11. Finally, be a sensitive, responsible and ethical inves-tigator at all times.

FINAL TIP

So there you have it – the basics of paranormal investigation. Perhaps the most important piece of advice we'll leave you with is this: if you want to have a go yourself, be as sceptical as possible. Always look for natural or man-made causes of any phenomenon. Remember that being sceptical doesn't mean having a closed mind: it means keeping an open mind about all possible explanations, including the paranormal. Never go into an investigation with pre-drawn conclusions. The above guidelines will aid you in reaching sound conclusions, but if there aren't enough data to reach a conclusion, don't.

Paranormal investigators attempt to find scientific evidence to explain what happens in haunted settings. So be objective about the things you encounter! Through the elimination of all other explanations, your evidence becomes stronger proof. Always try to find other, rational explanations for everything.

As an investigator you have to make sure that your final evidence will stand up to scrutiny. And if there is no other explanation for what you witness, you may just be on to something!

PART TWO

HAUNTING CASE FILES

INTRODUCTION

To prove something scientifically you need results that can be replicated over and over again under strict conditions. Unfortunately investigating the paranormal doesn't work that way. We can film, we can measure, we can record and we can document, but ghosts are elusive and rarely, if ever, perform on demand. That's why the majority of scientists, despite thousands of years of anecdotal evidence, the testimony of countless eyewitnesses and some supportive data, refuse to accept that hauntings are genuine.

If this is the case, why do we bother with paranormal investigation? We bother because paranormal investigation provides us with an opportunity to delve into the possibility, and again we stress that word possibility, of other realms. We bother because we believe there may be things out there that are beyond our current understanding. We bother because we believe it is up to those of us who are open to the possibility of the impossible to continue the search for evidence that can open up those understandings.

We also believe that it isn't enough to discuss ghosts: you need to actually experience hauntings at first hand. That's why this section of the book invites you to accompany us on five 'new' cases: The Farmhouse, Charter House, The Collingwood Pub, Cammell Laird and The Hex nightclub. To protect the privacy of those involved in some of the cases, exact details of names and addresses have been withheld, but all the cases are UK-based and were investigated and filmed by us during October and November 2005.

Two people can't feasibly investigate an entire building, so for each case that follows we were assisted by Steve and Ann, two experienced paranormal investigators from Para.Science (see Appendix A). Having a support team can be of enormous benefit, not just for safety reasons but also for their help in covering a large area, setting up monitoring equipment and recording and comparing experiences.

Each case will highlight what paranormal investigators like us routinely go through, but we deliberately chose a variety of cases, in order to illustrate the different ways to run investigations. These locations are also dynamically different. Four of them do not even look like your typical haunted house or castle. They're contemporary buildings. But it doesn't make them any less scary.

So, if you're feeling brave and would like to play the role of paranormal detective, just turn the page and prepare to meet the residents of Cold Creek Farm . . .

CASE ONE: THE FARMHOUSE

(DATE OF INVESTIGATION: FRIDAY 7 OCTOBER 2005)

Cold Creek Farm is located in rural Cheshire. It's joined to another house, the two houses forming one building, and this building is surrounded by farm outbuildings and an electrically powered milking parlour.

It's a two-storey house, built in 1954. On the ground floor are all the main domestic features but additionally a bedroom, now vacant, located at the front of the house. All the ground-floor rooms have reported paranormal activity, but the main areas of reported activity are the lounge, ground floor bedroom, stairs and kitchen. On the first floor are three bedrooms, the landing and a bathroom. Paranormal activity has been reported in all the bedrooms.

The farmhouse first came to our attention in November 2004, when Ciarán received detailed and florid accounts of amazing phenomena occurring there.

MEET THE FAMILY

A family of four currently occupies the farmhouse: Debbie and Neil and two of their children. A third child, the eldest daughter, now lives away from home and was allegedly anxious to move out as a result of her own unusual experiences at the farm. Two teenage children remain at home – a daughter, Helen, in her late teens, and a son, Ryan, in his mid teens. Ryan has a long history of chronic fatigue and illness.

Since moving in five years ago Debbie has reported continuous minor paranormal activity, although the level and nature of the phenomena are said to have increased significantly two years ago following the death of a close family member. All three children and Debbie have witnessed unusual activity in the farmhouse, but the activity isn't restricted to the house as the children and Debbie have also had unusual experiences outside. Debbie believes she is strongly psychic, although she is refreshingly open and down to earth about her claimed abilities, warning that the messages she gets from the spirits are frequently very difficult to interpret. According to Debbie, all three children share to a greater or lesser degree the same psychic abilities as her. Neil, Debbie's husband, does not share this claimed ability or the belief that the house is haunted in any way.

There is no desire on the part of Debbie and her children to have any of the phenomena stopped or changed. Although initially disturbed by the events, they are now curious as to the nature of their experiences. Debbie had first of all tried to investigate on her own with a video camera in the hope of documenting some of the activity – initially to convince her husband of what they were experiencing. Realising she would make better progress with a team of professionals, in 2003 she got in touch with an organisation of paranormal investigators called Para.Science (see Appendix A).

The farmhouse investigations conducted by Para.Science in 2003 and 2004 revealed possible links between both unusually high levels of, and complex fluctuations within, recorded EMF and the reported incidences of paranormal type activity in the front half of the house, in particular Ryan's bedroom. A natural cause for the high EMF levels was found in the form of some faulty electrical cables outside Ryan's room. As soon as the wires were replaced in early 2004 the activity in Ryan's room stopped, in addition to a dramatic reduction in his fatigue and illness. Despite this the activity hasn't stopped elsewhere as far as Debbie and Helen are concerned.

EXTRACTS FROM DEBBIE'S DIARY

When we first heard about the case we asked Debbie to keep a record of the almost daily occurrences, requesting her to note down even when things didn't happen. This wasn't a problem as she'd already kept one during the 2003–04 Para.Science investigation.

Debbie's diary runs from September 2003 to September 2005 and there are entries almost every day or at least every other day. In the diary H refers to Helen, R to Ryan and N to Neil. There is also B (Billy) and C (Charlie). The diary is detailed, and we have selected sample passages from September/October 2003, November/December 2004 and August 2005. These samples illustrate just how persistent the activity is and how much it is a regular part of Debbie's life.

1 September 2003

7pm R and N in kitchen and a man said "Hello". R heard it N didn't – I wish he would.

2 September 2003

Whilst cleaning the living room windows a man opened the door and sat on the small sofa. I called N to the window to see but he said no one was there. Still there after about 15 mins so I asked him who he was. 'Uncle Harry' he said. I thought I should tell B but didn't know why, then two of them were there. 'Tell him I've got his cousin' said Harry – OK I said – B said he had no Uncle Harry and didn't know of one – but Harry hung around for about 2 hours, I started to get a bit spooked but braved it out and did the cleaning no one here could claim Uncle Harry – C next door thought he might know him but I was sure it was for B. The milking parlour went wrong – standing joke – it's Uncle Harry! H sat on sofa and whilst leaning on it a bottle of spray stood itself upright – freaked H out.

3 September 2003

Al came today – used to work here and live in our house –
said they had no disturbances. The men told him about
Uncle Harry and me cleaning windows and that Harry
claimed to have his cousin. Al shut them all up – said he
had an Uncle Harry that died about 5 years ago and he
used to stand and look out of the living room window and
watch what was happening outside – he also had a cousin
that passed about 15-20 years earlier. Al is friends with B
and goes to see him regularly – that stops the men taking
the mickey out of me then.

4 September 2003

More interference with computer, I get it on and after a few
minutes I can no longer get it to cooperate but it's always OK
with R. Sometimes won't work for H either.

5 September 2003

R says two of them in his room tonight cold one side of him
and then both sides, pulled his T-shirt.
Computer problems again – I was trying to type and they
seem to be able to influence what I'm typing – the word
'shitty' kept appearing when I'm not consciously typing it –
not funny after a while. Took Mrs D a cuppa – something
knocked the cup – I thought I heard laughing, poor woman
got hot tea down her leg – I think it was the little girl.
R says the pencil rubber and ruler moved on their own but
Mrs D didn't notice – also said his arm went really cold.

6 September 2003

Phoned [Paranormal Investigators] said they will come –

probably in a few weeks – hope they don't get too spooked but hope we manage to get something on video.

7 September 2003

Went to bathroom before bed, the door shut itself when I left the bathroom.

8 September 2003

8pm H came out of her room – someone blowing in her ear. Sensed a presence in the living room – saw lights on curtains and tapping on side of TV, cold hand on my leg. N said he didn't notice anything – maybe he's too frightened to or just won't admit it. Had more PC problems today – odd words keep appearing – takes forever to type anything. Man in bedroom when I went to bed at 10pm, didn't bother me though slept all night till 2.30am. 11.30pm A cold spot on R's side in his room, felt definitely watched and a pen hit the PC stand near floor. 2.30am Knocking on outside of bedroom window – [have to keep changing pens – they keep running out!!!]

9 September 2003

8am Someone hanging about in kitchen – feel watched. 8.30am Took H to school, felt that we had a car full – Mum, Uncle P, Auntie P, Angel, R, C and more – trying to tell me something? Hair played with – still happening now 9.05am Struggled to write, someone is influencing what gets written, like when I'm on the PC.
12noon Papers flew off sofa in lounge next to Richard. They are obviously here all the time. Microphone got knocked off top of PC speaker next to me – someone playing with my

hair again and I got my face stroked in R's room, busy day.
Kept getting chills and here's a first – there's a smell of farts
that keeps coming and going.
Late pm [11'ish] H heard clock ticking or tapping on landing –
sounds more like odd clicks.
10pm Can smell strong perfume in R's bedroom for about 5
mins.

10 September 2003

R sitting with tutor – about 10-11am moving cold spots, later a
puff of white smoke appears by the tutors leg about 6cm
big, then more cold spots, bag handle on her bag then
starts to wobble then could smell crap for 2 mins, then ghost
stuck their finger up my nose!
12.30pm Can smell fruits in my room and can feel cold spot
while playing PS2.
12.30pm TV hisses at delivery woman, then video turns itself
off . Turned the TV off.
Video camera came – it's got night vision.
Put camera in H's room overnight tape will last 90mins.

11 September 2003

Someone woke me up at about 2am – pulled quilt over my
head and went back to sleep.
N came in and said he saw someone sitting on the chair by
the window in the kitchen, said it was me but I was upstairs.
3pm Smell of aftershave upstairs.

12 September 2003

Slipped up with camera last night – no date and time and
no night vision – got sounds only but lots of it. We notice that

no matter where we record the sound always seems to come from elsewhere – I've also noticed that thuds and whispers come together.

7.12pm Smell strong perfume, lasts for about 10 seconds.

7pm H was in living room and heard sounds of furniture being dragged across the floor in my room above her so we'll put the camera in here tonight.

8pm – someone behind me on the landing.

Woke me up again during the night – don't know what time – had to tell them to shut up – around 1.30am I think.

13 September 2003

Not a huge amount on video – disappointing but the lights were on – they don't seem to like the lights on – didn't bother putting it all onto video cassette – waste of tape.

14 September 2003

1pm somebody shouted my name next to me really loud.

2pm somebody shouted 'Oi' when I turned the PC off.

9pm Went into my bedroom, as I entered – a ball of white mist about 2ft wide raised up from dressing table and floated toward ceiling – before reaching ceiling it gradually faded away over about 2-3 seconds – I felt that I was being watched and felt it was my Mum – she's been gone for 16½ years now.

15 September 2003

Nothing on video. I'm starting to feel disappointed when nothing happens. Still no word from investigators, someone called me a bitch today – or at least I think they did [upstairs].

16 September 2003

R had his hair stroked / played with when in bed, nothing else to report, activity decreased for some reason.

17 September 2003

I had my hair tickled today – but not for long. Small light in living room.

18 September 2003

It's been a strangely quiet week – I wonder why. No cold spots, chills, movement of things or much at all. [How odd] or are we just not noticing it anymore.

PC problems – struggled to type – AGAIN – wording being influenced but not too bad today.

Mobile disappeared from living room.

[S left message]

19 September 2003

Had a chat with someone from Para.Science just hope activity has not gone altogether by the time they get here, but a woman saying 'June' did come to me when I was on the phone and someone watching me write this down [11.20am]. Mobile turned up inside dish in kitchen.

6.30pm   lights in living room.

20 September 2003

8.50am – woman's voice in hallway.

H's watch gone missing, she says she very often sees spirit lights now but she's not bothered by them. Saw a large light on my hand but didn't feel anything.

Someone woke me at 4.15am – don't know what for, followed to bathroom.

21 September 2003

7am Kitchen door closed itself, someone telling me –
'Tomorrow, tomorrow'??? What's tomorrow? We shall see.
9am kitchen door opened itself.

22 September 2003

Maybe the tomorrow means they will be back today – we
shall see.
Someone watching me paint in H's room.
8pm – smell of baby powder in living room – twice.
R in bed – one foot went really cold, then someone knocked
him on the head.

23 September 2003

I was painting in H's room when I heard a knocking on front
door, sent R to answer it – no-one there.
4.30pm 2 glasses moved together on kitchen work top – moved
about 2 inches, heard gate open 3 times but no-one there.
Movement by TV but N didn't notice.
Man in blue T-shirt and blue jeans in kitchen – tidy not
scruffy. Getting back to normal – H being annoyed by a
woman in her bedroom whilst trying to get to sleep – talking
to her and insistent she wanted to talk. H told her to go
away so she knocked on the wall.

25 September 2003

Went to bed – whispers for over an hour.

26 September 2003

7am – bumps inside wardrobe – no one there.
8am spirit lights in living room and what looks like a heat
haze by fire place – no fire lit.

6.30pm someone moving about behind me in R's room.

11pm Voice next to H's room, woman called R's name as he walked past.

27 September 2003

1pm fell asleep on sofa – got woken up by a man walking past me, he said 'Oh your asleep again are you?'

10.15pm bumping about in office.

29 September 2003

H heard someone walking down the stairs – no one to be found.

10.15pm Had my face stroked and hair tickled when in bed.

30 September 2003

8am Legs in front of living room window again [by TV and sofa]

10.15am Talking to Para.Science on phone and TV turned itself on. 4.30pm I turned radio on it hissed and S's voice said 'Hello' then the channel went back to normal.

10pm feeling of being watched on landing.

1 October 2003

A strangely quiet day!

Not that quiet! Because somebody was in my room! Haze, cold spots, faint banging every now and again, feeling being watched and followed. Thought I saw a mist [like on the phone and my stereo] but looked again – gone? So don't know about that one!

2 October 2003

H's watch still missing – maybe it will take a year like my

rings. Went into H's room and bumping / movement started coming from inside the built in wardrobe, went to get camera but when I came back it stopped. Left video camera recording whilst cleaning but got nothing although the cold spot kept coming and going – also felt watched.

Took camera into my room and left it recording whilst cleaning – didn't see anything or hear anything – but video got whispers and someone snoring!!! Nothing whilst I was in the room – they waited till I'd gone downstairs [who's sleeping in my bedroom?]

Put camera in my bedroom again at bed time – it turned itself off after 10 mins – R's room has gone really quiet.

3 October 2003

Feeling of being watched in kitchen
Went to bed – 10.15pm Man and woman standing by bed.

4 October 2003

7pm Movement and shadows on landing whilst I was using computer – being watched. Put video camera on and left to run. Got poked in the shoulder.

9pm Rubbish moving about on it's own in living room fire, then large light appeared on curtains by TV approx 3ft long and 1ft wide lasted 2-3 seconds.

6 October 2003

11am Kitchen door opened itself – then slammed shut.
10pm man and woman standing looking at us in bed, got my hair played with.

Odd clicks in different places in bedroom. Thumps and bumps coming from office.

7 October 2003

Feeling of being watched most of day.

10pm H was lying in bed with her arm raised over her head and someone poked her underarm twice. Felt a man's presence in bathroom doorway – went very cold when I walked through it.

3am presence on landing. Large lady called Karen told me her weight killed her.

8 October 2003

11am someone knocked on bath panel twice whilst I was in bath and thud on window sill.

1.20pm Strong smell of aftershave in car [S's] lasted 10 mins.

5pm kitchen door opened and slammed shut again – R's room gone really quiet.

11.30pm H went to bed and someone pushed their unseen finger into her ear.

9 October 2003

8.20am Sitting at the kitchen table someone said 'Mind if I join you' – woman's voice I think – keep being given the name Margaret.

8 November 2004

7am, in the kitchen and heard a loud thump in the hall door – frightened the life out of the cat.

2pm large lump of modelling clay rolled about 6 inches across the kitchen worktop.

3.30pm, in the living room with my friend and we both saw a pink mist form and fill the whole room. It made us feel very sleepy.

9 November 2004

9.30am, I'm once again being told that people are trying to contact us but were not answering the phone. They say they have left messages but just like before the phone doesn't ring and there are no messages.

4.15pm, lots of flashes of light around today, seen in various places, kitchen, living room and hall.

12 November 2004

Seen lots of lights around today and had a peculiar occurrence. Soaking in the bath around 11am and had a spinning feeling in my stomach, thought it might have been that I have taken on too much energy and I needed to calm it down as every time I get this feeling I have trouble with the telephones. I cut people off. I drain batteries, fully, charged ones go totally dead. This morning I even affected my mobile and I could not send messages for three hours. So I jumped into the bath to try to relax and discharge some energy. Whilst I was in the bath I found that I could use the phone okay with no problems at all but I pushed energy out through my hands into the bathwater and the water began to turn white. Not milky, but foggy – incredible but true, but as I lifted my arms over my head, with the energy still coming out, my arms got pinned to the wall above my head. It took me a good few minutes to get them to move. That really freaked me out. I will have to try and find someone who can explain what's happening. There was no presence felt, no ice cold hands and no lights from spirits around. I honestly believe it was my energy levels that pinned me to the wall. Also problems with the PC have started again and typing is a nightmare.

13 November 2004

11pm went to bed, 2 spooks with us, one by the window and one by the wardrobe.

14 November 2004

More phone problems. Lots of lights again, living room and kitchen.

5pm. Left pasta cooking in a pan and a wooden spoon on the worktop. 10 mins later the wooden spoon landed to the right of the cooker on the floor – about 4 feet away. It had to go around the fridge to do this!

6pm, more lights in living room (blue ones) some watching me. More computer problems again.

10pm, went to bed. At 11pm someone kissed my face and woke me up. It was my dead brother in law.

18 November 2004

Someone having a laugh, every time I put the bin back under the work top in the kitchen they pull it back out again

19 November 2004

At work and once again the smoke alarm kept going off. It happened about three times this afternoon. I also heard someone knocking but I couldn't find anyone around.

20 November 2004

At work and once again heard the knocking but nobody there.

22 November 2004

At work and a voice behind me said, 'Excuse me would you mind explaining just what it is that you think you are doing?'

It was the old lady that used to live here but I couldn't help but laugh at her tone.

26 November 2004

Lights on living room wall.

28 November 2004

Smell of aftershave keeps coming and going.

1 December 2004

H woke to find an ice cold hand stroking her face.

3 December 2004

9pm, flash off light by the TV in the living room.

4 December 2004

Seven of us in kitchen and twice the bin was pulled out from under the work top – but no one saw it move.

5 December 2004

Smell of aftershave in kitchen at work, it's the brother in law.

7 December 2004

H took her driving test today and while driving she says her left hand went ice cold and she heard a voice say, 'Don't worry, love, I'm here.'

10 December 2004

6.45 am in kitchen I can hear a muffled conversation coming from the room above – but from the landing doorway there is no sound at all. The conversation lasted for over 30 mins. Really strong smell of aftershave again, keeps coming and going, also felt a cold sensation all down my left side as if someone sitting next to me. It also disturbed the cat enough to move her to another seat.

7am bent down to pull washing from inside machine and someone poked me in the back four times.

12 December 2004

At work and I keep hearing knocks on the front door but no one was there. It happened half a dozen times then I Ignored it till they got fed up.

13 December 2004

5.40am. Woken up by the sound of someone pulling the bathroom light cord over and over again. Told them to sod off! But they kept it up for about 10 mins, not funny at that time of day as everyone else was asleep.

15 December 2004

I've been watched and followed for most of the day today and I managed to cut someone off the phone again. I do try not to but my tummy flips and then the phone goes dead.

16 December 2004

Bin pulled out in the kitchen again.

17 December 2004

Let the dogs out at 6am, checked the gate was closed but 2 mins later the gates were open and unbolted and the dogs were gone. Fetched them back but the same thing happened again.

24 December 2004

Very odd we have had a quiet week.

24 August 2005

Got up at 6am. In the kitchen half an hour later and a girl's voice said hello right behind me.

7.45am heard the same female voice again in the hall. I thought it sounded as if she was up stairs but I did not bother to look. I've fallen for that trick before and when you go to look the sound always comes from somewhere else. 5pm strong smell of after shave in the hall.

25 August 2005

H's boyfriend stayed the night and when H returned from having a bath he asked, 'do you always sing in the shower.' H pointed out that although she had been in the bathroom, she had not been singing and we don't have a shower as ours is broken. Boyfriend was adamant he had heard singing whilst a shower was being used. After that he did not want to talk about it.

I felt definitely watched today, so I put the video camera on but did not manage to catch anything on it. The brother in law was here again but thought it was funny that I could not catch him on tape.

3pm. I had a visit from my sister in law and her three children. When we were in the kitchen I felt my mum's presence and when one of the children started to play with the digital camera I heard mum say, 'It's alright if she wants to take a photo.' I sent the child off around the house to take photos and we got some interesting results from the ones in the kitchen – I think there are faces on a couple of them.

26 August 2005

I'm told that if we want to take photos we need to ask

permission from the spirit concerned and its then up to them if they want to make an appearance. That information came from my spirit guide John.

H got up this morning asking me if I've been rummaging around inside the kitchen cupboards as she was woken up by the sound of things being moved around as if from inside the cupboard. I have not been inside the cupboards and have not been making enough noise to wake anyone when I got up at 6.30am.

Feel watched again today, there's someone hovering about but I can't tell who it is.

H tells me that her abilities to see a mental image of spirits is growing and she can describe spirits in good detail as she comes into contact with them. She went off to town today to get the photos developed and purchase a new mobile phone. She reports that earlier in the week when she went to the seaside with her boyfriend on a day trip, she saw the spirit of a man dressed in a dark suit wandering around in one of the amusement arcades, she said she felt sorry for him as he was lost.

The photos of the kitchen show faces over layered one on top of the other. I can see three faces in one photo and can clearly see the face of my gran who died three years ago in another. The third photo shows an odd form of light reaching up from the TV and the fourth one shows some form of light that does not make any precise shape at all.

Went to bed at 10.30pm but was woken by the sound of breaking glass just before midnight. I jumped out of bed to see if someone was trying to break into the cars from my bedroom window but there was no one there. I had another look outside and looked around the house but there was no one around. The only thing that I could find was that all of the ornaments from on top of the lounge TV had been knocked to the floor, the odd thing was that they were all in a pile so I knew the cat had not knocked them off as they were not scattered. I just told them, 'I'm not playing that game,' and went back to bed.

27 August 2005

N off work this week so I'm not expecting much to happen as they tend to hide when he's around.
6.45pm, in the living room watching TV. N actually mentioned being able to smell gas. There is no gas supply in this area. And I couldn't smell it.

28 August 2005

7am, sitting in the kitchen with N and an old man's face appeared at the window. I thought he would go away so I ignored him, but five minutes later he was still there. I got up and went to the window. As I did the old man backed away a little and started pointing across the yard. 'Over there,' he said over and over again. 'Over there.' I said, 'You are gonna have to explain more mate coz I can't get what you are on about.' With that he puffed in frustration and vanished. He was late 60s in age, wearing an old greenish, beige suit jacket and a check shirt. I have not a clue who he was but may be he's the one who walks across the yard at night. He seemed friendly enough but p'd off because I would not follow him to find out what he was drawing my attention to. I got the feeling that he will be back just as most of them are if you don't do what they want you to.

H tells me that when she got into bed last night and closed her eyes she got the impression that there was a spirit right in front of her face. When she opened her eyes there was a woman standing in her room. She had long curly, red hair that was tied back and was wearing a long dress that was pulled tight around the waist. She said the woman was very friendly and as she was not worried by her presence so she just smiled at her and went to sleep.

29 August 2005

H reports being woken again by the sounds of someone moving things around, this time they were inside her wardrobe. I find it funny that H has the same attitude as me and if she thinks they are being annoying she will just tell them to bog off! I wonder how many other households are like this where the ghostly visitors are treated just like any member of the family and they are also missed when they are not around.

THE INVESTIGATION BEGINS

We arrange to visit the farmhouse and conduct a full investigation on 7 October 2005.

We pass through the heavy gate that Debbie says opens and closes by itself. The family welcome us into their home. Also present are paranormal investigators Ann and Steve who have been investigating the house for the last few years. Ciarán has investigated the house before but this is Yvette's first visit.

The first place we settle in to introduce ourselves to the

family is the kitchen. It's a homely and inviting kitchen. We all sit around a dining table and notice amid the inevitable clutter that goes with every family kitchen a black bin that looks like it needs emptying and bowls of food for Debbie's two dogs and cat. We chat with Debbie and her family over a cup of coffee and detect no obvious signs of tension. The relationship between Debbie and her children, Helen and Ryan, seems natural, humorous and warm. Helen and Ryan are supportive of their mother and both say they have experienced the same phenomena as their mother. This immediately makes the case stand out for us. We're not just dealing with one eyewitness account here but at least three. And from our initial assessment these three people all seem genuine. They don't appear to be attention seekers.

Debbie is a property developer. The house isn't a mansion but it is clear that the family are comfortably off and an initial assessment suggests very little motive for fraud.

Debbie comes across as a very level-headed, down-to-earth woman who genuinely believes she is psychic. In many paranormal investigations you find yourself dealing with a person or group of persons who believe they are psychic and can see things other people can't. The method we prefer to use for these kinds of cases is as follows: eyewitness interviews, walk around and environmental checks to rule out natural causes, filming of 'hot spots' to rule out the possibility of fraud and possibly a séance if it fits in appropriately with the witnesses' belief systems, though especially if the witness claims some sort of ability.

It's a good way to assess the situation in terms of how much the claimed ability 'feeds' the reported phenomena.

INTERVIEW WITH DEBBIE

Debbie's eyewitness account is central to the investigation. You've seen samples from her diary and in the following extracts summarised from our hour-long interview with her you'll see that particular key events are consistent with her diary. She also supplies some fascinating details. Read it and see what you think.

Q: Can you tell us about your experiences here?

A: Where can I begin! There are so many different things. The gate outside swings open and closes on its own, the bin in the kitchen moves backwards and forwards. The practical jokes are the most annoying. I'll be working on my computer and the words won't come out right or they'll be split and altered. Once the word 'shitty' kept appearing on the screen. Objects will be moved. The bin liners will disappear and they'll reappear in the linen cupboard. Neil's fleece disappeared and then reappeared three weeks later in the place it disappeared. My jewellery vanished for three weeks and then I found it hanging from light hooks – not a place you'd leave them. Another time I took my rings off when cooking. They vanished for a month until I found them behind the silk in an old silk case. I had to rip the silk out to get them.

I'll get pinched and stroked. I'll wake up and find I've

been pulled down the bed by six inches. I'll see them.
Recently I keep seeing a young girl around the bathroom
door. She's about six years old and she looks wet. She's
wearing an old apron over a shabby blue dress. I'll hear
them say things. I was in the kitchen once writing a letter
and I heard 'Hello.'

Q: *Can you tell us what happened to Ryan?*

A: Yes, last year Ryan ended up sleeping in my bed. He was
so scared and I knew this wasn't just teen hormone stuff.
He'd be listening to music and his headphones were pulled
off. He was touched by ice cold hands. They'd pull rubbish
out of the bin. They even followed him to his friend's
house and came back with him. He got really upset. On
one occasion he came to me and we could hear scratching
on the door outside.

Q: *How did you feel about all this happening to your son?*

A: I got angry. I was having none of it. One day I just went
into his room and threatened them. I told them I wasn't
frightened of them and they were to leave Ryan alone. I got
really angry as he has been very ill and didn't need this. He
was being pestered. It's stopped now.

Q: *How do you cope with it all?*

A: The more you notice them the worse they get so most of
the time I just ignore them. Like when the bin comes out
and moves three feet. If I put it back again it moves out

again. I just ignore it now. I've got used to it. It's part of our daily lives.

Q: *How long has this been going on?*

A: A couple of months after we moved in here. We came here in early 2000.

Q: *How often does it happen?*

A: Daily. The whole house is active 24/7. It doesn't happen in Ryan's room now.

Q: *Are you worried about it all?*

A: I'm not worried as the spirits are friendly, sometimes too friendly. They'll touch my head and stroke my nose and ears, waking me up when I really need to sleep. There was one time when I did get a little scared. I was on the landing and something ran at me. We all sleep with the bathroom light on. Our two dogs sense things and start barking. George was nasty the first time I saw him but now he is nice.

Q: *Who is George?*

A: I think George is from the 1800s, he has leather riding boots that are black and brown. George hangs around in the hallway. One night when I fell asleep on the sofa he was angry and woke me up to ask me what I was doing sleeping there. He called me a Judas. I told him I live here. I'm not going anywhere. Then he calmed down.

Q: *How do you see him?*

A: I see him in parts. Sometimes I just see his boots or his hands. He's getting braver and I'm seeing more of him.

Q: *Has everyone in the family seen spirits?*

A: Ryan and Helen have but Neil hasn't. He's a sceptic.

Q: *Do the apparitions appear outside the farmhouse?*

A: Oh yes. Tom often wanders in from the yard across to the dairy. Tom I think is from the 1930s – I get glimpses of a trilby sometimes. He tries to get my attention from the kitchen window and wants me to follow him to the barn but I take no notice of him. If you listen too much to them they'll take over your life.

Q: *What do your friends and family and other people think?*

A: Apart from Helen and Ryan they're scared. Neil isn't interested. I'm so used to it that it's funny if it happens to others. I had a workman in the house once. He saw the spirit of my brother-in-law lift his bucket handle up, throw a bread bag in the air and flip the radio on and off. He never came back and sent someone else to do the job. Friends and family won't come. My eldest daughter couldn't wait to leave. She'd feel them plucking her hair in the car.

Q: *Why do you think the spirits are here?*

A: Is it the place or is it us? I don't know. My guides have told me I am here for a reason. I'm just not sure what it is. Perhaps I lived here in a former life. Although I wasn't born here, it's always felt like home.

Q: *Has anything happened today?*

A: Yes this morning there was a naval guy hanging around waiting for you to arrive. He's got a naval outfit on. At 2 a.m. this morning I was woken with sea shanties and talk about Nelson's Column. He's come through one of my guides and he has a strong presence. He's waiting for you as he's got something he needs you to know. He wants nothing from me. He's waiting to see you. He's here now. I'm getting hot and you can hear my voice is croaky. That's him trying to take over. He says there is something you are going to find out at the end of the month. He has a pendant he wants to give you. He likes your attitude. Your compassion and humility and, Yvette, he likes short women.

Q: *Do you know anything about the history of the house?*

A: Not really, we only got back to 1958. Although there is the rumour that it was a station for the land army during the war.

Q: *Can you tell us about the time slips?*

A: Yes. I lose time. Once I left the bedroom and came downstairs and 40 minutes had vanished. This morning I woke up and saw the time was 6.20 a.m. I got up and it was 6.45 a.m.

Q: There could be a natural explanation for that. What about the historical playbacks?

A: Yes I've seen glimpses of two different lives. I'm wearing a different outfit. In one I'm a servant. I'm always in this place or near it.

Q: How many spirits are there here now?

A: I can sense, not see four. George is here. Rosemary, the girl, is here. Helen and I have both seen this young girl. She's wet and we think she may have drowned. The brother-in-law is here and then there is Arlene who lived here or near here. She was killed by a car when she got out of a car outside her school, perhaps in the 1970s. Oh and, of course, the naval guy is here too, so that's five of them.

Q: Do you ask the spirits about the afterlife?

A: They won't tell me much. I do know George has crossed over. Not sure why he has come back. There are halls of sleep on the other side. The halls of sleep are a bit like a hospital with rows and rows, millions and millions of beds stretching endlessly. You can rest in the halls of sleep and you are taken care of. The idea is to give your soul time to get over the shock of losing your physical body and only having the astral body. I don't really know much else and the spirits aren't likely to tell me. It's too personal. It's like me coming up to you, Yvette, and saying, 'Tell me what's in your handbag.' You wouldn't want to tell me, would you? You'd say it's none of my business.

THE WALK AROUND

Before filming begins we explore the whole house. We open all doors and latches to see if they can open on their own. We check each room and corridor for draughts coming through the doors, windows or gaps in the floorboards. We check for loose floorboards, airlocks in the central heating and pipe work, as well as noise levels in the farm next door. Basically everything is noted down on a checklist, ready to be consulted if anything strange happens during the night.

Ciarán sets up EMF meters in every room that is to be filmed and takes careful baseline measurements from the rest of the house, as unusually high EMFs had previously been measured at several locations within the house during the Para.Science investigation. As we've seen in Part One, there has been some research linking fluctuations in the electromagnetic field with paranormal phenomena. According to psychics this is because ghosts are an energy force and can disrupt our electromagnetic field. EMF fluctuations may also cause symptoms such as a sense of being watched or, in susceptible people, visual and auditory hallucinations. A normal EMF reading is between 0.1 and 10 milligauss: anything more than that is unusual and the source, which is most often a domestic appliance, needs to be established.

Debbie informs us that currently Helen's bedroom, the landing and the kitchen tend to be focal points for activity to occur, so we decide to focus our efforts there.

THE CHILDREN'S BEDROOMS

Ryan is working on his computer with his headphones on as we enter his bedroom. We ask him how he feels about the paranormal activity in his house and he just shrugs his shoulders and says it doesn't bother him any more. His room is of interest to us because the poltergeist activity Debbie mentioned in her interview used to be reported there.

The 2003–04 Para.Science investigations found a logical cause for the poltergeist activity in Ryan's room that Debbie mentioned in her interview. EMF readings taken at the time were extremely high. Whenever high or fluctuating readings appear during a paranormal investigation man-made causes are always looked at first. Household appliances such as fridges or microwaves can affect EMF readings if they are within two or three feet of the meter, as can nearby electric utility cables. In this case the dairy farm across the road from Ryan's room was obviously a possible source of electricity. However, an environmental monitoring agency inspected the house and found considerable cause for concern.

Poor wiring is a possible cause of high EMF readings, and in many allegedly haunted locations we've been to the experiences have stopped after the electrician paid a visit. This is exactly what happened in Ryan's case. When electricians replaced the faulty 1950s cables that ran above his windows and bed, not only did the activity stop but his health improved dramatically. This gives us a natural explanation for the activity reported previously in Ryan's bedroom, but it doesn't explain why Debbie and Helen continue to report activity. The rest of the wiring in the house is more contemporary.

Once the activity stopped in Ryan's bedroom, Helen's bedroom has become one of the most active 'hot spots'. Helen regularly reports seeing apparitions here, in particular a young girl aged about seven called Rosemary. We leave Ryan and go into Helen's room. It's a typical teenage girl's room with a stuffed tiger toy on the bed and posters on the wall. Yvette asks Helen how she copes with the experiences. Helen is a little more enthusiastic in her response to our questions, but in general has the same accepting, dare we say 'cool' attitude as Ryan. It's been going on for so long that it's become the norm for her. Most of the time the experiences don't bother her, but she does tell us that if she ever feels scared in bed at night she pulls her bedclothes over her head and hopes for the best.

FILMING BEGINS

At 11.18 p.m. Yvette and Ciarán begin filming upstairs. Yvette goes to Helen's room and Ciarán goes to Ryan's room and the master bedroom. Para.Science remain downstairs preparing equipment and taking some initial readings.

Yvette feels apprehensive from the start and isn't sure

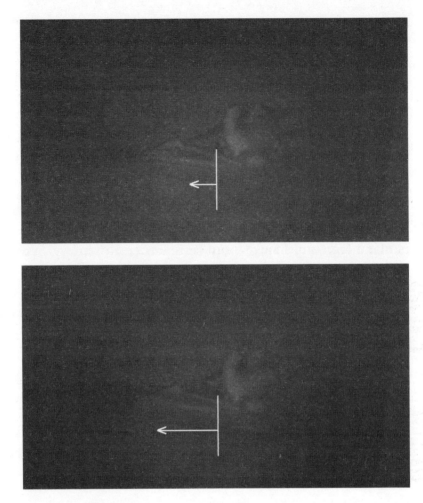

Light over Helen's bed

why. Almost immediately she thinks she hears a humming sound behind her at the doorway to Helen's room. She calls out to Ciarán who joins her in Helen's bedroom. During filming what appears to be a flickering light hovers briefly over Helen's bed and then disappears. As Yvette wonders out loud how anyone can live in this house she starts to feel very hot and sweaty.

Yvette asks if there are any spirits in the room and, if there are, for them to make themselves known by moving an object or making a sign. The only response is silence, but Yvette does get a sudden start near the door of Helen's bedroom. She feels as if someone is behind her. Ciarán asks what it was and she says it was definitely someone tall and most likely male.

Yvette moves from Helen's room to the landing, where Debbie has told her she sometimes sees an apparition called George. Apart from a creak on the floorboards and some interesting shadows on the landing, nothing unusual occurs.

The master bedroom and Ryan's room yield no results. The overnight kitchen vigil with Steve and Ann is also unproductive. Steve tells us that he has noticed in previous investigations at the house that unusual things tend to happen just after one of Debbie's two dogs bark – but the dogs remain fast asleep and the bin which Debbie says moves backwards and forwards stays put. We 'fish' (to use Steve Parsons' term) for a while to see if we can catch anything useful, but nothing occurs.

OUR INITIAL THOUGHTS

Yvette: *For me the most striking result was the presence I felt outside Helen's bedroom and the humming sound. I got very hot and sweaty at one point and I'm not wearing a thick coat. There was also an unexplainable light anomaly and the creak on the landing. I almost wish I hadn't read Debbie's diary or heard Debbie's and Helen's stories before we did the filming as there were moments up there when I felt very, very scared and I'm not sure if that was because I knew the history of the house.*

Ciarán: The most interesting results for me are the fluctuating EMF readings and Yvette's response to the question I asked her about the presence she felt. She was convinced it was a tall presence not just any presence. The shadows on the landing can be discounted because they were caused by my night vision camera. The creak in the floorboard could have been because Yvette was shifting her weight or because someone was opening a door and the light anomaly was very probably dust, an insect or a cobweb. The humming sound Yvette heard could have been someone downstairs or even the toilet flushing. As for Yvette feeling jumpy and hot I can't dismiss the power of suggestion. Here we are in a house that has a history of haunting. It's the middle of the night. Imagination is going to run wild.

THE SÉANCE

Everyone agreed that it would be a good idea to hold a séance and see who or what might come forward. We like to hold séances when we have witnesses like Debbie who believe they are psychic, as a séance fits in with their belief system and increases the likelihood of evidence or useful information coming forward.

Yvette, Ann, Helen and Debbie sit down in a circle. Ciarán and Steve are in the room filming and witnessing the séance but not taking part in it. Before the séance Ciarán sets up lock-off cameras in the landing and Helen's bedroom in case any audible phenomena are captured upstairs.

The Séance begins

The way Yvette does séances is to sit everyone on the floor with their hands placed on a table with their fingertips touching. (Sometimes she will have everyone sit on chairs in a circle holding hands, in which case both feet are placed on the floor.) She asks everyone to relax and visualise energy flowing through their left arms and across their bodies to their right arms and into the next person. The lights are dimmed and eyes are closed until the séance is in full swing.

During the séance Yvette talks sincerely as if she is talking to someone alive. She likes to keep asking questions and to ask the 'spirits' to make a sign that they're there. After the visualisation Yvette takes a deep breath and asks if there are any spirit persons present who would like to make themselves known to her. Almost immediately Debbie senses a presence. Helen thinks something touched her arm. Debbie calls out and asks George or Rosemary to come forward. Yvette thinks she hears a tap.

Nothing much seems to be coming through, but Debbie is convinced the spirits are present and the group round the table decide to try glass divination. This is a technique that involves each person resting a finger on a glass in the middle of the table and inviting spirits to move it. The glass begins to wobble slightly when Yvette asks if there is anyone there. Debbie says it is the naval officer who is blocking the others out. She asks him to step aside. The glass moves slowly towards Helen. Debbie asks if Rosemary is present. The glass moves vigorously and startles everyone. Debbie asks Rosemary if she drowned. The glass doesn't move. The glass moves again and Debbie says her guide John is here. John is a monk with a scarred face and Debbie believes he died in a fire at his monastery. Rosemary, John and the naval officer are present, and Debbie believes there is someone else.

Yvette thinks she knows who this someone else might be and she asks if they are related to her. The glass moves violently. She then asks if the spirit's name is Diane. The glass doesn't move. She asks if it is Mary. The glass doesn't move. She asks if it is Anna. The glass moves. Yvette thought it might be her grandmother Mary.

Rosemary takes centre stage with the glass again and there are lots of violent dramatic movements in response to questions. A picture of Rosemary is built up. She's about nine years old, someone hurt her and she lies underground in a quarry in Wales where there is water. Her murderer is still alive. She wants her body to be found. Her mother and father are not alive. Yvette wonders why she is alone and not with them. Debbie asks Rosemary if she wants to cross over. Helen starts crying, as the glass moves in response to questions. She is feeling for Rosemary.

Moving the glass

The atmosphere in the room goes flat and all in the séance agree to close down the séance with words of thanks and peace.

Ciarán asks Debbie how much time she thinks has passed and what she thinks the temperature is. Debbie thinks it is around 60F and that around 30 minutes have passed. Helen thinks it is hotter but admits that this may be because she has been crying. She thinks about an hour has passed. Ann thinks the temperature is comfortable at around 60F and that 45 minutes have passed. Yvette guesses 40 minutes and around 60 to 65F.

The séance lasted exactly 40 minutes and the temperature remained constant at around 65F.

OUR CONCLUSIONS

Yvette: *Tough one for me to sum up. When I first met Debbie it became clear that she believes she is a sensitive or psychic, someone who sees things most other people can't. The activity seems to be linked to her as she has had unusual experiences outside the home as well, which makes me think that perhaps it is her rather than the house that should be the focus of investigation. She's very convincing and has a sense of humour. She seems like the kind of woman you could trust. When we did the séance I also realised that Helen believes she is a sensitive too. She plays a big part in the manifestation of the phenomena. But I did wonder if the mother and daughter were feeding off each other? Were their energies creating the haunting? Was this genuine? I'm just not sure.*

I did sense something in the house and it's a place I'd like to revisit. I was genuinely scared outside Helen's bedroom when I thought I felt a presence and I did get very hot on several occasions. Although there were some intriguing bits for us, overall I'm slightly disappointed as Debbie repeatedly told us that things happened every day and we didn't really pick up anything tangible. The séance and the information about Rosemary just didn't overwhelm me.

Ciarán: This isn't the first time I've visited Debbie and I'm more familiar with the case than Yvette. The difficulty is that Debbie reported a lot of stuff, daily activity, but when we visited nothing much happened. I'm inclined towards the psychological explanation, the mother and daughter feeding off each other. Debbie's diary also shows an increase in the experiences in the last few years. It is interesting to me that she is a fan of paranormal shows, like Most Haunted, *which have emerged in the last few years, and a lot of what Debbie reports matches what she has seen on television. She seemed accepting, almost amused by the activity.*

Ryan's illness and alleged poltergeist experience have possibly been explained by the faulty electrical wiring uncovered in an earlier investigation. The séance didn't yield anything really ground-breaking, and although it all looked pretty genuine with fingertips lightly touching the glass, not pressing down on it, we can't rule out the possibility of subconscious 'micro' movements. We didn't capture anything significant on film, and all we really have to go on are slightly fluctuating EMF readings and eyewitness reports of alleged paranormal activity which are always very difficult to assess as evidence.

To conclude: we found the farmhouse case both intriguing and frustrating. The atmosphere in the house is intense, and well suited to a small team of investigators. There's no doubt Debbie and Helen are convinced that what they see and sense is genuine, but did they convince us? No! But the phenomena Debbie reports show no signs of going away and the farmhouse is one of those cases that definitely needs further investigation. We want more. That's paranormal investigators for you. We always want more.

CASE TWO: CHARTER HOUSE

(DATE OF INVESTIGATION: THURSDAY 3 NOVEMBER 2005)

In the summer of 2005 we were contacted by the owner of Charter House, a bed and breakfast in Warwick, with reports of strange activity. Intrigued, we decided to conduct an investigation. When we arrived it felt a bit like a one-night stand, as none of us had ever visited or investigated the venue before. We really didn't know what to expect.

According to the owner the old Tudor venue used to be a look-out post in the Civil War. In the last few years the apparition of a Civil War soldier had allegedly been seen on a regular basis both by the owner and by several guests. On one occasion the ghost was seen disappearing into a wall where a door once was. Those who had seen the ghost described him as short – only about five feet – and wearing a suit of chain mail. Heavy footsteps had also been heard regularly by the owner when no guests had been around, and guests had reported the footsteps too, thinking it was the owner.

Other guests said they had felt a presence, as if they were being watched. In addition there were reports of lights and radios being turned on and off. One guest thought that there was a problem with the electricity and bought a battery-powered radio alarm. It too was turned off in-explicably. Cleaners also reported an indentation on the edge of the bed in one particular bedroom. The bed looked as if it had been sat on, but nobody had been in the room.

The owner agreed to block off 3 November 2005 for our visit, as she would be away and no one had booked in. We could have the place to ourselves. As we only had the one night we decided to use the traditional vigil method to investigate. The venue was small and ideally suited for one person in each room to report anything they saw, heard, felt or sensed.

FIRST IMPRESSIONS

It's 9 p.m. and pitch dark outside. It takes us about ten minutes to turn off all the lights in the house; surprising given the fact that this is a small property with three floors,

The staircase at
Charter House

including an attic and five bedrooms. This makes us think that perhaps some of the activity and feelings of unease reported here may be caused by all this electricity.

As we walk around the first floor we see that the place is beautifully and carefully decorated with a Tudor theme. It doesn't feel scary at all. There are exquisite ornaments, paintings, furnishings, decorated cushions and antique dolls everywhere. 'I feel like we should be having tea and cakes,' says Yvette. We all agree that the atmosphere is comfortable, elegant and homely. 'Perhaps not for long,' says Ciarán. 'According to the owner phenomena are reported almost every week. With such unusual regularity and frequency the chances are good that something will happen.' 'Why did you say that?' Yvette replies. 'I was feeling OK until you said that.'

We move upstairs to the bedrooms, where most of the

phenomena have been reported. The first room we enter is called the Dressmaker Room and it has a creepy, almost Gothic feel to it. There are china dolls with enigmatic smiles wearing period costumes. On the wall we see three children's night-dresses hanging up. Both of us start to feel a bit uneasy. We aren't sure why, but it's creepy in here with dolls staring at us, the frilly furniture, the period paintings and those white dresses hanging on the wall.

Yvette starts to call out gently. She asks if there is anybody in the room who wants to talk to her. She asks if there is anything she can do to help. All is quiet. We decide to separate.

Yvette: *I'm in the Dressmaker Room, the one with the dolls and night-dresses hanging on the wall. The room is creepy but I think I'm all right. I'm sitting here on the bed that indentations are said to occur on. There is a mirror in front of me. It's a strange mirror, you can see lines that probably glue the mirror to the wall through it. As I sit on this bed I imagine what it must be like to wake up or fall asleep here with those dresses hanging on the wall and the dolls glaring.*

We know from research that the chances of seeing a ghost are greatly enhanced if a person is sitting or lying down and in a relaxed state. Could the activity reported in the bedrooms in this house be explained by hypnagogic or hypnopompic hallucinations that can occur in the few seconds/minutes before and after waking up or falling asleep?

The hypnagogic state is the period when the brain is

*falling asleep after being awake, while the hypnopompic
state is the period when the brain is waking up from
sleep. We know that a person can awake, often with a
start, to find that they can see, hear, feel or smell
something in the bedroom that either disappears or is
later found not to have happened. Common
hallucinations are: thinking that a name has been called
out or that the phone is ringing; bright or dark
amorphous blobs that hang in mid-air and slowly fade; a
feeling that somebody has touched the face, feet or hands;
the appearance of a person by the bedside who rapidly
disappears.*

*Hallucinations happen in that fuzzy, confused period of
time between sleeping and consciousness when the brain is
neither fully asleep nor fully awake. During this time
dreams may intrude into our waking world, producing
hallucinations through all the senses. Our brain can also
misinterpret signals it receives from the senses and create
hallucinations from these as well. For example, a shirt
hanging on a wall can, in the first few moments after
waking, be misinterpreted as a ghostly figure. Or in the
case of the Dressmaker Room the three dresses could be
misinterpreted as a moving figure, the dolls' faces as
nightmare images. There are so many ornaments and
paintings and furnishings here to stimulate the
imagination.*

*We're not saying this is definitely what has happened
here, but whenever a phenomenon is reported in a
bedroom we need to consider the possibility of
hallucination as a person eases into or out of sleep.*

I'm going to call out again and ask if anybody is in here with me. Please show yourself. Tap if you can hear my voice. Move the dresses or the curtains. Wait. I heard something, a dripping noise. There it is again, and again. I'm getting scared. It seems to be coming from the wardrobe. I'm going to call out again. Please show yourself and let me know you are here. I've come in search of you and am trying to figure out if there are ghosts here or not. Could you help me? I can hear a tiny drip again to my left. I've checked the sink to see if it is dripping, but it isn't.

Ciarán: *Yvette and I have decided to separate. I'm in the Kingmaker Room which is a really comfortable room. I'm not picking up anything on my camera. I'm not hearing any sounds or sensing anything. I'll sit quietly and film the room for a while.*

Half an hour later, with nothing to report in the Kingmaker Room, I head upstairs with Yvette to the attic bedrooms. In the first one we enter, as with all the other rooms in the house, the TV is on standby. I can't help thinking again about the overload of electrical appliances in this house. Could this have something to do with the phenomena reported here?

We look around the room and all is peaceful and quiet. We don't pick up any negative vibes at all. In fact it seems a perfectly pleasant place. Yvette feels a draught, but a small window is open. Curiously one of the rooms in the attic has a dripping tap. This is surprising, as when we walked around earlier to switch off all the lights we didn't notice any dripping taps.

The Kingmaker (left) and Dressmaker bedrooms

Apart from the tap dripping everything is so quiet that we decide to take a break and let Ann and Steve do a walk around and check the EMF readings. Once we've done that Yvette suggests a séance in the hope that it will create some energy.

IT'S ALL ABOUT ENERGY

Mediums and psychics believe that is through energy that we are able to communicate across the boundary between the earth and the spirit planes. Energy separates and links the physical and spiritual worlds. It is the essence of all existence, although it takes countless forms. You are energy, this book you are reading is energy, the chair or floor you are sitting on is energy.

This isn't as strange as you may think. The principles of science – well, physics actually – substantiate what the psychics are saying. Scientists believe that all objects, tangible and intangible, visible and invisible, audible and inaudible, are matter, and all matter is comprised of energy structures – atoms, molecules, electrons – that vibrate at certain frequencies. The rate or speed of the frequency determines the matter's tangibility.

Low-frequency vibrations produce tangible or visible representations such as everyday objects, and high-frequency vibrations produce energy that we can't quantify with our physical senses. For instance, the energy of matter that forms an object we think of as solid, say this book, vibrates so slowly that we are able to physically see it. The energy of matter that we cannot see, such as the air we breathe, vibrates very fast.

According to some psychics, energy on the spirit plane vibrates so fast that it doesn't have an appearance or presence at all, unless a spirit somehow chooses to represent itself in a tangible way. The energy of the physical body is not capable of vibrating at a high enough energy rate to exist on the spirit plane. So if spirit contact occurs it is the spirit that must come down to the earth plane. To make its presence known, the spirit must slow down its vibration while the medium raises his or her vibration so they can meet and communicate. At a séance the aim is to raise energy vibrations in the hope that a spirit will slow down its vibration and that communication between the living and the dead can take place.

If the basis of a ghost's existence is energy, then perhaps the answer to the question of an afterlife is staring us in the face.

Could the laws of physics that exist for us also apply for ghosts, making them a part of our reality? After all, what we are and everything around us is fundamentally energy.

The energy theory is one reason why we like to film and conduct vigils in the dark. It isn't to get that eerie effect on camera with pupils huge and white and the background shadowy. The theory is that spirits find it easier to come into the atmosphere when it is dark, because it slows down their vibrations. That's why we also use infra-red cameras that can capture images in total darkness. Sometimes we use a torch to see where we are going, but most of the time the only available light we have is the dim light of our infra-red.

THE EMF READINGS

At around 10 p.m. Steve and Ann do a walk around the house to check both the temperature and the EMF in each room. The temperature seems to be steady and comfortably warm. The EMF readings, however, are far from steady. Hardly surprising given the fact that all the lamps, TVs, clock radios are on standby and the house has more light switches than we have ever seen before – these still affect the reading even though they are off.

In the Kingmaker Room Steve and Ann are particularly interested in the area around the bed, which has an abnormally high EMF reading – as much as 30mG, which is the level you would expect near a household appliance. This 30mG reading was traced to a source beneath the bed in the room above where EMF readings exceeded 80mG. It's debatable, but if you were to sleep in that bed you

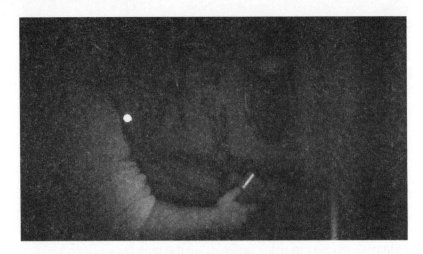

Steve taking an EMF reading

might experience physiological changes and interpret them as being the result of a haunting presence; or you might even be subjected to such a magnitude of EMF that it could potentially damage your health. They look under the bed in the room above and find some cables under a black box that are switched on. They are so concerned about the EMF readings that they make a note to recommend to the owner that she turns off the appliance under the bed.

As we've seen in Chapter Eight, when using highly accurate EMF meters the field shows minuscule fluctuations, and it is these that researchers are particularly interested in. For it is these, and abnormally high readings not normally found in domestic environments, that may be affecting the brain. This is what we found in the Kingmaker Room. The concern with such a high reading is that there is a proposed link between high ambient EMFs and increased reporting of paranormal activity in some witnesses. It is always our responsibility to ensure that any logical or plausible explanation is explored before declaring the witness experiences to be attributable to a ghost or spirit energies.

It is incorrectly accepted amongst some groups that spirits are a form of energy and that EMF meters detect that low level of so-called ghostly energy accurately. At Charter House we did get high EMF readings in various rooms. However, before we suggest paranormal activity independent of these EMF readings we first of all need to rule out other possible causes. The high number of electrical appliances in the house, the TVs and radio alarms on standby, the cables under the bed and all the light switches give us a strong indication that other sources may be the cause. To prove this conclusively, however, we would need to visit the house again, run more checks, investigate power supplies in the area and spend a few more nights there.

THE SÉANCE

At 11.30 p.m. Yvette, Ann and Steve take part in the séance while Ciarán films. They begin with their hands on the table. Yvette asks if there are any spirit people or astral beings in the house and if they want to make themselves known to her. Yvette hears a dripping sound again. She asks if the spirits can make a sign. Perhaps they could move the table or blow the candle out or effect a change in the temperature.

Ann and Yvette suddenly feel very cold. Yvette's hands go icy cold, but Ciarán isn't picking up any draughts on her hands with his thermal imager. Yvette insists she is getting colder by the second. She definitely senses a presence in the room. The table moves slightly. The team try to move the table themselves but find it very difficult to move even when all three try to lift it. Thin, creaky sounds are heard from upstairs. Steve goes upstairs to check, but nobody is there. He then puts on amplified earphones which boost his hearing considerably. In response to Yvette calling out, Steve hears faint knocks and sounds. Steve questions if what he is hearing is the traffic, people walking past, the wind – or his imagination?

Yvette, Ann and Steve all place their hands on a glass in the hope that it may move in response to Yvette's questions. After a while the glass does move. Yvette asks if anyone is standing close by and if it is a male spirit. The glass moves again. She asks more questions and the movement stops. Yvette decides to change her approach and pretends to be angry. She tells the spirit to move the glass because everyone has travelled a long way to meet him. Nothing happens. She asks the spirit to push the glass to where he is or to tap to indicate if he can hear her. Nothing happens. A few taps, thuds and creaks are heard, but eventually the team decide they aren't getting anywhere and they agree to end the séance.

TRIGGER OBJECTS

During the séance lock-off cameras are set up on the stairs where the footsteps have been heard and in the Kingmaker and Dressmaker Rooms. Trigger objects are also placed in various positions in the bedroom to see if they move during the séance. Ciarán ensures the 'trigger-object' room is locked, and is witnessed doing this by Ann.

At most locations we investigate we like to set up trigger objects in a sealed room with a camera running for one hour. We choose the rooms that have had the most activity reported in them and select an object that might have significance for the spirit supposed to haunt there. For example for a child we might use a toy. In this case we couldn't find a personal possession, so we left objects that the spirit might easily recognise such as a cross, a ring, a ball and an old coin.

An image taken by the lock-off camera

We only leave the trigger objects for one hour, because any more than that can make very, very tedious viewing afterwards, even though there are analysis techniques for examining hours and hours of footage of a trigger object for any movement. An alternative that we sometimes use is a camera hooked up to motion sensor software on a laptop, which means that the camera will only record if there is movement. You can set it so that even the slightest shadow movement would cause an alarm to go off and the footage to be dumped on to the hard drive. We usually leave the object during the séance when a huge effort is being made to raise spirit energy.

After the séance we checked all our trigger objects, but there had been no movement. Before ending the investigation we decide to do one more vigil.

POST SÉANCE VIGIL: 1 A.M. TO 2 A.M.

Yvette: *I always feel a bit apprehensive after a séance as you can never tell what you have unleashed. I'm in the Kingmaker Room and I've got goose bumps. It's so dark in here. The key is constantly swinging on the door, but that could be a breeze. I'll try calling out again. As I do, Steve interrupts me to say that he is hearing some gentle thuds. I can just about hear them too but they are so very faint. Steve puts on his headphones to amplify his hearing. As I call out he gives me the thumbs up and tells me he is hearing tiny taps and bangs in response to my calling out.*

If the theory that spirits exist on a higher, faster vibration than the one we exist on is correct, it might be a good idea to speed up our voices with a PC and play them on sonic speakers during a séance. It's something we should certainly think about. I'd like to try.

Ciarán: *This time I'm in the Dressmaker Room and I'm feeling slightly sick, which is unusual for me. It could be*

278

due to the late hour and the amount of coffee I've been drinking to stay awake. It will be interesting to see if this coincides with anything the others are experiencing, as our cameras are in sync. I've been thinking about the bangings, taps and creaks we've been hearing. Certainly in the part of the house Yvette is in now it could be due to the new timbers expanding and contracting in response to changes in the temperature. I'm in the older part of the house right now, where the timber would be harder and less affected by the temperature changes.

I'm no longer feeling sick, but I am frightened. I feel as if I'm being watched from the corner of the room where those dresses are hanging. They look a bit macabre there, and that could be causing my apprehension. I'm not alone in here. There is a pinprick of light dancing about near the door. I'm going to follow it with my camera. It doesn't look like an insect.

I'm feeling an intense calm now, in contrast to my feelings of unease earlier.

INFRASOUND

During and after the séance Steve used earphones to enhance his hearing. He thought he might have been picking up very low-frequency sound responses to Yvette's calling out.

We know that low-frequency sound has been known to cause a feeling of uneasiness, and because of this we certainly cannot rule the possible influence of this as an explanation for some of the activity reported at Charter

House. However, if it was genuinely low-frequency sound at infrasonic level (i.e. below 20Hz), Steve wouldn't have been able to actually hear it, only 'feel' it. We've got tentative evidence of a repeated low sound here, though, and we are certainly not going to ignore or discount it. At times, according to Steve, it didn't appear to be random. It seemed to respond every time Yvette's called out and to be at its most intense during the séance, suggesting the possibility of paranormal activity. On the other hand it could have just been the result of vibration caused by passing traffic. This is unlikely, as there was hardly any traffic when we held our séance (we're talking after midnight), but the passing traffic explanation is something that does need further investigation. We make a note to ensure we test for infrasound (low-frequency sound) on a future visit and also to guarantee similar testing on subsequent investigations for the book.

OUR CONCLUSIONS

Yvette: *I liked the creaks and noises during the séance and the freaky drops in temperature. What the entity may have done here is draw the energy, the heat, from the room to it.*

We spent a lot of time in bedrooms during the vigils, and it did make me think that perhaps some of the phenomena reported here may have been due to sleeping and waking hallucinations. If we get to visit again we must make a conscious effort to look for reported cases of strange phenomena occurring to guests in the bedrooms who have just woken up or who are very relaxed or falling asleep. It might even be a good idea for us all to spend a night here. Ideally we would have liked to spend a few nights at this venue, but unfortunately as it's a busy bed and breakfast this isn't possible. We were lucky to get this one night.

I thought the house, despite looking so pretty, was very creepy. But what intrigued me most about this case was the way it affected Ciarán. He's usually the one who stays calm, but this time he was the one who got a definite sense of being watched and I was the one who kept my cool. Welcome to my world, Ciarán!

Ciarán: *Watching the tapes of my experience in the Dressmaker Room still makes me feel uneasy. I can't explain what happened exactly. I was scared, and convinced I was being watched. This kind of thing doesn't usually happen to me.*

Thinking back, I was feeling very tired when it happened. It's possible my brain was playing tricks on me. The human brain is a far more extraordinary organ than most of us imagine, and the degree to which the human brain assists in the generation and understanding of paranormal experience has been a hotly debated topic for over a century now.

Sceptics would argue that all paranormal experiences are generated by the scientific workings of the brain and are therefore not 'paranormal' but simply cases of misinterpretation. Some parapsychologists generally believe that the brain is capable of producing completely unknown powers, such as extra-sensory perception and psychokinesis, which may be involved in a range of paranormal phenomena such as crisis apparitions and poltergeists. Psychics, on the other, believe that many paranormal phenomena are generated totally outside the brain through the intervention of discarnate entities such as spirits of the dead, angels or demons. As always there's no way yet of proving who is right or wrong. All I can say is that for a few moments in that room, for reasons I can't fully explain, I was terrified.

The fluctuating EMF readings in the bedrooms and the possible low-frequency responses picked up by Steve may explain some of the activity and my feelings of anxiety. If we are invited again these two things would definitely need to be investigated further. As for the clearly audible thuds, creaks and knocks we all heard – even though from our perspective inside the house natural explanations don't seem likely – we can't rule them out. There could be any number of reasons, from the new timber in the house creaking to the vibrating hum of cars passing outside.

All in all this investigation really emphasised the merit of spending longer or additional nights to get a feel for the bumps, bangs and atmosphere of an allegedly haunted house. We only got a fleeting glimpse. We all left with the sense that unless we spent more time getting to know it better, this house wasn't going to tell us its secrets.

CASE THREE: COLLINGWOOD

(DATE OF INVESTIGATION: THURSDAY 10 NOVEMBER 2005)

This pub in Rotherham interested us immediately when owners, Jane and Keith, contacted us in the summer of 2005. They told us that they weren't the only ones experiencing unusual phenomena there. Their seventeen-year-old son, Michael, and certain members of the bar staff as well as a customer had also seen, heard and sensed things they couldn't explain.

Jane gave us a list of strange happenings reported at Collingwood in the last six months:

- Jane says she saw the apparition of a man approach the bar. He looked so real that she asked him for his order, but as soon as she began to speak he disappeared. The chef and barmaid have also seen the same man on different occasions. They told Jane he looked like a young man who used to be a regular a few years ago but had died in a motor cycle crash. Every year on the anniversary of his death a memorial event was held at the pub, and it was after the latest memorial that the apparition allegedly started to appear.

- Upstairs above the bar where the owners and their son live, a small animal, possibly a cat, has been seen and sensed by Keith. It flashes in front of him as he is about to step on it.

- Both Jane and Keith say they often hear their names being called by unknown people.

- A large black figure has been following Michael. At one point it scared him so much that he asked his mum to help him. This dark figure has also been seen by dad Keith, but only out of the corner of his eye.

- If Jane and the barmaid are having a drink at the end of the evening they often notice that certain drinks, typically pints of lager and blackcurrant, disappear.

- The barmaid seems to think that the new owners are the reason there has been an increase in activity: Jane, who has an interest in the paranormal, is convinced that they were meant to buy the pub, early in 2005, but doesn't know why.

- The pool room appears to be the most atmospheric room in the pub: it has the largest amount of cold spots and the most oppressive atmosphere. Voices have been heard coming from the room when no one has been in there, and it is thought to be haunted by the spirit of a boxer who died there sitting in front of the fireplace. A customer has reported being pushed by an unknown force in this room. The push was so hard that he fell over.

• In the cellar lights come on and doors open when no one is down there. The presence in the cellar also seems to be drawing attention to problems before they can cause any damage.

With so much activity reported and with not one but several credible and independent witnesses, we simply had to set up a date to visit. So on a very cold November evening we arrived at the pub to begin our investigation. The pub has a cellar, a ground floor and an upstairs floor where Jane, Keith and Michael live. The ground floor is typical of many pubs, with a bar, juke box, tables, stools, a pool table and separate rooms for storage and office work.

For this investigation we decided to use a different methodology. In addition to interviewing, monitoring, recording and doing overnight vigils we asked David, a medium we know and respect, to accompany us.

THE INTERVIEW

We'd spoken with Jane many times on the phone, but to help set the scene prior to the vigils and to see if there had been any new developments we decided to interview her again. We also wanted to hear what husband Keith and son Michael thought about it all.

Q: *Can you remind us about how and why you decided to contact us?*

Jane: I met Ciarán at a conference and told him about the pub and what has been happening to us here. He told us he'd get back to us, and a few weeks ago we were contacted asking if we would be a case study for a book. We were happy to agree as we'd love to find out what is happening here.

Q: *Please could you tell us about what has happened to you since you've been living in the pub?*

Jane: It started about two weeks after we had moved in earlier this year. I was serving drinks at the bar. A man came up to me. He looked so real. He was tall and he wore a T-shirt, jeans and trainers. He had blond hair and dark glasses. I asked him if he wanted a drink and then he disappeared. I've seen him about six times since. I've been told by my staff that they have seen him too and he looks like an old pub regular who died in a motor cycle crash about four years ago. I've also smelled flowers and most recently a strong smell of tobacco. It's not cigarette smoke, which we get in this pub, but old-fashioned cigar smoke which I haven't seen anyone smoke here. One day it was so strong on the stairs I could hardly breathe.

Q: How about you, Keith?

Keith: I've seen and sensed a small animal. I think it's a grey or white cat. We have a cat and a dog but I know it's not them. Sometimes I feel as if I am about to trip over something and I see movement near the door. It freaks me out. Also when I come down at night there are temperature drops even when it's warm outside.

Jane: Don't forget, Keith, about the voices. We have both heard them. Sometimes when I'm shutting up for the night and everyone has left the pub I hear voices in the pool table room, but when I go in nobody is there. Some nights I feel a little scared and I just don't want to go into the room. I've been told there have been two deaths in there. One was a boxer who died by the fireside after a blow to the head. I've also found out that the pool room used to be an old boys' room where gents would go to play cards and smoke cigars.

Q: Michael, how about you? What has happened to you?

Michael: I'm being followed. There's a man with a dark face and clothes who stands over me while I sleep. He's tall and I can't see his face. He's like a shadow. One night I woke up to see him watching me. I don't know why I think it's a man. It just feels like a man.

Q: How do you feel about all this?

Jane: I'm OK because I think they want us to be here. Once Keith and I both heard what sounded like 'Well done' coming from the empty corner of a room. I think they approve of us and even want to help us. For example, once we found the barrels moved for us in the cellar and the lights on even though nobody had been down there. The doors were left open once too when they shouldn't have been, and I was furious with Keith because he said he had locked them. It was a good job they were open as a gas leak was found. Yes, I do think they want us to be here. You see when we came to the pub it has been closed for a while and had a bad reputation – drugs and things. We took it over and turned it around, and people tell us it's like the old Collingwood.

Keith: Yes, it was a huge risk taking this on and not really what we had planned. I was an engineer and Jane was a nurse before we became pub owners. When we were looking to buy and set up a pub we looked at several, but Jane was determined we'd have this one.

Jane: I know. When we first visited the place it was in a terrible state – so dirty and run down – but I remember standing in the bar area thinking we were meant to buy this place. I can't explain why, I just felt it was right.

Q: What you are saying to us is very interesting, because there are some common phenomena such as whispering and a sense of presence but also some unusual activity such as the helping and a full-bodied apparition. Can you tell us what you'd like to get out of this investigation?

Keith: We'd like to know who the spirits are and why they are here. We're not that worried about it as we think they like us. We'd like to see if we can help them.

Q: David, who's a medium we've brought along to help us, might be able to explain something and we might be able to offer you explanations for some of the activity, but perhaps not all. Are you OK with that?

Jane: Definitely. It would be fantastic to chat with David and see if he can pick anything up.

Keith: Sure, of course.

Q: Have any of you had any previous paranormal experiences?

Jane: When I was about eleven I saw my grandmother who had passed away. I do have an interest in the paranormal but I've experienced nothing like the activity here before.

Keith: I've also had visions of people moving past me, but as Jane says, nothing like this.

Jane: Our barmaid is convinced it's the two of us who have kicked things off.

During the interview Jane and Keith seemed to be very relaxed about the whole thing. They came across as likeable, warm and genuine witnesses. Although they don't claim to be psychic, they did admit to having a strong interest in the paranormal and psychic experiences in the past. Michael on the other hand seemed tense. During the interview he was very quiet, talking only when a question was directly addressed to him. At this stage we weren't sure if this was due to shyness or reluctance to open up. We also couldn't help wondering if he was being carried along by his parents' fascination with the haunting.

THE ROLE OF MEDIUMS IN PARANORMAL INVESTIGATIONS

This is a subject that is in constant debate amongst many paranormal investigative groups: should mediums/ psychics help during an investigation? It's a difficult question for us to answer, and one we look at in Chapter Eight. One thing we have found is that in cases like Collingwood where witnesses have a strong belief in the paranormal, bringing in a medium fits in with their belief systems and encourages them to open up. It can also be a source of comfort. We believe that if a medium or psychic follows the protocol below, he or she can be useful to the group as a whole.

Protocol:

1. We give our medium or psychic no information at all about the area to be investigated. Going in cold is very important.
2. When we arrive at the scene of a haunting we first of all let the medium/psychic survey the house with a trusted group member or members. We bring a tape recorder

or camera to record all that the medium senses in each room.

3. We then withhold from the rest of the group and the witnesses all the information that has been gathered by the mediums/psychic until after the investigation. During the investigation we do not want the group or the witnesses to be influenced by what the medium/psychic may sense or say.

4. How a medium conducts himself or herself is important. Generally, we pay a gratuity or donation towards expenses, but we avoid mediums who charge high fees for their services as it increases the likelihood of fraud.

5. A healthy balance in approach is also important for us when we work with a medium. We need to be sure that our medium is going into an investigation not with the intent of looking for paranormal activity but with the intent of looking for the possibility of paranormal activity. Possibility is a balanced approach.

As mentioned above for this case we decided to ask a medium to join our team. We've worked with David before and know that he meets the above criteria.

HOW MEDIUMS WORK

When mediums enter an allegedly haunted site, the first thing they are likely to do is sense any residual energies to help build a picture of what may have happened there in the past. For example, they might sense that it was once a hospital, a school or a church and so on.

Once a medium has got a feel for the energies of the place, he or she will now try to sense any spirits who for one reason or another may have stayed behind on earth after they have left their bodies behind. Mediums believe there can be any number of reasons for this, but the most common reason is fear of the light: if they have been evil or done terrible things in their past life they may be afraid to pass over to the afterlife. According to mediums, another reason a spirit may remain grounded is if they committed suicide or died very young. In the latter case these spirits may stay grounded because they simply don't know that they are dead. They could have died suddenly or been involved in an accident or even been murdered. They are still around their family and loved ones and trying to be noticed. Another reason could be that there are scores to settle; for example, some injustice was done to them when they were alive. In some cases mediums believe that they can help spirits who can't cross over: that if the spirits want to be released, mediums can help them to find light.

Not all spirits that mediums see and sense are 'grounded spirits'. They may be in visitation from other realms and have different ways of making their presence felt. Mediums believe these spirits come into the earthly realm through hot and cold spots which are like doorways, known as vortexes.

According to mediums in most cases spirits are unlikely to haunt graveyards or cemeteries. This is because once they have left their bodies behind they are far more likely to visit places where their loved ones are, places they were fond of during their lifetime or places they are associated with some reason.

Mediums say that when they feel a spirit in the atmosphere what they sense is a person's essence, which is a kind of map or picture of that person's whole life and personality. Many mediums are clairvoyant, clairsentient and clairaudient. This means they can see, sense and hear a spirit presence. Some mediums can smell a spirit presence too. Some mediums work through spirit guides. Guides are spirits who have the ability to pass on messages and information to a medium from spirits who have not yet learned how to communicate with the living.

Spirits allegedly use the energy of the medium to communicate and this is called channelling. Mediums say it is an exhilarating but draining experience. There is always the danger of being taken over or possessed, and it is important to have safeguards in place to ensure that this doesn't happen. Mediums believe it is possible for non-mediums to become possessed by spirits. This is the reason why they typically advise against playing around with séances and Ouija boards if there isn't a medium present or if you aren't aware of the correct procedure.

When spirits take possession of a medium's voice-box this is known as direct voice communication or DVC. When DVC happens a medium's tone of voice and vocabulary may alter. Transfiguration is the term mediums use to describe the process when a spirit takes control of their face and posture. If this happens it's very dramatic to watch and it can often seem as if another person is present speaking through the body of a medium. When spirit communication is over, mediums all have their own way of shutting out the spirit world, for example through visualisation, a relaxation technique where scenes or pictures that induce a relaxed state are visualised, and meditation, so they can get on with their normal everyday life.

We're fascinated by the way mediums and psychics work. We aren't a hundred per cent convinced that they are actually communicating with the dead, but on numerous occasions we have found them to be invaluable and helpful additions to our investigative team.

David the medium at Collingwood

THE CELLAR VIGIL

At 10 p.m. Ciarán, Yvette and David make their way down to the damp, dark cellar. Typical of a pub, the area is filled with boxes, crates, glasses, ashtrays and bottles. There are several storerooms and a generator room.

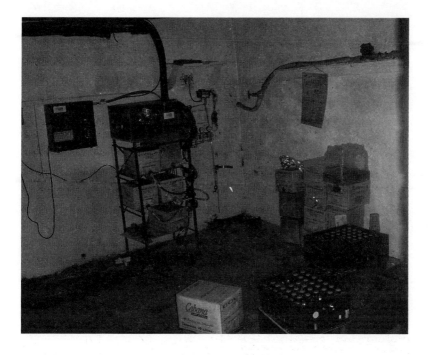

Inside the cellar

As soon as he steps inside the cellar David stops and tells us he senses dark energies, perhaps to do with witchcraft and old women. He says that before this was a pub something was going on here that shouldn't have, although he isn't yet sure what. He tells us that he can sense a male presence. When we ask him to describe that presence he tells us that it is a labourer type, someone who uses his body more than his brains. David goes on to say that routine is built into the building. The building is telling him that it has an institutional feel about it: perhaps it was once a school, a hospital or a factory – somewhere where routine was important.

Yvette calls out to ask if there are any spirit people or astral beings. David tells her someone is definitely there.

Yvette calls out again and as she does she smells something sweet – like roses. It seems to be getting darker down here, our eyes aren't adjusting. We all feel very cold.

We move further into the cellar and into a storeroom which is the oldest part of the building. The door is tight and only one person can fit through at a time. Yvette says she is feeling apprehensive. Ciarán tells her he wishes she wouldn't use that word as it is so loaded. As David enters the room we all feel a bit warmer. He tells us that it isn't witchcraft that he sensed earlier but old women doing washing. He says this place was a laundry once and he can sense nothing violent or nasty.

Ciarán inspects the wall in the storeroom and there is a hole in it. We all suspect that there must be a sealed room or secret area behind the wall of this one. It's intriguing. Yvette calls out but there is no response. We move out of the room and back into the main area of the cellar. Yvette calls out again. This time we all hear what sounds like a grunt coming from the darkness. Before we have time to recover Ciarán is shocked when a door he firmly closed with a latch suddenly opens. The atmosphere is tense and heavy for everyone. We don't like it down here at all.

We explore a little while longer, but when David says he is feeling a bit sick we decide to call it a day. The place does reek of something horrible. Perhaps it's gas. We just don't know. As we leave David stops and tells us he thinks someone – a man – died down here of a natural death, perhaps a heart attack.

THE BEDROOM VIGIL

David, Yvette and Ann head upstairs while Ciarán and Steve do a walk-around of the whole pub with their monitoring equipment.

At the top of the stairs Yvette strokes the family dog, who is sleeping peacefully there. David says he can sense a presence again but this spirit is very different from the man in the cellar downstairs. He is tall and dark with a lean and haggard face. He's intelligent and has a fanatical quality about him. David says he can feel him all around him. He is moving between the bedrooms and his name is Alfred or Albert. He's angry for some reason. He's from a pre-Victorian era.

We go into Michael's bedroom and David calls out to Alfred or Albert, asking him to make himself known. We hear the dog whining outside and a few creaks on the floor. There is movement in the hall but when we check the dog is sitting down.

David sits on Michael's bed and tells Yvette he can feel the spirit pressing on him. He asks the spirit to use his energy but not to take him over. David says the man is about fifty years old and the date he is getting is 1820. David wonders why he hasn't moved on and why he is so angry. David tells Yvette that Alfred or Albert isn't happy about what has happened to the building since his day. He tells her that he will see the building in his own time, not ours.

Yvette, Ann and David go into Jane and Keith's bedroom. David thinks the spirit could have been a teacher at

Everyone felt apprehensive

a school as he has that discipline quality about him. 'He's a watcher,' says David. 'He likes to watch people sleep.' Yvette feels heat in her hands, and David says that this man is wrapped around them all.

David tries to link with the spirit to find out how he can help him. Perhaps he did something wrong and that is why he can't cross over to the other side. David tells Yvette that he may have murdered someone, as he can feel the violence of the act.

Yvette calls out and everyone hears a couple of thuds coming from the stairs, as if someone is walking up them. David feels cold even though the temperature in the room is warm. Everyone feels apprehensive and jumpy, but then the atmosphere suddenly goes flat.

Yvette suggests a séance to get some energy going.

VISUALS, EMF, TEMPERATURE READINGS

Before and during the séance Ciarán and Steve do a walk around to take temperature and EMF readings and also to set up some lock-off cameras to film rooms, such as the pool room, where activity has been reported. They put a coin in the middle of the pool table as a trigger object. The coin, which dates back to 1936 and shows signs of use, belongs to Michael who says he found it in his room one day. He has no idea how or why it got there.

In the pool room Steve takes some temperature readings and discovers something very interesting that he believes might explain some of the phenomena reported here. It could be due to the temperature difference across the room. One side of the room has a low temperature and another side of the room has a higher temperature. Not only does this happen across the room (i.e. horizontally) but also up and down (i.e. vertically). So, for example, a person walking across the room would experience a drop in temperature but also experience a difference in temperature between their head and their feet. This, coupled with the knowledge that the pub is supposed to be haunted, could explain why some people have felt a sense of presence in this room. Steve points out that it is temperature drops and sudden fluctuations that are far more interesting to paranormal researchers than the actual temperature itself. In some cases there is no explanation for them and paranormal activity is suspected, but in this case Steve believes he has found a natural explanation.

In the cellars and bedrooms Ciarán and Steve discover

no unusual EMF activity, even though there is loads of electrical stuff everywhere. The EMF readings remain steady; again, like the temperature readings, it's always the fluctuations that interest us. Steve and Ciarán do discover what they think might be an electrical fault in one of the cellar rooms and make a note to point this out to the owners. The fault was a faulty earth on the mains supply. This manifested an EMF of over 700mG directly at the main earth cable and could, if someone was close enough, possibly 'trigger' some brain activity that they might interpret as being paranormal if they knew the pub's reputation.

During the walk around Steve sees something, or some-one, out of the corner of his eye. He turns, thinking it might be Ann coming to assist him with the EMF readings, but nobody is there. This occurs while he's on Michael's bed demonstrating the possible cause of the dark male figure that stands over Michael when he's in bed. Ciarán and Steve surmise that it might be the shadow cast by the pottery head sitting on the wardrobe, when lit by the colour-changing lamp.

THE SÉANCES

A few minutes after midnight Yvette, Ann, David and Jane sit down around a table with hands placed on the table and fingertips touching to begin a séance. Steve and Ciarán record the séance with cameras and thermal imagery equipment. David leads and asks the group to imagine a protective white light all around them. He asks them to visualise energy moving through their body and to the person on their right, so that the circle is a moving ball of energy while a light of protection and attraction surrounds them.

The group sit quietly for a while as David calls out for any spirits to make themselves known. Yvette hears a faint tap. David asks the spirits to use the energy of the group. He says a little girl is present in spirit and that she is skipping around the circle. There is also a young woman and an older man and the girl is dancing between them.

Yvette calls out for Albert or Alfred to make himself known to the group. All is quiet. Sounds of traffic passing outside can be heard. Yvette suggests putting the TV on a channel which isn't transmitting. She asks the spirits to turn the TV off.

'Did you murder anyone, Albert?' asks Yvette again. Everyone around the table hears slow, heavy breathing. They decide to use a glass to see if it will yield some results. The glass vibrates slightly but there is no movement.

David asks Yvette to scream in a high-pitched voice as he sometimes gets results from high-pitched sounds. Yvette screams and everyone covers their ears. The glass still doesn't move. David says the atmosphere has gone flat and the group prepare to end the séance. Yvette looks around and notices that the TV has gone off.

We have been so preoccupied with watching the glass that we haven't noticed that at some point during the séance the TV went off. Nobody in the room turned it off. Jane tells us it's not the kind of TV to switch off when it is not transmitting images. (Repeated testing of this, however, by Ciarán and Steve shows that when 'untuned' the TV automatically switches itself off after 4mins 30secs.)

We're initially so excited about the TV incident that we decide to hold another séance. This time Michael takes part instead of his mum. Again David leads and eases the group gently into the séance. Ciarán, who is recording the séance, notices that the door is moving. He also hears thuds and knocks in the corridor and goes off to investigate with a camera. He can't find anything unusual and returns to the séance.

Meanwhile the séance is in full swing with a glass divination. Michael says that his right arm is freezing and the thermal imager confirms that the temperature around his arm has indeed dropped. David notices that the zip on his pocket flicked up and down for no reason. Yvette calls out to the spirit who haunts this house to make itself known. The glass finally begins to move.

Yvette asks if the spirit is a male, and the glass moves, to indicate yes. Yvette asks if the spirit can move the glass to where it is standing and it moves towards Michael. In answer to the questions did you live here and did you die here, the glass moves to indicate yes.

Yvette feels very cold, and the thermal imager shows a temperature drop around her legs. She asks the spirit if there are other spirits here too and the glass motions towards yes. Yvette asks if this is the spirit who watches over Michael and the glass suggests yes. She asks if Michael looks like somebody the spirit knew in life and the glass indicates yes. She asks if he looks like his son and the glass motions yes. Finally she asks if the spirit's name is Albert, and the glass moves quickly towards yes.

David interrupts to say he is sensing and feeling for Albert. He says that Albert is happy here with Michael and means him no harm. In fact he wants to protect Michael and that is why he watches over him when he sleeps. David asks Albert if he wants his help to move to the other side, and the glass moves towards yes. After making sure that Albert will not harm Michael, David uses his energy to release Albert to the light so he can rest in peace. David then shuts down the séance.

As we end the séance Michael tells us that his hands are hot and they are extremely red. The thermal imager confirms that they are overheated. None of the trigger objects have moved during the séance, and the lock-off cameras in the hallways where the dog and cat are sleeping show no unusual activity.

Ciarán tells the group that while the séance was going on there were slight temperature drops and creaks upstairs as well as bangs in the corridor and a door that opened by itself. He didn't want to tell the group at the time as it would have interrupted the séance.

OUR CONCLUSIONS

Collingwood is one of those cases where we were able to provide some but not all the answers. The electrical cable fault in the cellar was interesting and we'd like to see if the events continue to occur after that is fixed. The temperature gradient may also help explain some of the experiences.

The pub sits on a main road and we can't discount passing traffic as an explanation for the unusual creaks and bangs we heard. We also can't discount the fact that since Jane and Keith own a dog and a cat some of the alleged activity may be caused by them without anyone realising it.

We did consider whether this might be a classic case of poltergeist activity, perhaps triggered consciously or unconsciously by Michael. During our investigation this seemed unlikely as it was Jane and Keith, rather than Michael, who seemed to be experiencing most of the phenomena. Michael also seemed honest and decent, like his parents, and we did not suspect him, or them, of fraud in any way.

We do acknowledge that Jane and Keith have a strong interest in the paranormal. It's conceivable that being highly sensitive individuals they could be imagining things that aren't there. This doesn't, however, explain Michael's dark figure or the reports of apparitions by Jane and the bar staff. Accurate descriptions of full-bodied apparitions by several independent witnesses are very rare; most of the time we investigate isolated sightings by one witness. There are also the alleged attempts by an unseen force to be helpful in the cellar. In most cases of alleged haunting the phenomena reported to us tend to be random without any agenda.

All these things make Collingwood stand out for us. Some of the fascinating readings in the pool room, the various creaks and bangs and the temperature drops during the séance as well as Michael's burning hands were also remarkable and inexplicable. We'd certainly like to keep in touch with the owners at Collingwood and see what happens in the months and years ahead.

David really helped kick things off during the vigils and the séance. Even though David had no idea that Michael had seen a dark figure in his bedroom, he picked up the dark figure of a man upstairs and built up an interesting picture of this figure and the reason why he couldn't cross over. He also gave the whole family peace of mind by reassuring them that the dark figure meant Michael no harm. But do we believe David? Do we believe in Albert?

A lot of what mediums tell us during an investigation is either inaccurate or doesn't make sense. Sometimes, though, mediums can and do provide us with astonishing insight and information. How they do this we simply don't know. They could be play-acting and faking in a remark-able way. To avoid the possibility of this we make abso-lutely sure that we only work with mediums we know to be honest, who aren't doing it purely for the money and who have a good track record. That leaves us with three other possible explanations. The medium is people reading (psychological explanation that Ciarán tends towards), or mind reading (explanation that intrigues us both), or genuinely talking to the dead (explanation Yvette tends towards).

Are mediums genuine? We simply don't know. It's a loaded question and perhaps one that deserves a book of its own.

CASE FOUR: CAMMELL LAIRD

(DATE OF INVESTIGATION: THURSDAY 20 OCTOBER 2005)

In 2004 paranormal activity was reported at the derelict Cammell Laird shipyard in Birkenhead. The activity reported included: sightings of apparitions, movement of objects, unexplained noises and ghost lights or light balls. The shipyard owners were so concerned that they called in a team of paranormal investigators. On Monday 31 January 2005, BBC Merseyside ran a feature on the Para.Science investigation on their website. The journalist assigned to the case described the incidents reported there as 'very strange'.

Ex shipyard calls in ghost hunters

The owners of a former Merseyside shipyard have called in a team of ghost hunters following a series of haunting experiences. The Wirral-based paranormal group Para.Science hopes to find out what is behind the sighting of mysterious strangers. The former Cammell Laird shipyard, in Birkenhead, is earmarked for a multi-million pound redevelopment. Its owners want to convert it for retail, commercial and residential use.

'Very strange'

The 140-acre site was one of the biggest shipyards in the world for 170 years, but the ghost hunt centres on an office block built in the 1960s, which is now being used by its owners, Reddington Finance. Site manager Mike Rider said: 'You can walk down the corridor, it's cold even in summertime and feel your hair stand up and tingles down your spine; quite a lot of times, when I've been sitting here at the desk, you see something in the corner of your eye.'

His daughter, Amy, says she regularly finds the same glass fallen from a tray in the canteen. She said: 'Every morning when we come in there's normally a glass fallen off that tray. It's always that glass and it's never, ever broken. It's very strange.'

(http://news.bbc.co.uk/1/hi/england/merseyside/4220979.stm)

According to the Para.Science investigation in early 2005 most of the sightings at the shipyard came from security guards and people working in the offices or on site, but strange things also occurred during an all-night vigil. In one case the apparition of a man was spotted by two independent witnesses at different locations at the same time. Intrigued by the previous investigation and the activity reported there, we decided to take a look ourselves. Here's what happened.

OUR OVERNIGHT VIGIL BEGINS

At 8.30 p.m. we meet in the reception area of a huge and virtually derelict office building. Steve, Ann and Ciarán have all investigated the location before and are familiar with the history and geography of the place. Yvette has not visited or investigated the venue before and she immediately notices how uncharacteristically nervous everyone is. Ciarán is keen to brief her on the case, but Yvette decides she would rather not know about what has happened or what has been reported until after the vigil has finished. She doesn't want to be influenced in any way by prior knowledge.

We decide to split into two groups to cover as much ground as possible. Steve and Ann head outside into the work yard and we decide to concentrate on the office building first. We leave the relative comfort of the reception area and walk through some swinging doors. As we climb a set of creaky stairs we're struck by the dramatic change between the warmth and light of the reception area and the darkness and cold of what lies ahead. The place feels unpleasant for both of us. The smell is rank and stale. The first room we enter with our torches, walkie-talkies and night vision cameras is a big meeting room.

THE MEETING ROOM

The room has a *Mary Celeste* feel. It looks as if it has been occupied but the residents have simply upped and left with no attempt at tidying up or organising. We see chairs abandoned in the middle of the room, filing cabinets with doors open, desks scattered with items. There are so many things lying about – pieces of paper, wires, cloths and so on – that it would be hard for us to know if anything had been moved. It's untidy, run-down and chaotic.

The meeting room

We move slowly to another room. It's pitch black but we can just about see that it is an area used by a group of actors. Alongside the chairs, tables and filing cabinets there are posters, scripts, tape recorders and artwork. There are side rooms with sewing machines and a clothing rail with names above each costume. One costume hanger carries the ominous name Derek Fear!

Yvette thinks she hears a footstep. We know it can't be Ann and Steve, and security have promised us they won't be doing their normal patrol while we are investigating. We both feel a cold blast of air. Ciarán thinks he sees a figure, but he soon realises it is a filing cabinet that, in the dark, he took for a figure. Yvette sees the blinds move, but then we notice an open window. Yvette wonders out loud if the naval guy that Debbie had predicted in our first investigation for this book is waiting for us. For no particular reason we both find the idea of this amusing and it takes some of the edge off our fear.

We decide to split up. Ciarán stays in the theatre room and Yvette goes into the big room. Yvette calls out to ask if there are any spirit people or astral beings who would like to talk to us, but she gets no response. Despite a nervous start both of us feel calm, and the only thing that we find remarkable is how very, very quiet and still the place seems. There is the odd creak from above, but we put this down to the creaking of the building.

THE SHIPBUILDING YARD

At around 9.30 p.m. we decide to go outside into the back yard. We put on our safety helmets. The yard area outside is massive again and has that *Mary Celeste* feel. It's full of stacks of wood, tyres, tools, equipment and what Yvette calls 'garage boy's bits'. There are trucks and abandoned cars with very dusty windows. Everything looks as if it has simply been left, without any attempt to tidy or create order. Yvette calls out and a remarkably long echo answers back.

The yard area, now completely deserted

We walk around the area. It's dark, it's dirty and we feel apprehensive. A few minutes later we hear a low moaning sound followed by a whistling sound. It's bizarre and very frightening as we don't think it's windy enough to make those kinds of noises. Yvette thinks she's being watched.

We move further into the work yard and into an area that was formerly a bus depot. We look up to see the office buildings surrounding us. The place is simply huge. There are shelves, boxes, wires, old PCs, rags and broken glass scattered everywhere. There is also some writing smeared in paint on the walls. This is the area where an apparition has been reported by two independent witnesses at the same time in different places. Yvette didn't know about the apparition and isn't surprised. It looks like a scene from a ghost film.

We hear a loud bump and for a second we are absolutely terrified.

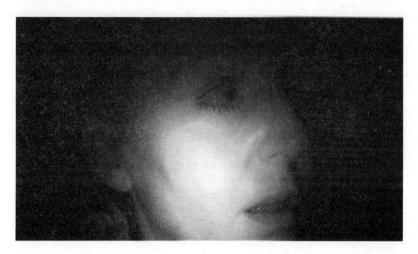

Were we being watched?

THE BOARDROOM

We go back to the office block, and as we are walking along the corridor Yvette is convinced she sees a white flash of light cross the hallway. We enter the boardroom and in contrast to most of the office building it looks lived-in, cared for and comfortable and is obviously still very much in use. There is a large table surrounded by chairs, a sink and tea- and coffee-making facilities. There is also a television.

We decide to turn the television on and leave it running, as in some cases we have investigated we have known televisions and radios to go off and on by themselves. Apart from a cold feeling in her legs Yvette feels happy in the room and is surprised to discover that a cleaner refuses to enter this room because she has seen a full-bodied apparition in it. There have been other reports of apparitions both half- and full-bodied in this part of the office building, in the corridors and in the kitchen. What's especially interesting for us is that there have also been reports of light flashes in the corridor. Ciarán knew about this but Yvette, who witnessed a flash of light, did not.

THE LONE VIGILS

Once again we decide to split up. Yvette goes to the giant meeting area and Ciarán investigates the rest of the office block.

Yvette: *I'm feeling more relaxed now. If I felt scared I wouldn't have agreed to go on a lone vigil. I've tried calling out and asking if there is anyone here who wants to make themselves known to me, but there has been no response. I do think I can hear banging doors, though. There is also what sounds like a high-pitched whistle.*

Ciarán: *One deserted room leads on to another. One room is of particular interest to me as it has lights with cords. Apparently these lights went on and off by themselves during a recent BBC news feature on the fate of Cammell Laird. I can see for myself that the only way to turn the lights on and off is to walk around and give the cords a big tug.*

As I shine my torch around certain rooms I notice that there are double shadows of myself. This is spooky and I can see how it could give someone the fright of their life. Also, when I turn off my night vision camera I can see shadows which are in fact my own reflection.

THE STAIRWELL

Yvette, Ciarán, Ann and Steve gather by the stairwell as both Steve and Ciarán believe they can hear muffled footsteps and voices. Yvette and Ann also hear the voices and the footsteps and what sounds like a door banging. Ciarán goes downstairs to see whether a door is banging by itself. He opens the swing door and then about ten seconds after, as he is walking away, he hears it bang shut. Thinking that is the explanation for the door banging sound he walks upstairs, only to hear the same bang again. It's highly unlikely that it is the door, as it wouldn't shut twice. The group attempt to repeat the experiment but this time there is only the one bang.

An explanation is eventually found for the barely perceptible voices and the sounds of shuffling. Steve opens a window and notices that there is a parcel depot across from the yard. Some guys are loading a van and they have the radio on. However, this doesn't explain the banging doors that we all heard at some point during the overnight vigil.

Banging doors were heard, but nobody was around

Later we return to the boardroom. The TV has gone off. Nobody has been in the room. There could be a natural explanation so we turn the TV on again. This time it stays on.

THE INFRASOUND TEST

Prior to and during the vigil at Cammell Laird we conduct environmental infrasound tests. This is to check the frequency of sound below normal range. Infrasound equipment is difficult to use, and to explain, but what we are looking for is a frequency of sound below 18 hertz.

We mentioned this briefly with reference to an interesting finding at the Charter House investigation, but to elaborate further: in scientific jargon, infrasound refers to low-frequency standing waves, and, for the rest of the world, audio frequencies below 20Hz. Humans can naturally detect audio frequencies between 20Hz and 20,000Hz, so it means sound which is there, but which you can't really 'hear' in the normal way.

About sixty years ago in the middle of the twentieth century, experiments were conducted on developing weapons based on resonance, or the frequency at which an object will vibrate. Through research, it was determined that body organs vibrated in the infrasonic spectrum, below 20Hz, and by manipulating sound, it was thought these sounds could be used to invoke sickness, incapacitation, possibly death.

During the 1990s university lecturer Vic Tandy was experiencing paranormal activity while working in his Coventry physics laboratory. These included visions, chills, strange feelings, etc. He decided to investigate this phenomenon, and discovered that the activity wasn't caused by spirits but by a faulty motor that was emitting a frequency between 17 and 19Hz. As soon as the motor was fixed, the phenomenon stopped. After this discovery, he visited various haunted sights in England and found two that had high levels of infrasound.

In May 2003, Ciarán and others conducted an experiment to investigate infrasound at the Purcell Room, London. This involved incorporating 17Hz frequencies intermittently into one of a pair of orchestral concerts.

Around 700 people attended the two concerts and they were all given questionnaires regarding their feelings and emotions throughout the event. The surveys netted a significantly greater intensity of heightened emotions, anxiety and chills with the infrasound than without.

Some scientists were quick to declare that an explanation for paranormal activity had finally been given, but had it? Out of all the areas that Mr Tandy visited, we need to emphasise that he only found that two of them had infrasonic activity, not all of them. Also, the infrasonic theory doesn't explain apparitions and all such phenomena associated with paranormal activity.

As paranormal investigators we need to be aware that the infrasound theory is out there and to take it into consideration when we investigate. Sceptics often assume that paranormal investigators and believers will ignore this information, saying that ghosts cause infrasound, or perhaps scoff at this groundbreaking evidence of non-existence. As paranormal investigators we take on board and respect every theory that attempts to prove or disprove the existence of the afterlife, and as much as possible we try to incorporate such theories in our investigations so that we can either rule them out or use them as an explanation.

We look for low-frequency sound because it has been suggested that infrasound can create cold chills, a sense of paranoia and distress, and even hallucinatory figures glimpsed in peripheral vision. In 1967 researchers at the University of Salford who tested subjects' ability to hear low frequencies asked them what they experienced.

Subjects described the sensation of infrasound as 'rough', a 'popping effect'. Infrasound below 5Hz was described as a 'chugging or 'whooshing', a sensation that they could 'feel'. Tandy, the Coventry physicist we mentioned earlier, discussed the idea that the human eyeball has a resonant frequency of 18 cycles a second, and will vibrate in sympathy with infrasound waves that have a similar frequency. Under such conditions, a person might – and we stress might, as this is preliminary research – experience a 'smearing of vision' that could result in evanescent hallucinations in the periphery of their visual field. This effect is reminiscent of the theories of neurologist Michael Persinger (see box below) who has suggested that electromagnetic waves can interfere with brain activity and lead people to think they see ghosts or aliens.

Both Ciarán and Sarah Angliss, who was the project leader on the Purcell Room experiment, were equally fascinated by the wild and wacky stories about infrasound research. As part of their writings on the subject they noted that interest in the dangers of infrasound was fuelled in the Cold War by the search for non-lethal weapons. In this respect, one of the strangest and most memorable research programmes was carried out by the French physicist Dr. Vladimir Gavreau. After experiencing an infrasonic wave that made him feel uncomfortable, Gavreau embarked on a research programme to make an infrasonic 'beam weapon'. His prototype, a scaled-up version of a Parisian police whistle, could supposedly immobilise or kill anyone who heard it.

Gavreau claimed that his whistle caused most problems when it was heard in a room that resonated at the so-called 'death frequency' of 7Hz. Later researchers have tried to replicate Gavreau's work – with little success. But this hasn't stopped his death whistle becoming the stuff of legend – a favourite among the internet's fringe science community.

FRITZING

Michael Persinger is the Professor of Psychology and head of the Neuroscience Research Group at Laurentian University, Ontario, Canada. His theory is that the sensation commonly described as 'having a paranormal experience' is merely a side-effect of both sides of our brain trying to work together. Simplified, the idea goes like so: The right hemisphere of the brain, the seat of emotion, is stimulated in the cerebral region that is presumed to control notions of self, using a weak magnetic field generated in a contraption worn on the head, also known as 'God Helmet'. Then, when the left hemisphere, the seat of language, is called upon to make sense of these notions, the mind generates a 'sensed presence'. Dr Persinger believes such cerebral 'fritzing' is responsible for almost anything we might describe as paranormal such as apparitions, ghost lights, poltergeist activity and so on. Experimental subjects who were exposed to a specific series of pulses from TMS (transcranial magnetic stimulation) described feeling an invisible presence near them or feeling connected to the whole world.

Infrasound could account for the 'presence' of ghosts. For example, infrasound could be caused by wind blowing past a cracked window in a long, narrow corridor. This type of low-frequency sound generation is similar in principle to the deep tooting sound a glass bottle makes when you blow across the top of it.

Archaeologists have discovered that a number of neolithic tombs in England and Ireland may have been built with the infrasound concept in mind. Some experts believe they may have been deliberately designed to make sounds bounce off walls and create an effect that's, well, scary. The tombs uniformly create this acoustic environment through the familiar construction of a long, narrow entryway with an opening to the outside at one end. The ancient architects of these tombs may not have understood infrasound frequencies, but eeriness was a desirable feature for a tomb, for the purpose of instilling reverence for the dead and discouraging grave-robbers. They might, through trial and error, have struck upon the most sonically foreboding design possible, and stuck with it.

This is a great theory for sceptics to fling at believers but true believing ghost hunters remain undaunted. Some even claim wildly that it is the ghosts themselves that produce subsonic sounds, thereby hijacking all the salient facts over to their side of the argument.

The readings we are getting at Cammell Laird are consistently below 18. Could these findings explain the eyewitness reports of apparitions and our experiences of cold draughts during the vigil? Could the paranormal activity here simply be the result of people responding to 'normal' factors in their surroundings? It's certainly worth taking into consideration, but it isn't proof positive for us as it doesn't explain the whole range of paranormal phenomena reported. For example, at Cammell Laird it doesn't explain the door banging or the independent reports of, ostensibly, the same apparition.

YVETTE'S EXPERIENCE

A damp, unpleasant, gloomy place. I didn't like it. Although I got no response when I called out, I did hear bangs, creaks, whistles and moans. They could have been caused by the building. The most interesting thing for me was the ball of light in the corridor which appeared for a brief second. I had no idea this kind of phenomenon had been reported before. The boardroom surprised me as, apart from feeling a little cold, it was a room I felt comfortable in. Ciarán tells me apparitions have been spotted there. The TV turning off by itself was very spooky, though it didn't turn itself off the second time we switched it on.

CIARÁN'S EXPERIENCE

Not a lot to report. I'm intrigued by the infrasound test in particular, but this doesn't account for the noises or the movement of objects that has been reported. I think for me the most fascinating thing about this particular investigation is the history of the place. It's incredible and as you can see from the section which follows that if any place was going to be haunted surely it would have to be Cammell Laird.

THE HISTORY OF CAMMELL LAIRD (1824–1993)

Cammell Laird shipyard in Birkenhead was built on the site of a Benedictine monastery that dates back to 1150. We know that because bones of monks have been found buried in the walls.

Birkenhead is a seaport and industrial town in the Wirral, Merseyside, on the west bank of the Mersey estuary opposite Liverpool. Cammell Laird came about following the merger of Laird, Son & Co. of Birkenhead and Johnson Cammell & Co. of Sheffield at the turn of the nineteenth century. The company made, among many other metal products, iron wheels and rails for Britain's railways. The businesses of Messrs Cammell and Laird merged to create a company at the forefront of shipbuilding in the nineteenth and twentieth centuries. In its heyday Laird shipyards covered the whole river from Woodside Ferry Terminal to Tranmere.

During the nineteenth and twentieth centuries Cammell Laird was one of the most famous names in British shipbuilding and more than 1,100 vessels of all kinds were launched on Cammell Laird slipways into the River Mersey. Cammell Laird built its first vessel at Birkenhead as long ago as 1828. A number of Cammell Laird's products are still sailing or preserved, including more recently built vessels such as the RFA tankers

Brambleleaf and *Appleleaf* of 1979, the Type 42 destroyer HMS *Liverpool* and Type 23 (Batch 3) destroyer HMS *Campbell Town*. The years following the Second World War were turbulent ones for Cammell Laird, and despite the efforts of a workforce which helped create one of the UK's largest commercial ship repair, conversion and shipbuilding companies, its Birkenhead operations were suspended in 2001. The company has not built a new vessel at Birkenhead since 1993. Ship repair and conversion work continues to expand at Birkenhead under the A&P Group, but given the general state of the British shipbuilding industry it seems unlikely that shipbuilding will ever return to the legendary Cammell Laird shipyard at Birkenhead. It seems that this chapter in the yard's history has now closed for ever, and for the past five years there have been plans to redevelop it completely as, among other things, a shopping mall.

Cammell Laird has a rich and fascinating history. So fascinating in fact that books and DVDs have been published about it. Of particular interest to us is *Old Ships and Hardships: The Story of a Shipyard* by David Roberts. This DVD brings the shipyard to life. You see the history of Cammell Laird from its earliest days to the tragic day when it was finally shut down. You see how it served the nation through two world wars, building world famous vessels like the *Rodney, Hood, Mauritania, Ark Royal, Windsor Castle* and many more. Even more fascinating for us, however, is how the story of the yard is told through the voices of the men who worked at Lairds: welders, crane drivers, electricians and plumbers. They tell of the hardships of building ships in all weathers, as well as the lighter moments that were provided by some of the 'characters' of the yard.

The DVD helped with the investigation because it reminded us that when the shipyard was up and running people lived and died there. In the early days workers were recruited as young as fourteen and many devoted their whole lives to the place. The hours were long and the work was strenuous and dangerous. There was plenty of suffering on the part of those who devoted their lives to the shipyard. Accidents, injuries and deaths on site were inevitable. Not to mention the spooky stories and grisly rumours of a welder who was accidentally welded into the hull of a ship. They say his body was only discovered when the ship was opened up for repair.

There are some who say that ghosts are replays of past events. This is what is known as a residual haunting. Could the apparitions at Cammell Laird then be some kind of time/space instant replay? We know from the work of Einstein and other scientists that it may indeed be possible for events of the past to exist in the present in a sort of time/space warp – see Part One. This gets into some very complicated notions, but the idea is that some 'ghosts' are not ghosts at all but an instant replay of a past event. In such cases what one sees is the ghost performing a certain scene over and over again. For example, a ghost of this type may go from the top of the stairs to the bottom and then disappear. This may happen over and over again. It never changes. The ghost never interacts with anyone, and we cannot interact with it. It never changes facial expression nor does it ever acknowledge anything around it. Thus the phenomenon is exactly like an instant replay on TV. These ghosts are like spirit-level recordings – residual energies – that replay over and over again.

As opposed to a traditional haunting, the residual haunting is believed to be the result of psychic energies being imprinted upon the environment and replayed time and again in a seemingly endless cycle. Is it possible then that some people's lives were so wrapped up with Cammell Laird, or that certain shipbuilding tasks were repeated so often, that they somehow imprinted their energies on the shipyard?

The residual haunting theory is interesting, but as we have absolutely no proof for now it has to remain just that – a theory. Besides, as far as we are concerned the idea that people can imprint their energies on a place for later generations to view is just as incredible and exciting, and tough to prove, as the idea that ghosts exist.

OUR CONCLUSIONS

Cammell Laird is a huge venue and impossible to cover with a small group. Traditionally you would have a larger group and divide it up to focus on different areas, and if we investigate again we'd certainly approach it that way. It's a fantastic site to visit, especially in the light of its history and the fact that most of the phenomena reported tie in with previous history. But is Cammell Laird haunted?

It certainly has all the right credentials. Given its history and the eyewitness reports we were disappointed we didn't see anything, but not surprised. If ghosts were going to appear it's unlikely that they would appear to us during a short and intense investigation for the purposes of this book. All the previous sightings at the shipyard occurred when people were either going about their daily business, as the security guards were, or doing mundane activities. Para.Science reported phenomena during night-long vigils, but they occurred when people were chatting amongst themselves and not particularly looking out or listening for something. In short, as far as Cammell Laird is concerned, paranormal activity is more likely to occur when you least expect it.

The chaotic, run-down and massive scale of the place should also not be overlooked. The building is bound to creak, wind is bound to rattle through, and there could be perfectly natural explanations for the door banging sound we heard. We simply can't rule that out.

Today Cammell Laird is earmarked for a redevelopment. This is heart-breaking in terms of the loss of investigative opportunities in the building, but very exciting in terms of the prosperity and other benefits that whatever stands in its place will surely bring to the area. It's a wonderfully spooky place with an incredible history. We've never been anywhere like it before. We will definitely continue to keep our eye on it, as the gloomy, intense *Mary Celeste* feel, smell, sound and look of the place really gripped us, and weeks later we still find it hard to shake off. At this stage, though, without sufficient evidence, the only conclusion we can make is that Cammell Laird is haunted; possibly by ghosts, certainly by memories.

CASE FIVE: THE HEX NIGHTCLUB

(DATE OF INVESTIGATION: TUESDAY 25 OCTOBER 2005)

This was our last investigation for the book and it proved to be the most dramatic. Apparitions, dark moving shapes, unexplained fires, a strong sense of presence, objects being moved and the sudden opening of a locked fire escape that was captured on video have all been reported at the Hex nightclub. On 25 October 2005 we arrived to investigate and see for ourselves.

The club is situated over two floors of a large building.

There is a basement – which is divided into a number of rooms of various sizes that are currently used for storage and for dressing-rooms of visiting bands – and a ground floor which houses the dance floor and several smaller bars. The entertainment area on the ground floor is split into two levels, the main dance floor being the upper level.

The décor is fairly typical of a Gothic Rock venue – subdued lighting, black paint, dark furnishing and more black paint. Not surprisingly the club has a satanic, black magic theme and this is reflected in a number of motifs and artwork with Gothic symbols and images throughout the public entertainment areas.

FROM CHURCH TO NIGHTCLUB

Like many allegedly haunted locations the Hex nightclub has an interesting history and an association with religion. The site was first noted in the 1860s with the building of St Paul's Chapel, United Presbyterian. It was described as a 'neat structure with a finely proportioned tower and spire'. It seems also to have been known as 'Ebenezer Baptist Church', which may have been a local nickname.

In August 1903 the chapel was sold to the Shaftesbury Boys' Club for £1,259. It opened as a youth club on 15 October 1903.

In 1934 the former chapel building was demolished to make way for a brand new purpose-built youth club. The building was of brick and reinforced concrete construction. It had an activity room, called the 'Romping Room', and classrooms in the basement and a games room, kitchen, library and toilets on the ground floor. The first floor was a gym complete with a stage area.

During the Second World War the reinforced concrete basement was turned into a public air raid shelter. About three hundred local residents regularly slept in the shelter during the winter and spring blitz on Merseyside in 1940–1. Only a few incendiaries ever hit the club building, with just one starting a small fire on the pitch pine block floor of the billiard room, and that was extinguished without serious damage being caused.

From early 1941 the whole of the ground floor and later parts of the upper floor were taken over by the Ministry of Food for use as a British Restaurant, feeding more than 400 local residents and workers at every sitting. This use continued until the end of the war.

In 1974 the building was finally closed as a youth club and sold to the Beehive Social Club, who reconstructed it internally at very great cost. Elaborate furnishings were used and no expense was spared. A large stainless steel tank was installed in the former 'Romping Room' as a beer reservoir, with an ingenious system of plastic pipes taking the beer to the many pumps.

In 2004 the building was transformed into a family-run nightclub. When the Hex opened it soon established itself as a venue popular with youngsters, holding regular band nights and music workshops for the under-twenties. The club attracted more than three hundred teenagers to its Teen Demons night every Wednesday evening.

EYEWITNESS TESTIMONY

In late 2004 Para.Science were contacted by the owners of the Hex following a series of inexplicable events that had occurred while the club was being renovated. These events had continued in the weeks following the opening of the club and had increased dramatically after members of staff began conducting séances using a Ouija board.

According to eyewitness accounts given to Para.Science, apparitions had been seen in the bar area. Descriptions of the apparitions varied, but some believed they saw a man dressed in clothing from the 1940s. There were also reports of dark moving shapes, objects being moved and a sense of being watched. Perhaps the most interesting of all was the sudden opening of a locked fire escape that was apparently captured on the club's CCTV security system. The video footage was seen by Para.Science on their first visit to the club, but despite their repeated requests for a copy of the tape they were subsequently told it had been lost. According to staff it was probably taken by another staff member to show to friends and family.

The footage was shot from a static CCTV camera located in the dance floor area and trained on a fire escape double door. The door was seen to open quickly and then swing partially closed again. There were no obvious persons visible in the picture and although it was fairly grainy and low resolution, the overall quality of the recording was perfectly watchable.

After viewing the footage Para.Science conducted a

visual inspection of the door and the camera location and it was clear that although possible it would be extremely difficult for a person to have opened this door without appearing on the footage or else using cords or strings. The door was strongly secured and appeared the same as it looked in the video footage – it was not possible to simply or quickly open the door either from the inside or the outside. The door was locked and barred from the inside except for public events.

Initially Para.Science had concerns that the accounts of paranormal activity might be merely for publicity. They also discovered in their initial conversations that some staff members were initiated into 'the craft' and were skilled in the 'black arts'. One staff member believed she was psychic and had effected some protective charms against an 'evil presence' that had entered via the Ouija board. Despite these concerns Para.Science decided to investigate. As well as the fire door incident there did seem to be a number of unusual features worthy of an investigation.

Key activities reported included audible phenomena – those most often included the sounds of a 'kitchen with lots of plates being clattered and voices' and separate distinct voices that sounded like 'people talking in the adjacent room'.

The eyewitness accounts of a member of the security staff sounded intriguing. He revealed how during one evening at the club while it was being renovated he encountered the ghost of a little girl in the basement. She appeared real, but her sudden appearance and disappearance a few seconds later had shaken him badly and he had refused to enter that part of the basement alone since his encounter.

All members of staff had their accounts of cold spots, dark shadows and the feeling they were not alone. There was also a second apparition sighting, this time on the ground floor near the entrance. It was the apparition of a man, described as being in his middle years and wearing old-fashioned clothes, 'like from the war'. Two witnesses apparently saw this apparition, although one of them was no longer employed by the club and attempts to contact him proved fruitless.

The staff seemed unaware of the location's history. They knew the building had been a youth club but seemingly didn't know about its use in the war years as a British Restaurant and as a rescue centre during the Merseyside blitz, or that there had previously been a church on the site.

THE OUIJA BOARD SÉANCE

Club staff informed Para.Science that although there had been a number of unusual events since they first occupied the building, the main activity had started immediately after a Ouija board séance conducted one evening by eight staff members.

During the séance, which lasted several hours, various spirits came through with information – including the threat that the building would be burned down. Mean while a number of non-participants claimed to have seen dark shadows moving around the room. They also claimed that the temperature in the room dropped suddenly, and they all felt that something evil was near to the small stage area. It was the following day that the fire door was opened suddenly – the event captured on CCTV and described above.

The staff believed that the increased activity within the location was due to the séance and agreed to take part in another séance with Para.Science observing. The repeat séance was conducted using the same staff members who had attended the original séance. However, there were also a number of curious additional staff and their friends who wanted to see what might happen second time around.

The repeat séance was not satisfactory, as there was clear evidence of pushing of the glass by several people. After an hour or so the whole séance dissolved in chaos, hysteria, argument and tension. Nothing unusual was noticed or observed by any of the Para.Science team, although members of the club staff did report sense of presence and a drop in temperature.

THE INVESTIGATION PROPER

After much discussion Para.Science decided to proceed with the investigation. There was a feeling of unease in the group about some of the conditions. There was also a strong suggestion that some staff members were playing along with the events and even indications that some were simply joining in with tales of paranormal activity. Despite this the investigators were impressed by a small number of the witnesses and their accounts of experiences, and it was for this reason that they decided to continue with the case.

A series of visits were made to the club in early 2005 to corroborate the seemingly genuine experiences and try to determine their causes. At the time of the investigation the club was still undergoing renovation and other building works, and this meant that parts of the basement level were full not only of old items of equipment and other junk but also some building materials. The ground floor was functioning as a night club and music venue and was fully accessible. One female member of staff was living on site in a basement room which was set up as a bedsit. The club therefore was normally occupied 24 hours a day. The Para.Science visits were made when the club was closed to the public and with only a few staff members present.

During these visits the basement area was highlighted as being of particular interest with a number of the team reporting temperature fluctuations and 'popping' of the ears. Two team members also reported a partial sighting of what they described as a 'figure' and at the same time another pair of team members reported a strong sense of presence at an adjacent location.

During one visit some team members reported that a photograph was apparently turned over several times during the day. Video camera evidence confirmed that the photo had indeed turned over several times but didn't record the actual turning. The exact correspondence of the camera's time code and the timing of the witness reports make at least one of the 'turning' incidents impossible for anyone to have approached and turned the photo over themselves. There are two possibilities for what happened: 1) the witness misreported the incident; 2) by some mechanism, as yet unknown, the photo was turned over without direct human contact.

The team also recorded one audible anomaly that they found hard to explain. During the same investigation visit two video cameras recorded the sound of what is best described as a voice saying the word 'stop'. The sound was clearly recorded and computer analysis confirmed that it was identical on both recordings. The location of the cameras in the basement meant that it is fairly certain that the word was not spoken by any team member as they can all be seen at the time of recording. It is also clear that no member of staff was close enough to have inadvertently been recorded speaking. Comparison of the word with recordings of team members using a computerised analysis programme also allowed Para.Science to feel confident that no explanation of the event can be offered.

Subsequent visits by Para.Science after their third visit began to prove difficult to arrange, due to the opening hours of the club, and the investigation was put on hold.

WE CONTINUE THE INVESTIGATION

A few months later we are contacted by the club owners, who ask if we can continue to investigate as the unusual activity hasn't stopped. We were told that several staff members have left and that the club's opening hours have been reduced, making it easier for us to carry out our work.

We review the case and visit the owners prior to our investigation. We are impressed by some of the witnesses and decide that there are clearly a number of unusual events that are worthy of investigation, in particular the fire door and over thirty unexplained fire brigade call-outs at the club since 1975. Like the previous investigative team, however, we do feel uncertain about whether or not the 'paranormal' activity is fuelled by a desire for some publicity for the venue – the name and décor suggesting a link with the occult and paranormal.

In October 2005, a few weeks before our first investigation is scheduled, our concerns are heightened when we hear that a fire has taken place. Just as 'predicted' in the first séance the club has nearly been destroyed by fire. The foyer was gutted and there is severe damage to the rooms and offices in the building. Property and equipment worth thousands of pounds has been lost or damaged. The heat from the suspected arson attack burst water pipes and melted computers and musical equipment. Following severe damage to the electrics much of the building needs to be re-wired.

No apparent cause for the fire has been found, or motive, although the police suspect arson. The owner is currently appealing for help from the local community in getting the popular venue up and running again. We can't help thinking that we are being drawn into something 'sinister,' but not for paranormal reasons.

After discussing our concerns with the owners we are

reassured that this certainly isn't a publicity stunt. The sincerity of the witnesses appears genuine. However, before our investigation begins we stress the absolute necessity of putting additional safeguards in place to ensure the integrity of our investigation at all times. Only a few members of staff will be allowed to take part in the investigation, and lock-off cameras will be placed in every room to ensure against fraud. Satisfied that our criteria to protect against fraud will be met by the owners, we decide to continue.

We agree that the best way to investigate is first to record the environment, approaching it methodically, then to carry out vigils and walks around and finally to hold a séance with recording equipment and cameras up and running.

RECORDING THE ENVIRONMENT

At 10 p.m. Ciarán, Yvette, Steve, Ann and three of the club staff meet up in the main dance floor area of the nightclub for a couple of hours before the actual vigil begins to conduct some baseline tests. This is the area where apparitions have been reported and the fire door mysteriously opened. The idea is to get a real sense and feel of the place.

This is Yvette's first experience of investigative methodology. We use floor plans, question sheets and recording equipment to establish a baseline. The floor plans have been drawn up previously and if any of us experience or sense anything unusual we must immediately record where it happened on the floor plan. This will reveal whether there are focal areas of activity. EMF and temperature recordings are taken every ten minutes or so to see if there are any unusual fluctuations. There are also questionnaires to record impressions and establish a baseline, which will enable us to see if those feelings change during the vigil.

Yvette: *I'm not as familiar with the Hex as Ciarán, who has investigated it before. I don't know that much about the place, except that apparitions have been seen, it has been burned down a few times and was built on a church. The fires could of course be down to faulty wiring. My initial impression is that it is dark, depressing and sad. Although I feel slightly tired I don't at this stage feel anxious or nervous. It's sad to see how much damage the fires have done to the place. It's got a really gloomy, seedy feel about it. I'm intrigued that the club is built over a church. I don't think the ghosts would be too happy about the satanic theme.*

I'm feeling a shiver run down my spine and now a cold draught. Look, everyone, at the fire door we shut with the chair. It's opened. How could that happen? I'm going to set my camera on it. There is nobody around and the wind isn't strong outside. Look. I'm sure that is a light anomaly? I'm glad I was filming. The comfortable feeling I had earlier this evening is slowly fading. I'm getting scared now. I'm dying for the loo but won't go. I'm too scared.

Ciarán: The temperature on the floor is averaging about 15.5 to 16. In a place like this the best way to begin in my opinion is to 'fish' for a while to assess the atmosphere and get accustomed to the sights and sounds of the place before we begin our vigil. I'm not easily scared but it is creepy here. We've just noticed that the fire door with the chair has moved. That is hard to explain naturally. Yvette has seen a light anomaly. Steve also recorded it on his digital.

THE FIRE DOOR

After we've conducted our baseline tests we get ready for the overnight vigil. We're all feeling a bit jittery right now as the incident with the fire door has shaken us. Before we met in the dance floor to conduct our tests we shut and locked all the doors for security reasons. To be extra sure the fire door didn't swing open we pushed a chair through it. It took two of us to push the chair in place and you'd need to be very strong to dislodge it. Opening the door from the outside would be virtually impossible. It would also make a lot of noise.

How could the fire door have opened without any of us seeing or hearing anything? True we were all busy conducting our baseline tests, but we were working quietly so each of us could get a sense of the place. It's not a large room and we would have noticed or heard if someone had tried to open it from inside or out. It wasn't windy outside, so the wind couldn't have opened the door, and also a table tennis ball placed on a shelf near the door didn't move (you can see it on the left of the second photo).

Somehow the chair was pushed up and the door opened without any of us noticing it or hearing anything. When or how it happened is a complete mystery. We can't stop thinking or talking about it. Have a look at the photos below to see for yourself.

The locked fire door with chair (left) and partially opened door (right)

THE OVERNIGHT VIGIL

We now split up into groups. Steve and Ann remain upstairs and we head downstairs into the basement.

Yvette: *As we climb down into the darkness of the basement I'm getting a strong smell of horses. A wet, animal-like smell typical of stables. Now the smell has gone. How weird! It's pitch black down here. With my torch I can just about make out storage rooms with barrels and lots of junk lying around. I'm no medium, I'm not psychic, but I'm convinced we aren't alone down here. There is something or someone with us. I can hear a low rumble sound. Ciarán hears it too and we aren't sure what it is.*

Ciarán is taking me through some rank-smelling corridors to the area where you can see the original foundations of the church on which the Hex is built. I

wonder what the priests think about it becoming a
nightclub? I bet they aren't happy about it. Could they have
started the fires in protest? Should I try saying the Lord's
Prayer? They might like that. Trouble is I'm finding it hard
to remember the words. Strange. That is odd. I used to
know it so well. I'm going to call out in the name of God to
see if there are any spirit people or astral beings here who'd
like to make contact with us. What was that? It sounds like
a rattling. Uncannily I think it started to rattle when I said
the word God. Ciarán hears it too and has called Ann
down to be an extra pair of ears.

We're going into another room now. It's so very dark
in here. I can't see anything and am worried about falling
over. It looks like a gym. There are punch bags and a
poster of Bruce Lee, very menacing. The gym might
explain the sweaty smell that was so strong earlier. There
is so much junk down here it would be hard to tell if
anything was moved. I can hear the odd creak and clank,
but the more I hear the more I think the strange sounds
probably come from the water pipes.

Ciarán: I can tell that Yvette isn't happy down here, and
I'm not either. It's a nasty smelly place and it's dank and
dark – very dark. I wouldn't want to be down here without
my torch. The Gothic furniture items discarded here and
there certainly help to create a macabre atmosphere. There
are plenty of strange sounds to interest us, but I suspect they
could be due to the water pipes clinking and clanking when
water passes through. The low rumbles Yvette and I both
heard could be from a passing train.

Yvette tries to speak but is unable to

Yvette is calling out and trying to say the Lord's Prayer. I'm struggling to remember the words as well. I can also feel a headache coming on. It gets worse when I'm near the old foundations of the church and clears the further away I am from it. Can't explain that. Perhaps it could be the low ceilings. I can hear the odd thud. Not sure where that comes from as we know nobody is down here with us right now. It can't be the people above as these ceilings are made of brick; they were protection against air raids during the war. There could be natural explanations for everything we've heard and the way I'm feeling, but even so this is a truly horrible place to spend time in. Again this is uncomfortable. I can't breathe properly. I'll be glad to get out of here.

SÉANCE WITH RECORDING EQUIPMENT

At 11.45 p.m. we meet back in the dance floor area of the club and, given the history of the phenomena reported, we decide to hold a séance.

Taking part in the séance are Yvette, Ann and three staff members who participated in the original Hex séance. We believe these women, one of whom claims to be psychic, are genuine witnesses. Yvette leads the séance, as she did in our first investigation at the Farmhouse. Ciarán and Steve don't take part in the séance but observe and film it and set up cameras at various points in the room to check for fraud. They also set up thermal imagery equipment to detect any temperature drops or fluctuations in the room.

The temperature fluctuates as the group receives different messages

A glass is placed on a table that has letters and numbers marked on it to form a makeshift ouija board. Each member of the séance places a finger on the glass. Yvette begins by asking the group to imagine a protective white light above, below and around them. She also asks everyone in the séance to imagine a white light passing through their left arm into the right arm of the person sitting next to them so that energy is pushed around the table in a clockwise motion.

Yvette calls out for spirits or astral beings to make themselves known. After a slow start the glass begins to move, indicating yes, there are spirits present. The communication is confused and Yvette, feeling frustrated by the lack of response, gets a little more aggressive in her calling out. She backs down but is encouraged by Ciarán and Steve to continue with this assertive approach as interesting things are happening on the thermal imagery equipment.

Another spirit makes its presence felt via the glass divination. The name Derek Higgins is spelled out. It seems that Derek is about 45 years old and wants to confess to starting the fire. The communication gets more and more confused, and so the group decide to abandon the glass and instead put their hands on the table with fingers touching.

One of the staff members who thinks she is psychic says a little girl called Elizabeth is present. She starts to cry as the girl wants to be held and kept warm. Yvette suddenly feels very cold and has to withdraw her hands from the table to warm them by rubbing. She then places her hands back on the table and as she does so she suddenly feels warm.

The séance ends when the group feel that the messages

are getting too confusing. Yvette and Ann are disappointed, but Ciarán and Steve aren't at all. They have got some fabulous readings on their thermal imagery equipment.

TEMPERATURE

Typically during investigations we take the temperature in each of the rooms where we will be videoing, and at different points in those rooms. Sometimes we use a weather station with transmitters inside and outside to give both readings at the same time. We may also use a directional laser thermometer to give readings up to fifteen feet away and then compare them with baseline readings. For this particular case, however, we decided to use a thermal imaging camera that can pick up hot and cold spots.

Cold spots or hot spots are often reported before and during paranormal activity, and some mediums believe that the phenomenon is caused by a vortex, a kind of portal that spirits travel through to get to another realm. Mediums believe that cold spots are number one on the scale of common types of haunting activity. They are a ghost's calling card. The feeling of a sudden mass of icy cold air or a cold draught from nowhere will often precede ghost activity. In a sense, these cold spots are considered to be ghost activity, as this change in temperature is the ghost trying to manifest. Instead of using its energy, it is drawing energy from people on this plane. This, mediums explain, is why sensitive people may feel cold or get a chill: the ghost is sucking energy away from them. Ciarán, looking at it from the viewpoint of a parapsychologist, says that even slight changes in temperature can alter the physiology of the body and trigger the adrenalin 'fear response'.

Thermal imaging cameras allow you the luxury of actually seeing what a thermometer picks up. They show and record temperatures and temperature fluctuations in the form of colours. With most of these units you look through them in much the same way as you look through a video recorder to view the image. Using infra-red technology, you can actually see the shape and size of cold spots.

During the Hex séance above Ciarán and Steve noticed on their thermal imaging camera that every time Yvette called out it affected the temperature readings on their imaging camera. Inexplicably it seemed as if the temperature was reacting to her voice. At certain times during the séance the group was also surrounded by a mass of green shapes on the imager – green indicating a drop in temperature. We have checked and double-checked the room and weather

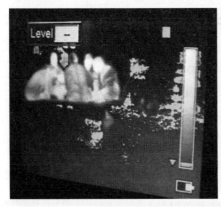

The green fog seems to close around the group

recordings outside, and there were no obvious signs of draughts to account for the sudden drop in temperature. It looked like a scene from the movie *The Fog* – as the séance participants were reporting a drop in temperature and apparently getting communication, a green fog on the thermal imager really did seem to close in around them.

OUR CONCLUSIONS

The amazing results on the thermal imaging camera during the séance are what impressed us most about the Hex.

At the back of our minds we still get niggling suspicions that some of the paranormal activity reported here in the last year or so may be fuelled by a desire for publicity and support for the venue to get it up and running again after the fire. If we hadn't got those reactive readings from the thermal imager the chances are we might well have decided to file this case as curious but lacking in credibility. But we did get those readings that appeared to be reacting to Yvette's voice, and they – along with our light anomaly, the fire door incident, the fact that we forgot the Lord's Prayer and the sound anomaly picked up earlier in the year by Para.Science – have ensured that the Hex case file stays wide open.

For us the Hex nightclub revealed some of the most inexplicable and bizarre temperature shifts ever. Yes, it's possible there's a natural explanation, but so far we simply haven't been able to find one. At present that just leaves us with possible unnatural explanations.

Could the energy created by the séance or Yvette's voice have somehow influenced the temperature in the room?

Could Derek's spirit, Elizabeth's spirit or something unexplained have showed up on our thermal imager?

Were ghosts actually present in the room with us when we held the séance?

The possibility of any of the above sends shivers (of fear, uncertainty and excitement) down our spines.

APPENDIX A:
INVESTIGATIVE GROUPS AND
SOCIETIES

The authors do not endorse any ghost group and are not in any way liable for the behaviour of a group during an investigation unless they are personally in attendance. For those interested in seeking a group to join, or to invite for an investigation, the authors recommend enquiring via national organisations such as the SPR or ASSAP.

Name	Information	Webpage
Society for Psychical Research (SPR)	The purpose of the SPR is to advance the understanding of events and abilities commonly described as 'psychic' or 'paranormal', without prejudice and in a scientific manner. The Society does this by promoting and supporting important research, and by publishing scholarly reports of a high standard. It acts as a forum for debate by organising educational study days and an annual conference.	www.spr.ac.uk [www.aspr.com] (American equivalent)
Parapsychological Association (PA)	An international professional organisation of scientists and scholars engaged in the study of 'psi' (or 'psychic') experiences, such as telepathy, clairvoyance, remote viewing, psychokinesis, psychic healing and precognition. The primary objective of the association is to achieve a scientific understanding of these experiences.	www.parapsych.org
Parapsychological Foundation (PF)	A not-for-profit foundation which provides a worldwide forum supporting the scientific investigation of psychic phenomena. The Foundation gives grants, publishes pamphlets, monographs, conference proceedings etc., hosts a lecture series at its facility on the upper-east side of New York City, and maintains a library with a collection of more than 10,000 volumes and 100 periodicals on parapsychology and related topics.	www.parapsychology.org

International Survivalist Society	Formed with the aim of publishing articles, books and photographs relating to survival after death and psychical research. It is an independent, non-profit organisation that regularly cooperates with many distinguished psychical researchers and parapsychologists across the globe.	www.survivalafterdeath.org
Survival Research Network	Dedicated to the impartial and critical scientific evaluation of reported phenomena suggesting the continuity of human consciousness after bodily death. Also provides information about the range and quality of the scientific survival research literature from the 1880s to date.	www.survival-research.net
The Parapsychologist (Dr Ciarán O'Keeffe)	Provides information about parapsychology. The aim is to disseminate information, to expose the facts and let you decide.	www.theparapsychologist.com
Para.Science	Paranormal Science - Para.Science - was established to conduct serious study, research and investigation into all types of paranormal phenomena. Based in North West England. The group makes extensive use of state-of-the-art photographic, video and sound recording equipment and techniques to undertake this study. All results of their investigations are made available for public and peer inspection.	www.parascience.org.uk

www.assap.org

The Association for the Scientific Study of Anomalous Phenomena

An association dedicated to discovering the scientific truth behind unexplained anomalous phenomena. ASSAP has no corporate beliefs and encourages an open-minded, undogmatic, scientific approach to its subject. The main activities of the association are research into reports of anomalous phenomena and the analysis and publication of the results of such investigation. Members are encouraged to actively investigate phenomena in a disciplined, responsible way through a training programme.

APPENDIX B: RECOMMENDED READING AND VIEWING

BOOKS

The following are just a selection of recommended books which have been written from various perspectives and focus on different aspects of survival research and haunting and poltergeist experiences.

Auerbach, L., *ESP, hauntings and poltergeists: A parapsychologist's handbook*, New York: Warner Books, 1986.

Baker, Robert A. and Nickell, Joe, *Missing Pieces: How to Investigate Ghosts, UFOs, Psychics and Other Mysteries*, Buffalo, NY: Prometheus Books, 1992.

Bayless, Raymond, *Apparitions and Survival of Death*, New Hyde Park, NY: University Books, 1973.

Bayless, Raymond, *The Enigma of the Poltergeist*, West Nyack, NY: Parker Publishing Co., 1967.

Carroll, R. T.,*The Sceptic's Dictionary*, http://skepdic.com/

Cheung, T., *The Element Encyclopedia of the Psychic World: The Ultimate A–Z of Spirits, Mysteries and the Paranormal*, London: Harper Element, 2006.

Fontana D., *Is There an Afterlife?*, London: O Books, 2005.

Gauld, A., *Mediumship and Survival: A Century of Investigations*, London: Heinemann, 1983.

Hines, T., *Pseudoscience and the Paranormal: A Critical Examination of the Evidence*, Buffalo, NY: Prometheus Books, 2002.

MacKenzie, Andrew, *Hauntings and Apparitions*, London: Heinemann Publishing, 1982.
Nisbet, B.C., 'The Investigation of Spontaneous Cases: Some Practical Suggestions' in I. Grattan-Guiness (ed.), *Psychical Research: A Guide to its History, Principles and Practices* (pp. 211–16). Wellingborough: Aquarian Press, 1982.
Roberts, R. and Groome, D. (eds.), *Parapsychology: The Science of Unusual Experience*, London: Hodder Education, 2001.
Rogo, D. Scott, *An Experience of Phantoms*, New York: Taplinger, 1974.
Rogo, D. Scott, *Life After Death: The Case for Survival of Bodily Death*, New York: Sterling Pub Co Inc., 1986.
Roll, William G., *The Poltergeist*, Garden City, NY: Nelson Doubleday, 1972.
Society for Psychical Research [SPR], *Guide to the Investigation of Apparitions, Hauntings, Poltergeist and Kindred Phenomena*, London: The Garden City Press, 1965.
Tyrell, G.N.M., *Apparitions*, Published under auspices of SPR by Gerald Duckworth & Co. Ltd., London, 1943 (revised in 1953, reprinted 1973).
Underwood, Peter, *Ghosts and How to See Them*, London: Caxton Editions, 1996.

FILMS

The Haunting (1963)
The Exorcist (1973)
The Legend of Hell House (1973)
Poltergeist (1982)
Ghostbusters (1984)
The Exorcist III (1990)
The Sixth Sense (1999)
The Others (2001)
The Devil's Backbone (*El Espinazo del Diablo*) (2001)
The Eye (*Jian Gui*) (2002)
The Grudge (*Ju-on*) (2003)
R-Point (2004)

ACKNOWLEDGEMENTS

On a ghostly hitch-hiking adventure such as this you meet an assortment of people willing to give you a lift or point you in the right direction. For their frequent investigative lifts and invaluable technical assistance along the way we owe a debt of gratitude to Steve and Ann from Para.Science. To the owners of The Farmhouse, Charter House, Collingwood, Cammell Laird and Hex, we will be for ever indebted to you for opening your doors to a pair of ghost hunters and providing such wonderful hospitality, free access and fascinating conversations. We would also like to thank the experts who provided insightful comments: Maurice Grosse, Guy Lyon Playfair, Paul Adams and David Fontana. For their unwavering support both whilst conducting other haunting investigations and for perfectly timed phone calls we'd like to thank Karl Beattie, Iain Cash, Jon Dibley, Richard Felix, Jon Gilbert, Cath Howe, Stuart Torevell, David Wells and Jo Whitestone. Theresa Cheung has been holding up the comforting road signs, providing key words and invaluable research as we've driven through this forest of facts. Thank you. And for those moments when both of us were travelling on different roads because of other responsibilities and needed to return to the investigative one we are eternally grateful to Tor O'Neil. Finally, we would like to say a big thank you to our literary agent Guy Rose. Without him we would not have been given this wonderful opportunity.

Ciarán: *Over the last six months preparing the book we have become the 'Scolded and Mouldy' of the ghostly world, supernatural siblings! Special thanks to my paranormal partner in crime – Yvette, merçi.*

I'd also like to express my greatest thanks to those people who may not have realised they helped, who, on those numerous long roads when it looked as though nobody would stop and offer a lift, pulled over in a luxury motor home with a full fridge, DVD collection and understanding ear: Mum, Dad, Bro and Sharon and Olly, Lol and Emily and Heath, Emma G, Andy and Chris, Ian B. Finally, to the driver of that luxury motor home who will continue with me on this life adventure, carry on giving me lifts and pointing me in the right direction beyond this book: I love you Pretty.

Yvette: *Firstly I would like to thank my family Karl, William and Mary, who have endured my long nights away looking for ghosts. I love you.*

I would also like to thank my other family, the team at Antix. They have all helped me laugh through some tough times.

Thanks to the Most Haunted crew, my wonderful husband Karl, David Wells, Gordon Smith, Cath Howe,

Stuart Torevell, John Dibley, John Gilbert, Jo Whitestone, Richard Felix, Iain Cash, Rachel Phillips. Long may we continue.

Ciarán, my friend and partner in scary places. You have made me look at the paranormal in a different light and I thank you for that. You are a true friend. Thanks for everything.

Thanks to Theresa for all your help and hard work. And big thanks to Nicola and all the guys at Hodder. Thanks for your belief in us and our ideas. The offer to come and investigate a haunted location with us still stands.

Picture acknowledgements

All images are copyright the authors except the following:

© Mary Evans Picture Library: 12, 21, 26 © Mary Evans/ Harry Price: 126 © Mary Evans /Peter Underwood: 129 © Fortean Picture Library: 96, 102, 106, 114, 130, 133 © Mari Huff: 132 © Graham Morris: 67, 68-69

Every effort has been made to contact copyright holders but if there are any errors or omissions, Hodder & Stoughton will be pleased to insert the appropriate acknowledgement in any subsequent printing of this publication.